CONTENTS

List of Maps & Diagrams 14

Acknowledgements 17

Introduction 18

Geology by *Noel Williams* 20

Landscape History 26

Wildlife by *Gordon Rothero* 30

Weather 38

Mountaineering History by *Noel Williams* 41

Environment, Safety & Technical Notes 44

Amenities 50

RÙM 54

    Barkeval 55
        1 North-West Flank 55
        2 Broad Buttress 55
        3 Narnia Arête 59
        4 Honeycomb Arête 59
        5 Descent Spur 61
    Askival 61
        6 North Ridge via Askival Pinnacle 61
        7 North Ridge Easy Route 63
        8 East Ridge 63
        9 South Ridge 64
        10 West Ridge 64
    Trollabhal 66
        11 East Ridge 66
        12 South Flank 66
        13 West Ridge 68
    Ainshval 70
        14 Forgotten Ridge 70

  15 North Ridge 70
  16 Harris Face 72
 Sgùrr nan Gillean 72
  17 Dibidil Face 72
Traverse of the Rum Cuillin 75
  18 Main Ridge Traverse 75

KNOYDART TO THE GREAT GLEN .76

a) Knoydart 77
 Beinn na Caillich 77
  19 South-East Slabs 77
 Ladhar Bheinn 79
  20 An Dìollaid 79
 Stob a' Chearcaill 81
  21 North-East Ridge 81
 An Caisteal 83
  22 South Face 83
 Meall nan Eun 85
  23 Cannonade 85

b) The Rough Bounds 88
 Beinn an Aodainn (Ben Aden) 88
  24 East-North-East Ridge 88
  25 South Face 90
 Garbh Chìoch Mhòr 92
  26 Coire nan Gall Slabs 92

c) Morar 92
 Cnoc a' Bhac Fhalaichte 92
  27 Tarbet Slabs 93
 Sgùrr an Eilein Ghiubhais 93
  28 Right-hand Rib 93
 Beinn Gharbh 95
  29 Ursainn Slabs 97
  30 North-West Face 97

d) The Loch Lochy Hills 99
 Sròn a' Choire Ghairbh 99
  31 Sean Mheall, South Face 100
 Meall na Teanga 100
  32 Meall Dubh, Central Buttress 100
  33 Meall Dubh, Right-hand Buttress 103

HIGHLAND SCRAMBLES SOUTH

Scrambles and Easy Climbs from the Cairngorms to Galloway

including

Cairngorms, Ben Nevis, Glen Coe, Etive, Knoydart, Ardnamurchan, The Cobbler, Rum, Mull and Arran

Iain Thow

SCOTTISH MOUNTAINEERING CLUB
SCRAMBLERS' GUIDE

Published in Great Britain by The Scottish Mountaineering Trust, 2017
Reprinted with corrections 2018

© The Scottish Mountaineering Club
All rights reserved. No part of this publication may be reproduced, stored in or introduced into a retrieval system, or transmitted, in any form or by any means (electronic, mechanical, photocopying, recording or otherwise), without the prior written permission of the publisher.

ISBN 978-1-907233-23-4
A catalogue record for this book is available from the British Library

Climbing and scrambling are activities with a danger of personal injury or death. Participants in these activities should be aware of and accept these risks and be responsible for their own actions and involvement.

Route descriptions of scrambles and climbs in this guide, together with their grades and any references to in situ or natural protection, are made in good faith, checked and substantiated where possible by the author. However, routes lose holds and are altered by rockfall, rock becomes dirty and loose and in situ protection deteriorates. Even minor alterations can have a dramatic effect on a route's grade or seriousness. Therefore, it is essential that scramblers and climbers judge the condition of any route for themselves, before they start. The authors, editors, friends and assistants involved in the publication of this guide, the Scottish Mountaineering Club, the Scottish Mountaineering Trust and Scottish Mountaineering Trust (Publications) Ltd, can therefore accept no liability whatever for damage to property, nor for personal injury or death, arising directly or indirectly from the use of this publication.

This guidebook is compiled from the most recent information and experience provided by the author, members of the Scottish Mountaineering Club and other contributors. The book is published by the Scottish Mountaineering Trust, which is a charitable trust. Revenue from the sale of books published by the Trust is used for the continuation of its publishing programme and for charitable purposes associated with Scottish mountains and mountaineering.

Production: Scottish Mountaineering Press
Layouts and typesetting: Noel Williams
Diagram and map graphics: Noel Williams
Printed and bound by Hussar Books
The Maps are derived from Ordnance Survey OpenData™
© Crown copyright and database right 2016

Distributed by Cordee Ltd, 11 Jacknell Road,
Dodwells Bridge Industrial Estate, Hinckley, Leicestershire, LE10 3BS.
(t) 01455 611185   (e) sales@cordee.co.uk   (w) www.cordee.co.uk

CONTENTS

ARDGOUR & ARDNAMURCHAN 104

a) Ardgour 104

Sgòrr Craobh a' Chaorainn 104
  34 Meall na h-Airigh, West Ridge 104
Sgùrr Ghiubhsachain 107
  35 North Ridge 107
Càrn na Nathrach 107
  36 Left Spur 110
  37 Right Spur 110
Sgùrr Dhomhnuill 112
  38 Druim Garbh, Left-hand Slabs 112
Beinn Beag 112
  39 East Face 113
Garbh Bheinn 113
  40 Eagle's Nest Slabs 113
  41 Great Ridge 116
  42 Pinnacle Ridge 119
  43 Sròn Lag nan Gamhna 119
Creach Bheinn 120
  44 Meall a' Bhràghaid, Holly Tree Slabs 120
  45 Coire Mheall Challuim Slabs 123
Beinn Resipol 123
  46 South-West Flank 124

b) Ardnamurchan 124

Creag an Airgid 124
  47 Western Flank 124
Sgùrr nan Gabhar 127
  48 North-East Rib 127
Meall Sanna 127
  49 West Flank 129
Beinn na Seilg 131
  50 Hebrides Rib 131

MULL 132

Beinn Chreagach Mhòr 133
  51 South-West Face 133
Ben More 134
  52 Northern Circuit 134
Ben Buie 135
  53 Sròn Dubh Spur 135
  54 Sròn Dubh Central Slabs 135
  55 Summit Buttress 137

    56 Juniper Buttress 137
Creach-Beinn 139
    57 Loch an Eilein Shoulder 141

CAIRNGORMS 142

a) Loch Avon Basin 143

Garbh Uisge Crag 143
    58 Feld Spur 145
    59 Feith Buidhe Slabs 145
Hell's Lum Crag 147
    60 The Escalator Right-hand 147
Stag Rocks 147
    61 Afterthought Arête 147
    62 Serrated Rib 150
    63 Final Selection 152
Stac an Fharaidh 152
    64 Broad Buttress 152
The Saddle 153
    65 Saddle Slabs 153

b) Northern Corries of Cairn Gorm 153

Stob Coire an t-Sneachda 153
    66 Pygmy Ridge 155
    67 Fingers Ridge 155
Cairn Lochan 158
    68 Fiacaill Ridge 158

c) Northern Làirig Ghrù 158

Lurcher's Crag 158
    69 Collie's Ridge 160
    70 Drystane Ridge 160
    71 Doorway Ridge 162
    72 Ptarmigan Ridge 162
    73 Sweep 165
    74 Summit Buttress 165
    75 Arctic Monkeys Ridge 166
West Side 166
    76 Lairig Ridge 166

d) Gleann Eanaich 169

Sgòr Gaoith 169
    77 Corner Ridge 169

CONTENTS

e) Braeriach & Cairn Toul Massif 171
Braeriach 171
  78 Near East Buttress 171
  79 The Black Pinnacle 173
Sgòr an Lochain Uaine 175
  80 Angel's Ridge 175
Cairn Toul 175
  81 Solitude Rib 175
The Devil's Point 176
  82 Corrour Slabs 176

f) Ben Macdui Massif 178
Carn a' Mhaim 178
  83 Creag Coire na Poite 178
Beinn Macduibh 181
  84 Coire Sputan Dearg, Crystal Ridge 181
  85 Creagan a' Choire Etchachan, Quartzvein Edge 181

g) Eastern Cairngorms 183
Beinn a' Bhùird 183
  86 Dividing Buttress 185
  87 Addition Buttress 185
  88 M & B Buttress 187
Ben Avon 189

LOCHNAGAR & GLEN CLOVA 190

a) Lochnagar Massif 191
Lochnagar 191
  89 Central Buttress 191
  90 Black Spout Left-hand Branch 193
  91 Black Spout Buttress 193
Càrn a' Choire Bhoidheach 195
  92 Stuic Buttress 195

b) Loch Muick Hills 197
Broad Cairn 197
  93 Broad Cairn Slabs 197

c) Glen Clova 199
Craig Mellon 199
  94 Craig Mellon 199

CONTENTS

CREAG MEAGAIDH & BEN ALDER 202

a) Monadhliaths 202
Beinn Sgùrrach 202
  95 North-West Ridge 202

b) The Creag Meagaidh Massif 205
Beinn a' Chaorainn 205
  96 East Ridge 205
Meall Coire Choille-rais 206
  97 East Ridge 206

c) Ardverikie 206
Binnein Shuas 206
  98 Ardverikie Rib 209
Creag a' Chuir 209
  99 Central Buttress 209

d) Geal Chàrn & Ben Alder 211
Geal Chàrn 213
  100 Aisre Cham Streamway 213
  101 Lancet Edge 213
Ben Alder 215
  102 North Buttress 215
  103 Long Leachas 217
  104 Short Leachas 217

NEVIS RANGE & MAMORES 218

a) The Grey Corries 218
Sgùrr Innse 218
  105 South-East Slabs 218
Stob Bàn 221
  106 Giant's Staircase 221

b) The Aonachs 224
Aonach Beag 225
  107 North-East Ridge 225
Aonach Mòr 227
  108 An Cùl Choire Headwall 227
  109 Golden Oldy 229

c) The Ben Nevis Massif 232
Càrn Mòr Dearg 232
  110 Càrn Dearg Mheadhonach, East Ridge 232

CONTENTS

Ben Nevis 232
   111 Castle Ridge 236
   112 Ledge Route 239
   113 Number 4 Gully Buttress 242
   114 South Trident, Upper Arête 244
   115 Creag Coire na Ciste, Central-North Route ... 244
   116 Garadh Buttress 244
   117 Raeburn's Easy Route 246
   118 Tower Ridge 246
   119 Observatory Ridge 251
Meall an t-Suidhe 253
   120 Central South-west Buttress 253
   121 Right-hand South-west Buttress 255
Glen Nevis 255
   122 Surgeon's Rib 255
   123 Scimitar Ridge 257
Meall Cumhann 257
   124 Traverse of Meall Cumhann 258

d) The Mamores 259

Mullach nan Coirean 259
   125 Gendarme Ridge 259
Stob Bàn 262
   126 North Buttress, East Ridge 262
Sgùrr a' Mhaim 265
   127 Ring of Steall 265
Binnein Mòr 269
   128 North-East Ridge 269

GLEN COE 270

a) Glen Coe North 271

Aonach Eagach 271
   129 Aonach Eagach Traverse 271
   130 Clachaig Rib 274
A' Chailleach 275
   131 South Face 275
Beinne a' Chrùlaiste 278
   132 Summit Buttress 278
   133 Split Buttress 278
   134 Pink Rib 281

b) The Buachailles 281

Buachaille Etive Mòr 281
   135 South Buttress 283

136 Chasm to Crowberry Traverse	283
137 D Gully Buttress	284
138 Curved Ridge	284
139 Crowberry Ridge Indirect	287
140 North Buttress	289
141 Great Gully Buttress	289
142 Broad Buttress	291
143 Lagangarbh Buttress	292
144 Creag na Tulaich, North-East Spur	292

Buachaille Etive Beag 294
    145 Stob nan Cabar 297
    146 Creag nan Cabar, North-East Buttress 297

c) Bidean nam Bian Group 298

Stob Coire Sgreamhach 298
    147 Sròn na Lairig 298
    148 Eilde Rib 300

Stob Coire nan Lochan 300
  Geàrr Aonach 303
    149 The Zigzags 303
    150 The Nose 303
  Aonach Dubh, East Face 306
    151 Barn Wall Route 306
    152 Far East Buttress, Right Edge 306
    153 Far East Buttress, Left Edge 308
  Coire nan Lochan 308
    154 Lochan Approach, Left-hand 308
    155 Lochan Approach, Right-hand 310
  North Face 310
    156 Summit Buttress, Left Flank 310
    157 Dorsal Arête 312
  Aonach Dubh, West Face 312
    158 Dinner-time Buttress 312
    159 A Minus Buttress 314
    160 Rhyolite Romp 314
    161 B–D Buttress 316
    162 B–F Buttress 317

Bidean nam Bian 317
    163 Diamond Edge 319

Stob Coire nam Beith 319
    164 Number 1 Buttress 319
    165 Number 3 Buttress 321

CONTENTS 11

APPIN 322
Beinn a' Bheithir 323
  166 Sgòrr Bhan, North-East Ridge 323
  167 Sgòrr Dhonuill, Sgòrr a' Chaolais 323
Beinn Fhionnlaidh 325
  168 South Face 325
  169 North-West Slabs 327
Beinn Sgulaird 330
  170 South-West Slabs 330

ETIVE & BLACK MOUNT 332

a) Glen Etive West 333
Stob an Fhuarain 333
  171 Bealach Fhionnghaill Buttress 333
Beinn Trilleachan 335
  172 Coire Crìche Slabs 335

b) Glen Etive East – The Starav Range 335
Meall Odhar 339
  173 Epiphany Arête 339
Stob Coir' an Albannaich 342
  174 Coire Glas Headwall 342
Beinn nan Aighenan 342
  175 North-East Face 342
Ben Starav 344
  176 Leac nam Fionn 344
  177 Red Man's Rib 345
  178 Slabathon 348

c) The Black Mount 348
Creise 348
  179 Sròn na Creise 350
  180 Inglis Clark Arête 350
  181 Stob a' Ghlais Choire, North-East Spur 352
Stob Ghabhar 352
  182 Aonach Eagach 352
  183 Lochan Buttress 353

d) The Cruachan Range 355
Ben Cruachan 355
  184 Stob Dearg, North Ridge 355
Stob Daimh 357
  185 Stob Garbh, North-East Ridge 357

CONTENTS

SOUTHERN HIGHLANDS 358

a) The Loch Earn Hills 359
Ben Vorlich 359
  186 South Face, Central Rib 359
  187 South Face, Right-hand Rib 361
Stùc a' Chroin 361
  188 North-East Buttress 361

b) The Arrochar Alps 363
The Cobbler 363
  189 South–North Traverse 363
Beinn Narnain 369
  190 Spearhead Arête 369
  191 Restricted Crack 371

c) Colonsay & Islay 372
Colonsay 372
  192 Beinn nan Caorach West Ridge 372
Islay 373
  193 Dun Athad 373

ARRAN 374

a) The Rosa & Sannox Hills 375
Caisteal Abhail 375
  194 Ceum na Caillich 375
  195 Little Broomstick Ridge 378
Goatfell 379
  196 Cioch na h-Oighe 379
  197 Bonus 380
  198 North Goatfell, West Ridge 380
  199 Am Binnein, South Face 383
  200 Coire nam Meann Slabs 383
Cir Mhòr 385
  201 Cubic Ridge Indirect 385
  202 Cubic Gully Spur 385
  203 Prospero's Prelude/Old East 388
  204 Lower South-East Slabs 389
  205 East Shoulder 389
A' Chir 391
  206 Boundary Ridge 391
  207 A' Chir Ridge Traverse 394

b) Pirnmill Hills 397
Mullach Buidhe 397
  208 North-West Ridge 397

CENTRAL LOWLANDS & SOUTHERN UPLANDS 398

a) Central Lowlands 399

b) The Galloway Hills 399
Milldown 400
  209 North-East Spur 400
Mullwharchar 400
  210 Tauchers Couloir 400
Dungeon Hill 401
  211 East Shoulder 401
Craignaw 403
  212 North-West Slabs 403
  213 North-East Shoulder 406
  214 Dow Spout 406
  215 Snibe Hill Rib 409

c) Other Southern Uplands Routes 409
Glenwhargan Craig 411
  216 Glenwhargan Craig 411

Index 412

List of SMC Publications 416

MAPS & DIAGRAMS

The Scottish Terranes - Map	21
Rùm - Map	54
Barkeval, South Face	56
Askival, North Ridge	62
Trollabhal, South Face	65
Ainshval, North-East Face	69
Ainshval, North-West Face	69
Sgùrr nan Gillean	73
Knoydart - Map	76
Beinn na Caillich, South-East Face	78
Ladhar Bheinn, Western Flank	80
An Caisteal	84
Meall nan Eun, West Face	86
Beinn an Aodainn (Ben Aden), South Face	89
Garbh Chìoch Beag, North Face	91
Sgùrr an Eilein Ghiubhais, North Face	94
Sgùrr an Ursainn, West Top, North Flank	96
Loch Lochy Hills - Map	99
Meall Dubh, South-East Face	101
Loch Shiel Hills - Map	105
Meall na h-Airigh, Sgòrr Choinnich, West Ridge	106
Ardgour - Map	108
Càrn na Nathrach, South Flank	109
Druim Garbh, North Flank	111
Garbh Bheinn	114
Garbh Bheinn, Great Ridge	117
Meall a' Bhràghaid, North Flank	121
Ardnamurchan - Map	125
Mull - Map	132
Ben Buie, North Flank	136
Ben Buie, East Face	138
Creach-Beinn, North-West	140
Cairngorms - Map	142
Loch Avon & Northern Corries - Map	144
Head of Loch Avon, Garbh Uisge Crag	146
Stag Rocks	148
Stag Rocks, Final Selection	151
Stob Coire an t-Sneachda	154
Lurcher's Crag, Southern Section	159

MAPS & DIAGRAMS   15

Lurcher's Crag, Northern Section	161
Sgòr Gaoith, East Face	168
Braeriach, Coire Bhrocain	172
The Devil's Point, Corrour Slabs	177
Beinn Macduibh, Coire Sputan Dearg	179
Creagan a' Choire Etchachan, Far Left-hand End	182

Beinn a' Bhùird & Ben Avon - Map   183
Beinn a' Bhuird, Coire an Dubh-lochain   186
Beinn a' Bhuird, Garbh Choire   188

Lochnagar - Map   190
Lochnagar   192
Craig Mellon, South Face   200

Creag Meagaidh & Ardverikie - Map   204
Binnein Shuas, North-East Face   207
Creag a' Chuir, West Face   210

Ben Alder - Map   212
Ben Alder, North Buttress   216

Grey Corries - Map   219
Sgùrr Innse, South-East Face   220
Stob Bàn, Grey Corries   222

The Aonachs - Map   224
Aonach Beag, North-East Ridge   226
An Cùl Choire Headwall   228
Aonach Mòr, West Face   230

Ben Nevis - Map   233
Ben Nevis, North-East Face   234 & 235

Ben Nevis (North Face) - Map   236
Càrn Dearg, Ledge Route   240
Number 4 Gully   243
Tower Ridge, West Flank   245
Observatory Gully   247
Tower Ridge, The Great Tower & Tower Gap   249
Meall an t-Suidhe   254

Meall Cumhann - Map   258

The Mamores - Map   260
Stob Bàn, North Buttress   263
Glen Nevis, Ring of Steall   266

Glen Coe - Map   270
A' Chailleach, South Face   276
Stob Beinne a' Chrùlaiste   279
Buachaille Etive Mòr, South-East Face   282

MAPS & DIAGRAMS

Buachaille Etive Mòr, North-East Face	285
Crowberry Ridge Indirect	288
Buachaille Etive Mòr, North Face	290
Buachaille Etive Beag	295
Lairig Eilde (Beinn Fhada)	299
Geàrr Aonach, North-East Face	301
Aonach Dubh, East Face	304
Stob Coire nan Lochan	309
Aonach Dubh, West Face	313
Aonach Dubh, North Face	315
Stob Coire nam Beith, North Face	320

Appin - Map 322
  Beinn Fhionnlaidh 326
  Beinn Sgulaird, Coire nan Capull 329

Etive & Blackmount - Map 332
  Stob an Fhuarain, East Ridge (Bealach Fhionnghaill) 334
  Beinn Trilleachan, Coire Crìche 336
  Meall Odhar, South Face 338
  Stob Coir' an Albannaich, Coire Glas Headwall 340
  Beinn nan Aighenan, North-East Face 343
  Stob an Duine Ruaidh, South Face 346
  Creise 349
  Stob Ghabhar, Coirein Lòchain 354

Ben Cruachan - Map 356

Ben Vorlich & Stùc a' Chroin - Map 358
  Ben Vorlich, South Face 360

Arrochar - Map 364
  The Cobbler, East Face 365
  The Cobbler, South Peak 367
  The Cobbler, Centre Peak 368
  Beinn Narnain, Spearhead Arête 370

Arran, North-East - Map 374
  Caisteal Abhail, Far East Top (Ceum na Caillich) 376
  Goatfell, Coire nam Meann 384
  Cir Mhòr, South Face 386
  Cir Mhòr, East Flank 390
  A' Chir, Boundary Ridge 392
  A' Chir Ridge Traverse, Le Mauvais Pas 395

Galloway Hills - Map 398
  Craignaw & Dungeon Hill 402
  Craignaw, North-West Slabs 404
  Snibe Hill, Point of the Snibe 408
  Glenwhargan Craig 410

ACKNOWLEDGEMENTS

This guide includes many of the country's best known scrambles, so around two thirds of these routes have been described before in various places, notably the SMC District and Climbing Guides. Some are also featured in previous guides by Noel Williams, Andrew Dempster or Dan Bailey, or are mentioned on the UKClimbing website. That the other third are unrecorded doesn't of course mean that they've not been done before. Some have traces of passage in many places. My thanks are due to my predecessors, known and unknown.

Most of these unrecorded routes have been selected by the simple expedient of walking past them and thinking 'that looks good' – an approach which has inevitably led to the occasional minor epic. Even in compact well-travelled areas such as Glen Coe or Arran there are still acres of exploratory scrambling available and this is even more the case in areas such as Ardgour or the Cairngorms. Many possibilities still await the adventurous and I hope they get as much enjoyment out of them as I have from those included here.

My thanks especially go to Noel Williams for doing the desktop publishing work, for technical advice, helpful suggestions and writing the geology and mountaineering history sections; and to Gordon Rothero for writing the wildlife section.

Thanks for company on the routes and for posing for photographs go to Paul Buchanan, Marco de Man, Paddy Earle, Nicky Gear, Jamie Hageman, the late Ben Lowe, Joanne Schwartz, Nate and Melissa Webb, Lucy Williams and Noel Williams.

Thanks for supplying photos go to Nick Bramhall, Paul Buchanan, Andrew Gifford, Jamie Hageman, Colin Moody, Scott Muir, Andy Nisbet, Tom Prentice, Peter Smith, Eric Taylor, Nate Webb, Robin Wallace, Noel Williams and Kevin Woods.

Suggestions for places to go (and sometimes to avoid) came from Alison Coull, Paddy Earle, Ben Lowe, Andy Nisbet, Tom Prentice, Stephen Reid, Nate Webb, Noel Williams and Bill Wright. Lastly my apologies to anyone I have inadvertently omitted.

'Crowberry Tower' by Jamie Hageman

INTRODUCTION

This guide covers a high proportion of the hill country of Scotland, with a huge variety of terrain, from the gabbro ridges of Rum to the spacious corrie faces of the Cairngorms and from the Alpine scale of the North Face of Ben Nevis to the knobbly peaklets of Ardnamurchan. Most of the routes can be done in a day but there are quite a few, in Knoydart and around Ben Alder for instance, where a longer trip will be preferred by all bar the ultra-fit. At the other extreme there are routes in Glen Coe and Glen Nevis that can easily be fitted into an evening – one only five minutes from the door of a well known climbers pub. The vast majority, however, are mountain routes with all that implies in the way of weather conditions, the possibility of some loose rock and the need to be able to navigate safely and competently. It is essential that anyone doing these routes carries and can use a map and compass.

Whether to use a rope comes down to personal choice. If there are inexperienced or nervous members of the party then a rope should certainly be carried, and the ability to abseil might well be useful in case of retreat (carrying a sling and a karabiner could well be invaluable). A few routes have a short pitch much harder than the rest of the route (The North-East Ridge of Aonach Beag or the traverse of A' Chir for instance), and the use of a rope may allow less confident scramblers to complete these.

Most types of scrambling are represented here; there are towering buttresses, narrow ridges, huge slabs and tumbling streams. Some routes find the easiest way up a big face, others look for difficulty on outcrop-scattered hillsides. In some places, particularly on the south side of Glen Coe, routes naturally link together to form the scrambling equivalent of a day's cragging. Descents have not usually been described, as virtually all the scrambles here finish on summits or hillsides from which there is an easy way off. This may be rough or pathless and it may be quite a long way, but the skills brought into play are those of navigation and map reading rather than scrambling.

The remoteness of some routes gives them an added seriousness, especially in the event of an accident or drastic change in the weather (not an unknown occurrence in these parts). Some routes involve river crossings which can be tricky or impossible in bad conditions, while in some places snow may linger as late as July or arrive quite early in October. On the other hand the sheer size of the area means that at any given time weather conditions vary across the region, so it should be possible to find good conditions somewhere. It should always be remembered, however, that **ALL SCRAMBLING IS POTENTIALLY DANGEROUS – MOVING UNROPED IN EXPOSED SITUATIONS CALLS FOR EXTREME CARE AND SHOULD NOT BE TAKEN LIGHTLY**. Even the easier routes can take you into impressive and committing positions. Allow a wide margin for error and always be prepared to retreat or traverse off if necessary. However, don't lose sight of the fact that scrambling should be fun!

Iain Thow
April 2017

GEOLOGY

This guide covers a large part of Scotland and so what follows is effectively a potted geology of the whole country. The routes described are situated on a wide variety of rocks which each have their own distinctive characteristics. This account can only give an outline of the main events behind how these rocks were formed, but it involves three main themes of i) folding, ii) fire and iii) ice.

The bedrock of which Scotland is formed is made up of five different blocks of the Earth's crust which geologists call terranes – see the diagram opposite. These terranes are bounded by major faults and thrusts, along which significant movement took place in the distant past. The classic example is the Great Glen fault which runs right across the Highlands from Fort William to Inverness. This separates the Grampian Terrane and the Northern Highlands Terrane. These two blocks of crust were at one time widely separated, but sideways movement along the fault some 400 million years ago brought the Northern Highlands Terrane several 100s of kilometres southwestwards relative to the Grampian Terrane.

This simple classification is further complicated by major episodes of igneous activity which caused new rocks to be intruded into the existing bedrock of each terrane. Three noteworthy episodes of igneous activity are worth highlighting. During these episodes volcanic activity caused lavas to be erupted at the surface and granite and other igneous rocks to be formed within the crust. The first of these occurred about 420–410 million years ago, shortly after the main phase of plate collisions that had created the mighty Caledonian Mountain Chain. This is when the lavas in Glen Coe and Ben Nevis were formed as well as the granites of the Cairngorms, Ben Nevis, Aonach Mòr and Ben Starav. The second major episode occurred a little bit later (about 300 million years ago) during the Permian–Carboniferous) when there was much igneous activity particularly in the Midland Valley Terrane. This is when the volcanic plugs we see today beneath Stirling and Edinburgh Castles were formed. The third episode occurred much later in the Palaeogene (60 million years ago), immediately prior to the opening of the North Atlantic, when Greenland was still joined to Europe. This is when the various igneous centres on Skye, Rum, Ardnamurchan, Mull and Arran were active.

These terranes are thought to have settled into their current relative positions by early Devonian times about 400 million years ago. Since then, as well as new igneous rocks being formed, new sedimentary rocks have been laid down on top of the older bedrock. These include deposits such as Jurassic shales which contain not only marine fossils, but also dinosaur remains.

Hebridean Terrane

This terrane has the oldest rocks in Scotland. It has a basement of extremely old metamorphic rocks, which are commonly referred to as Lewisian gneiss.

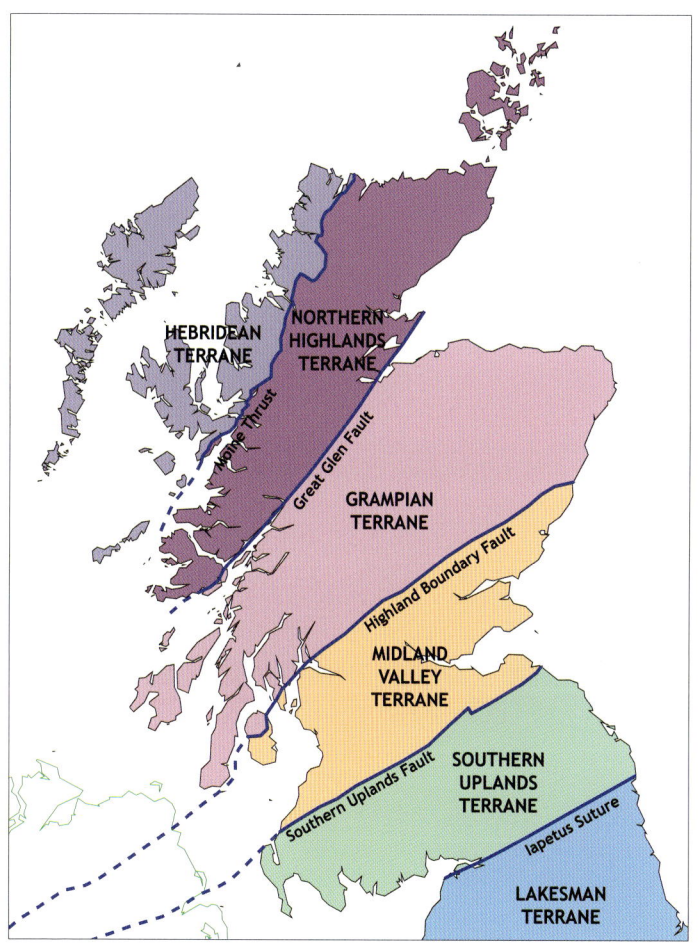

The Scottish Terranes

After the basement rocks were metamorphosed, this terrane was not involved in the later Caledonian mountain building events so the overlying Torridonian rocks, although very old (1000 million years), are still sedimentary in character. The island of Rùm is the only area in the guide representative of this terrane. Red Torridonian sandstone outcrops over large areas in the northern part of Rùm, although all the scrambling on the island is on the much younger (Palaeogene) igneous rocks.

A remarkable feature of the main Rum igneous centre is the layered intrusions of alternating gabbro and peridotite. One of the largest breeding colonies of Manx shearwaters in the world, takes advantage of the softer peridotite layers to create burrows for their nests on the upper slopes of Askival, Hallival and Trollabhal. Nearby Barkeval is largely built of peridotite, which the geologist Harker described in an early SMC Journal (1909) as

> '... the most considerable development of this rock in Britain; and its great toughness and hardness, coupled with the extremely rough surface of the rusty-looking slopes, makes this perhaps the best rock in the world for climbing.'

'Perhaps the best rock in the world for climbing.'

Narnia Arête, Barkeval.

Northern Highlands Terrane

The Northern Highlands Terrane is comprised largely of rocks belonging to the Moine Supergroup. These metasedimentary rocks were originally deposited as coastal marine sediments at about the same time as Torridonian sediments were being deposited by rivers on land now forming the Hebridean Terrane. The sediments are thought to have been deposited in a rift system which developed in an early supercontinent called Rhodinia, prior to its break up.

They were later caught up in several mountain building events which changed the original sandstones and siltstones into metamorphic rocks called psammites and pelites respectively. The original layers were squeezed and folded and great slices of crust were thrust up and over each other onto the rocks of the Hebridean Terrane along what is called the Moine Thrust zone.

The Moine rocks are generally less varied than the Dalradian metamorphic rocks in the neighbouring Grampian Terrane to the south-east. They are sometimes referred to as the 'monotonous Moine' being largely made up of psammites of very similar appearance. The rocks were intruded in places by granitic gneiss as well as numerous pegmatite veins and later granite plutons. Some of the rocks only partially melted and formed a rock called migmatite.

The rocks of Knoydart and Ardgour belong to this terrane. Most of the best scrambles in these two areas are found on psammitic rocks, although there are also some fine outings on the gneiss of Garbh Bheinn for example.

Also found in this terrane are the scrambles on Ardnamurchan and Mull. These are on much younger igneous rocks which were formed during the dramatic episode of volcanic activity which occurred down the west coast of Scotland some 60–55 million years ago. The volcano on Mull is estimated to have been some 2000m high. Vast quantities of lava were erupted from this volcanic centre and much of it spilled over onto what is now Morvern. Molten material also erupted from great vertical fissures which developed in the Earth's crust and extended huge distances from Mull right across southern Scotland to the North Sea coast of England. When the molten material in these fissures cooled it formed narrow elongate features called dykes. A good example known as the Wishing Stone, can be seen near Fuinary, west of Lochaline.

The lavas erupted onto a land surface covered in vegetation. On the west coast of Mull there is a remarkable fossil tree preserved within the lava. The original pine tree was at least 15m high and had roots which were sufficiently strong for it to remain in position when the lava flowed around it. The wood was turned to charcoal by the great heat of the magma. Much of this charcoal has eroded away, but early visitors were still able to collect it from the site.

Some of the magma remained within the crust and cooled to form large bodies of gabbro. Although the crags of this rock in Ardnamurchan are quite small, the quality of the rock is exceptional. Much of Mull is built of lavas which in contrast are not so good to climb on. However, there are also outcrops of gabbro on Beinn Buidhe which make enjoyable scrambles.

Grampian Terrane

The large area of the Highlands between the Great Glen and the Highland Boundary Fault is known as the Grampian Terrane. Most of the bedrock in this area belongs to what is known as the Dalradian Supergroup. This is a varied group of metasedimentary rocks which were deposited as marine sediments around 700 million years ago, sometime later than the Moine sediments. They are thought to have been deposited in a basin on the northwestern side of the Iapetus Ocean which in late Precambrian times separated Laurentia from Baltica and Gondwana.

Later in the Ordovician (about 470–460 million years ago) these sediments were strongly folded and metamorphosed when the Caledonian Mountain Chain was formed. This great chain extended from Svalbard, across Norway and Eastern Greenland to Ireland, Newfoundland and the Appalachian Mountains of Eastern America. The Iapetus Ocean it thought to have finally closed in the Silurian (some 425 million years ago). This in when the rocks of Laurentia (Scotland, Northern Ireland, Greenland and North America) finally fused with the rocks of Avalonia (England, Wales and Southern Ireland).

Most of the rocks in the Highlands were metamorphosed at a depth of some 20km or more. Subsequent erosion over more than 400 million years has removed all the overlying rocks. The remaining rocks we see today in the Highlands represent the eroded root of the Caledonian Mountains.

The original Dalradian sediments were more varied than the Moine. They included not only siltstones and sandstones, but also limestones, fine-grained mudstones and clean quartz sandstones called quartzites. A feature known as cross bedding in the quartzites has been used to work out the orientation

Spectacular folding in Dalradian quartzite, Stob Coire Easain, Grey Corries.

of the beds. Many of the rock units in the Mamores, for example, have been shown to be turned completely upside down.

Soon after Avalonia 'docked' with Laurentia there was a significant amount of igneous activity in the Grampian Terrane. Glen Coe in particular was the site of a spectacular caldera volcano. A smaller caldera volcano also occurred in the Ben Nevis area. Numerous large bodies of granite were intruded across the Highlands, including the Cairngorms, Ben Nevis, Rannoch Moor, and Ben Starav. Also included in this terrane are the granite hills of Arran, though these are of much younger Palaeogene age.

The largest proportion of the routes in this guide belong to this terrane. Scrambles can be found on all the main rock types ranging from metamorphic quartzites and schists to the older granites of the Cairngorms and Ben Starav as well as the younger granite of Arran.

Midland Valley Terrane

This terrane is made up of a series of smaller faulted terranes. Although it has an older basement, most of the rocks at the surface are of Devonian to Permian age (400–280 Ma). They include various sedimentary rocks such as coal measures and numerous examples of igneous rocks including, lavas, sills and volcanic necks. Few good scrambles are to be found here, although fun can be had on the volcanic rocks of Arthur's Seat.

Southern Uplands Terrane

The most southerly of the Scottish terranes is built largely of marine sediments of Ordovician and Silurian age. These include turbidites and mudstones as well as chert and pillow lavas. They were laid down in a spreading oceanic environment. Although they were deposited at about the same time as the Caledonian Mountains were being formed, they were not involved in mountain building and so were not metamorphosed. Then, some 400 million years ago, three large granite intrusions were formed in the Loch Doon, Cairnsmore of Fleet and Criffel-Dalbeattie areas. Most of the best scrambles in Galloway are on the first of these granite intrusions.

Glaciation

The final sculpting of the hills took place during the repeated glaciations of the last 2 million years. When glaciation was at its maximum all the mountain summits were covered in ice including Ben Nevis. In the very last minor glaciation around 12,000 years ago an ice cap built up mainly over the western Highlands. The major summits stuck out above the ice as nunataks. Freeze-thaw action on the exposed rocks created extensive areas of blockfield, notably on Ben Nevis.

When the ice melted the land started to rise up again after being depressed by its burden of ice. Raised beaches can be seen today in many places around the west coast with fine examples on the isle of Arran for example.

LANDSCAPE HISTORY

This guide covers a good two-thirds of Scotland, so a human history of its area would be a history of the entire country, of which there are already many excellent examples available. However, some sense of how the landscape has changed since the arrival of humans may add a perspective to a day on the hill, so a brief introduction is included here.

Scotland was free of permanent ice by around 11,500 BP and became covered in a tundra vegetation of mosses and dwarf shrubs, not dissimilar to that on the higher tops today. Gradually birch scrub worked its way up from the valleys, followed by other species such as pine, hazel and alder. About 7000 years ago the forest was at its most extensive, with a tree line at about 600m in the east, lowering to around 300m in the far west. By this time people had certainly arrived in the Highlands, mostly following the coast northwards feasting off seafood, and their middens still survive in places such as Oronsay and in caves on the NW coast of Jura. Probably some also hunted reindeer further inland, but the numbers would have been tiny and they have left no trace. It's estimated that the Mesolithic population of the whole of Britain was under 5000.

The small numbers meant that Mesolithic man's impact on the landscape was insignificant, but once stone tools became commonplace and people started to grow crops rather than just gathering wild fruit then numbers increased, more land needed to be cleared for fields and fuel and the wildwood started to be felled. Forest cover declined markedly between 6000 and 4500 years ago, as settled agriculture got going, and the first peat development also dates from around this time, as temperatures fell and the climate became wetter. To what extent felling the trees caused the fall in temperatures as against the fall in temperatures producing scantier tree cover is debated, with probably both processes operating. The main period of peat growth on the tops was rather later, around 3000 years ago, and this too has provoked suggestions that felling of the forest was a factor. Certainly there was a climatic deterioration at the time, but some blame the introduction of iron axes, which were both more efficient and much more widespread than the previous bronze ones as the ore was much commoner. Some of the more remote parts of the area remained forested throughout mediaeval times – Viking sagas report the locals taking refuge in the forests, for instance, but by then most of the Caledonian Forest was long gone.

In Iron Age times travel was much easier by sea than by land and this remained true until relatively recently, especially on the indented west coast. Few roads penetrated the hill country until the military incursions of the 18th century and the settlement pattern hugged the coast as a result – as indeed it still does. The big cultural influences were all sea-borne, the Celtic monks coming across from Ireland in the 6th and 7th Centuries, the Vikings raiding and settling down from Norway in the 9th and 10th and the dominance of the Lordship of the Isles from the 11th to 15th, all of which had a huge

LANDSCAPE HISTORY   27

Machrie Moor on the west side of Arran is rich in remains from the Neolithic and Bronze Ages between 5,500 and 3000 years ago.

Six separate stone circles can be identified. This photograph shows some of the impressive sandstone pillars in circle two.

Photo: Noel Williams

impact on the area. The place names still reflect these movements, along with an underlay of Pictish (which was related to Welsh) in the East, traces of Old Welsh in the South-west and more modern English additions.

Throughout this time the hills were used for hunting and for pasturing cattle in the summer, and the clusters of shielings where people lived while looking after the latter are seen in many of the upper glens (the path up Meall nan Tarmachan passes a good example). In the autumn the cattle were driven southwards to markets at Crieff and later Falkirk. The 'drove roads' that they followed were lines of travel rather than built features, with the only real trace visible today being the heavily grazed areas around the overnight stances. One of the few exceptions is Comyn's Road linking Blair Atholl and Ruthven, constructed in the 13th Century, parts of which can still be traced at 800m on Sròn a' Chleirich in the Forest of Atholl.

The first paved roads into the Highlands were built by the army under Generals Wade and Caulfeild from 1730 onwards to allow easy movement of troops to fight the Jacobites. These included routes from the south to Braemar and Speyside, with a link across the Lecht, the road across the Corrieyairack and the predecessor of the modern A82 via Glen Coe and Fort

William to Inverness. Ironically the first users were the Jacobites themselves in their rapid march to Edinburgh. After Culloden the military carried on building more roads until the job was taken over by public engineers such as Thomas Telford.

One of the results of both the easier access and the forfeiture of estates after the failure of the '45 was the exploitation of much of the remaining native woodland, particularly felling for charcoal to feed iron smelters such as Bonawe on Loch Etive (which at its peak consumed an acre of woodland per day). Commercial mining also took off around this time, the lead mines around Tyndrum and Strontian for example. On a smaller scale the search for the semi-precious stones known as cairngorms took adventurous locals into the wilder recesses of the eponymous range, and it is probable that some of the scrambles described here were first done by these crystal hunters.

In the late 18th and early 19th centuries the replacement of the cattle economy by a sheep one resulted in the removal of most of the population, the notorious Clearances. Initially many people left voluntarily, often in large groups, mostly to cheap or free land in the American Carolinas, then after the introduction of Cheviot sheep in 1792 (which had a fleece underlayer that the native breeds lacked, enabling them to stay out all winter) whole glens were cleared of people, usually by the clan chiefs they had followed for generations. Obviously this made the hills less frequented, but it also had a marked effect on the hill vegetation, with shorter cropped grasses replacing the coarser tussock grass.

Within a few decades a combination of overgrazing and the invention of refrigeration (which allowed the huge sheep farms in Australia to supply European cities) meant that raising sheep became uneconomic and a shift to keeping deer for shooting began. This radically accelerated once Queen Victoria bought Balmoral and a deer forest became the 'must have' status symbol for those made wealthy by industrial growth. Not entirely coincidentally the Highlands became much easier to get to from the south around this time, a classic example being the rail line to Ballater from Aberdeen, built to ease Queen Victoria's access to Balmoral. By 1848 railways had reached Perth and by 1894 trains ran to Inverness and Fort William, while steamships ran up the west coast to places such as Mallaig and the head of Loch Etive by 1847. These brought in the first tourists, mainly the wealthy arriving for shooting, but also a select few climbing the hills for their own sake. Numbers were still small and would remain so until after World War II.

During the middle decades of the 20th Century much of the Highland landscape was transformed by the twin developments of large scale forestry and hydro electricity. A shortage of timber during the First World War led to the formation of the Forestry Commission and over a million hectares of Scotland were densely planted, largely with sitka spruce. This led to repopulation in some areas, Cowal and Morvern for instance, but made the hills harder to access through the trees. The removal of the sheep radically changed the vegetation on the upper slopes too, Galloway in particular seeing a change from short cropped grass to coarser tussock grass in many places. After World War II many of the larger lochs were dammed and linked by tunnels, as Hydro schemes brought electricity to the glens for the first time. From a hillgoer's perspective this made areas such as the head of Loch Quoich much harder to reach, but also provided useful access roads in other places.

The Victorian mountaineers found isolated cottages still inhabited in most of the glens and were often able to obtain accommodation in them. The vast majority of these were abandoned during the first half of the 20th Century, leaving the hills at their emptiest for millennia. Visitor numbers increased during the 1930s as the onset of mass unemployment led to people seeking cheap ways of using their spare time and clubs such as the Creagh Dhu, Ptarmigan and Lomond were formed. Many of the abandoned cottages were used as free accommodation and the bothying tradition developed. The big jump in numbers came later, however, as the huge growth in car ownership and the building of motorways during the 1960s and '70s made the hills much more accessible to people in the big cities. Since then most well known hills have developed defined paths, particularly those over the magic figure of 3000ft, and in places path maintenance has been deemed necessary. Many argue that this has gone too far in places with built routes high on the Cairngorm plateau, for example.

Estimating the number of people on the hills is a fraught business, but it is estimated that Ben Nevis gets around 120,000 visitors annually, around 80% going to the summit. The number of Munro completions registered with SMC gives a rough guide to the growth, with 2000 by 1970, 3300 by the turn of the millennium and over 6000 by 2015.

One factor which has made a huge impact since the 1960s, in both visual and economic terms, is the growth in downhill skiing. The growth of Aviemore and the easing of access to the Northern Cairngorms produced by the road into Coire Cas is the most obvious example, but the Glenshee, Lecht, Glencoe Mountain and Nevis Range schemes all bring in large numbers of people, with the last named being particularly useful to scramblers heading for Aonach Mor and Aonach Beag.

In the last decade the two most obvious changes have been the construction of wind farms and their associated access roads and the felling of much of the sitka spruce planting of the 1960s and '70s, usually with the aim of replacing it with native woodland. The rockier hills of interest to scramblers are generally less suitable for wind turbines, but the changes in forestry practice are very noticeable in areas such as Ardgour and Galloway.

Despite all the human influence though, the Highlands remain a wild place, even if not a wilderness. There are many places where you are unlikely to meet another person and at times it is hard to believe yourself sharing a smallish island with over 60 million people. They may only be tiny by world standards, but the Scottish hills carry an impact out of all proportion to their scale.

WILDLIFE

This chapter gives an introduction to the varied plant and animal life which you might encounter whilst tackling these scrambles in the southern half of Scotland. Because the scrambles are widely spread across such a large area, it is not possible to give a detailed guide to each locality – so this is more of a general introduction to the mountainous parts. Also, the rocks most suitable for scrambling tend to be hard and stable, which makes them less conducive to plant growth than softer, more friable rocks. So, whilst a limited range of plant species will be encountered on the routes themselves, the approach to and descent from the scrambles offers a greater opportunity to observe some of the diverse plant and animal life for which the Scottish mountains are famous. The books listed under 'further reading' should be consulted for more detail on individual localities.

Different plant species are variously equipped to cope with the challenges of geology, climate and topography. The nature of the vegetation found at any particular place depends on the chemical composition and physical characteristics of the substrate, degree of exposure to wind, annual rainfall, duration of snow-lie and also the land management history. Biogeography also plays a part, with some common mainland species being completely absent from the islands. We will start at sea level and work upwards through the major habitat types.

Coasts

In the west of Scotland the coast is never far away, and sea views add greatly to the enjoyment of a day on the hill, particularly on the islands and in Ardnamurchan. Several plants of coastal habitats – thrift (or sea-pink), sea plantain, scurvy grass and sea campion, are also found in the mountains. Conversely, because of the severity of the coastal climate, some mountain plants, like the yellow and purple saxifrages, descend to sea level in the west.

The bird-cliffs of the north-west mainland are largely absent from the south but seabirds and particularly gulls are never far away, even far inland. On Rum, the tops of some of the hills provide the nesting sites for a large population of Manx Shearwaters. These birds spend most of their lives at sea, only making landfall to breed in burrows amongst the rocks. A night visit to the top of Askival as these birds fly in making their weird calls, is quite an experience. The coasts of Rum and Mull are also good places to see sea eagles, and peregrine falcons also exploit the nesting season bounty, hunting along the cliffs to feed their own broods. The sheltered sea-lochs along rocky coastlines from Arran to Rum, with their thick fringe of brown sea-weeds, small salt-marshes and yellow iris beds, provide ideal habitat for otters. Further offshore, you may be lucky enough to spot a basking shark, a minke whale or pod of bottle-nosed dolphins, but harbour porpoises or seals (grey or common) are more likely.

Left: Common Blue. *Right: Sundew.*

The buzzard is the commonest large bird of prey at lower altitudes and any 'eagle' perched on a fence post or telegraph pole is a buzzard! This bird has increased in numbers and range with lower levels of persecution but the fact that it is not a fussy eater, preying on anything from beetles to rabbits, also plays a part. Another common bird of agricultural and moorland landscapes is the crow and our area straddles the boundary between the southern carrion crow and the 'two-tone' version, the hooded ('hoodie') crow of the north. South of this dividing line, which roughly follows the Highland Boundary Fault, the magpie is common but is almost absent further north. Further inland, waders such as lapwing, curlew, oystercatcher, and redshank nest in pastures and arable fields in the cultivated glens, but retreat to the coast in winter. The short, steep river systems of the western seaboard are generally low in nutrients and support species, such as the freshwater pearl mussel and dipper, which require clear, sediment-free water, as do the commercially-important populations of Atlantic salmon and sea trout.

Woodland

Native woodlands are an important backdrop to many of the mountains in this guide. In the west, the broadleaf woodlands of oak and birch and the dense coastal hazel woods are remarkable for their profusion of non-flowering plants – lichens, mosses, liverworts and filmy ferns, which often festoon trees and rocks. These plants depend upon the level of humidity maintained by the woodland canopy but flourish best where it rains on more than 200 days per year, so you have been warned. This 'Celtic rain-forest' is an internationally important habitat with numerous lower plants that are very rare in Europe and some are globally rare. Typical birds of these woods are the redstart and wood warbler although today you are more likely to see an introduced pheasant. The Scots pine woodlands in the drier Cairngorms have a different character but are still very mossy; however plant interest here centres on the special flowering plants like juniper, creeping ladies tresses, the wintergreens and the elusive twinflower. The iconic birds of the pinewoods are the crested tit, the Scottish crossbill and the capercaillie, the threatened 'turkey of the woods'.

In the woodlands roe deer are widespread but wary, most often seen as a white rump bouncing away into the undergrowth, accompanied by a gruff bark of alarm. Many of the woodlands in the area have red squirrels and there is a very active campaign to enhance and expand these populations. Recent years have seen a significant expansion in the range and numbers of the pine marten in the south but sightings are rare, as they are of the more numerous stoats and weasels.

Bogs

The combination of high rainfall and acidic rocks makes western Scotland ideal for the growth of bogs, and the approach to many of the scrambles will involve a somewhat soggy walk-in. The colourful Sphagnum mosses which carpet the bog surface are also essential to its formation. Their growing-point is at the top, and as the lower parts die, the acidic water which they hold prevents decomposition, and the build-up forms peat, even on quite steep slopes. In these mires, familiar plants such as heather and deer-grass grow with bog specialists which are well adapted to the nutrient-poor, acidic and wet conditions. The carnivorous sundews and butterworts, which trap insects on their rosettes of sticky leaves, are found on bare peat and along the margins of pools and lochans. Unfortunately, the combined efforts of all these carnivorous plants still fail to make much of a dent in the midge population! In open water, bog bean and bottle sedge are 'emergent' plants – rooting on the loch floor but with leaves and flowers above the surface.

The hummock and pool mires provide an excellent habitat for damselflies and dragonflies, the large golden-banded dragonfly being the most spectacular. The greenshank is a rarity of the larger mire areas but the snipe and golden plover are more widespread, the latter inhabiting drier moorlands and mountain tops as well as the bogs. Both species winter in coastal habitats. Red-throated divers nest on islands in the smaller peatland lochans, whereas their black-throated cousins prefer larger lochs. Some of the lochs are home to the Arctic charr, a non-migratory member of the salmon family and Loch Lomond and Loch Eck have the Powan, a freshwater whitefish.

Wet Heaths

Intermediate between bog and moorland, wet heaths cover extensive areas in the west. Sphagnum mosses are still present, but occupy a smaller proportion of the surface. Heather and cross-leaved heath are the dominant dwarf shrubs, accompanied by deer-grass, common cottongrass, the yellow bog asphodel and the pink lousewort but this is a very species-poor habitat. Purple moor grass is also very common and walking through areas where the tussocks of this plant are dominant is not much fun. The aromatic bog myrtle prefers to grow where there is lateral water movement through the peat and is also worth avoiding if possible if your feet are still dry.

Moorlands

Where drainage is better and peat thinner, drier moorlands dominated by heather, blaeberry (bilberry) and bell-heather are found. Beneath the taller shrubs creep stems of tormentil, with its yellow flower with four petals, heath bedstraw, with clusters of tiny white flowers and the tiny trumpets of heath milkwort which can be white, blue or purple. Smaller evergreen shrubs such as the confusingly-named crowberry, cowberry and bearberry occur more sporadically. Under leggy heather, the tiny lesser twayblade orchid, with its paired leaves, may be found but more conspicuous flowers include the spikes of the common spotted orchid, which can occur in a range of colours from almost pure white to dark blotched purple and, later in summer, the pale blue devil's-bit scabious.

Red deer range over most of the moorlands in the highland part of our area, and deer stalking is an important part of the local economy. Rum and

Left: Moss Campion. *Right: Deer Ked (Glen Scaddle).*

Feral Goat (Rùm)

some other hills are renowned for their populations of feral goats. These shaggy beasts are the descendants of domestic goats allowed to run free in centuries past. Their exact antiquity is disputed. Of the smaller animals, mountain hare, common lizard, common frog, adder, and slow worm can be found on the mainland moors, although some are absent from the islands. The commonest moorland bird is the meadow pipit, and its nest, concealed in tussocky grassland is a favourite target of the cuckoo. The white rump of the wheatear is another familiar sight, flitting amongst the rocks with its characteristic call, like two stones knocked together. These small songbirds provide food for the merlin, our smallest moorland bird of prey. The hen harrier, which prefers lower, rolling moorlands, also takes larger prey items and is not popular with grouse-moor keepers in the east. Populations of field voles, although at lower densities than in grassland habitats, support predators such as the short-eared owl.

The sudden appearance of a green patch, in a predominantly brown moorland landscape, indicates an outcrop of more base-rich rock. These outcrops can present a colourful spectacle in early summer, with a proliferation of orchids, common birds-foot-trefoil, eyebrights, wild thyme, ladies mantle and fairy flax in their short turf. Later in the season, the flowers of frog orchid and grass of Parnassus may appear, along with fertile fronds of

Left: Starry saxifrage. Right: Northern haircap (Beinn a' Bhuird).

the tiny fern, moonwort. Montane species such as purple saxifrage, alpine bistort, alpine meadow-rue and alpine saw-wort may be seen at relatively low altitudes where there are outcrops of limestone and calcareous schist. Seepages of alkaline water across the ground surface form calcareous 'flushes', where plants such as the Scottish asphodel (a smaller, paler relative of the bog asphodel), black bog-rush, yellow saxifrage, and the worm-like moss Scorpidium scorpioides may be found.

On more acid soils, upland grasslands composed of bents and fescues may be poorer in flowers, but provide favoured grazing for red deer and domestic stock far up onto the hill. Viviparous fescue, in which the seeds germinate, forming little plants whilst still attached to the parent plant, shows adaptation to the harsh mountain conditions where setting seed is not guaranteed. The appearance of alpine lady's mantle, dwarf cornel and alpine clubmoss in these grasslands, is a signal that you are gaining altitude.

The water of most hill lochs and lochans is acidic and nutrient-poor, supporting a limited but characteristic range of plants, including shoreweed, water lobelia, water horsetail, bottle sedge, white water-lily and, in the most acidic, awlwort. Some hill lochs have distinct populations of brown trout which have survived in isolation since the last ice-age but many others have been augmented by stocking. The trill of the common sandpiper characterises the hill lochans in spring, when it arrives to nest by the waterside. Where acidic water seeps out of the ground, spring-heads with the bright green moss Philonotis fontana and delicate, white-flowered starry saxifrage dot the hillsides.

Crags
Moving on to the higher crags, the distribution of the scrambles in this guide admirably demonstrates the fact that the best rocks for scrambling are usually not the richest for mountain plants. There are exceptions; limited areas on Ben Nevis and Bidean nam Bian have a good flora with some rarities like Drooping and Highland saxifrages. There are bands of limestone at high level on both Aonach Beag and in the Alder Forest with a number of rarities like woolly willow, mountain avens, tufted saxifrage and rock speedwell but none of these areas match the rich montane flora of the soft, calcareous schist in the Lawers range. More acid rocks in the Alder Forest have a cluster of sites for the rare Blue Heath, quite close to some of the scrambles here, and on Rum, the gabbro around Loch Fiachanis has the rare Norwegian sandwort. Those plants growing on ledges but often visible from the scrambles include tall perennials such as globeflower, meadowsweet, wild angelica, greater woodrush, wood cranesbill, goldenrod, northern bedstraw, water avens and melancholy thistle. Where the rock is a bit more base-rich, there may be prominent stands of the grey-leaved downy willow and alpine saw-wort. These plants are generally palatable to sheep and deer, and benefit greatly from the protection offered by inaccessible ledges, where they grow and flower with a luxuriance unequalled in grazed situations.

Late snow lies
On the mainland, on slopes where snow lies late, a distinctive vegetation develops, with swards of mat-grass, and in more open areas, Sibbaldia, with its three lobed leaves and the grey-green rosettes of dwarf cudweed. The Cairngorms, the Ben Nevis massif and the Ben Alder area have large areas of ground over 1000m and have the longest lying snow in the country, our own small piece of the arctic. Under the longest-lying snow, the short growing season means that the vegetation is dominated by mosses, liverworts and lichens with the alpine lady-fern, parsley fern and a few flowering plants like least willow, stiff sedge and wavy hair-grass. The high corries provide secure nesting sites for golden eagles and ravens and secluded pastures for calving red deer hinds. On the mainland, the hill fox makes its dens in the high rocks, and may occasionally be surprised foraging (or even sleeping) in broad daylight. The ring ouzel is another summer visitor, and its fluting song epitomises the high places.

High summits
On completing your scramble in the higher hills, you may emerge onto a windswept ridge or plateau. Here the patchy vegetation will typically consist of low-growing woody shrubs such as dwarf willow, mountain azalea, and cushion plants including moss campion. In the Cairngorms and to a lesser extent elsewhere there are large patches of the spindly three-leaved rush up on the plateau, turning it brown in the autumn. On broader ridges and plateaux, the woolly fringe-moss can form extensive grey carpets,

Left: Lichen on quartzite (Grey Corries).   Right: Snow Bunting (Ben Nevis)

interspersed with plants of stiff sedge, alpine clubmoss and reindeer-moss (which, perversely, is not a moss but a lichen). On the more fractured and angular rock types, for example the quartzites of the Grey Corries or on the summit of Ben Nevis, the summits and ridges may appear practically bare of vegetation, but a closer look reveals an intricate crazy paving of tiny lichens covering the rock surface.

Of the birds whose breeding is restricted to the high tops, ptarmigan are widespread in the Highlands. They remain all year round, relying on their changeable plumage for camouflage (white in winter, mottled brown in summer). Snow bunting and dotterel have a more limited breeding distribution, using only the highest rocky summits and mossy plateaux respectively. Snow buntings are quite frequent in the Cairngorms and often seen on Ben Nevis and are quite approachable but dotterel are more elusive unless you are prepared to spend some time looking.

Further reading:

Raven, J & Walters, M (1971) *Mountain Flowers*. Collins New Naturalist, London.

Scott M (2011) *Scottish Wild Flowers*. Harper Collins.

Wrightham M & Kempe N Eds. (2006). *Hostile Habitats – Scotland's Mountain Environment: A Hillwalkers' Guide to Wildlife and the Landscape*. Scottish Mountaineering Trust.

WEATHER

By far the dominant characteristic of the weather over the area of this guide is its unpredictability – cyclonic systems moving in off the Atlantic hit the rugged mountains of the indented west coast and don't always do what you (or the forecasters) expect. Some general trends can be picked out, however, although year by year variation is huge. Most obvious is that the west is wetter, annual rainfall being over 3000mm in Knoydart but only 1000mm in Glen Clova. Many people's perception is that things are drier south of the Central Belt but this is only true of the east, the wettest main recording station in Scotland being Glen Dee in Galloway. Snowfall, however, is usually higher in the East, with the higher parts of the Cairngorms usually covered until July, and even down at Derry Lodge snow lies for about 100 days a year. The exception to this is Ben Nevis, which usually has snow on its summit for around 200 days a year. Snow patches remain on some high north facing slopes all year – 300 patches were recorded on 1 August 2014, for instance.

Temperature changes drastically with height, 5°C in the glen will be below zero at Munro level even when the effects of wind chill and/or snow cover are discounted. The exception is during temperature inversions, common in autumn and winter, when cold air pools overnight in sheltered hollows, sometimes dropping temperatures to as low as −28°C. Both over the year and within the day the temperature varies less in places closer to the sea, especially on the west, and in April or May areas such as Knoydart, Ardgour and Arran may be virtually snow free when Lochaber and the Cairngorms are still in full winter garb.

Wind speeds can be very strong indeed, with 281km/hr recorded on Cairngorm, and even down in the Cairngorm car park 150km/hr is not unknown. The windspeed on the tops is usually at least double that in the valleys and often much more. An 80km/hr wind will stop most people in their tracks and 120km/hr will pick you up. The current writer was once thrown 10m by an equinoctial gust. Even in less extreme conditions it pays to try and avoid walking into the wind on the more exposed parts of your route. On the positive side a good wind at least has the advantage of keeping the midges down!

The Ben Nevis Observatory operated from 1883 to 1904 and collected a vast amount of weather information. Average annual temperature was 0.3°C at the Observatory, compared with 8.4°C in Fort William, and varied from a mean of −4.6°C in February to +5°C in July. The summit was clear of cloud 50% of the time in June, but only 20% of the time in December. Mean annual rainfall was 4.08m and the greatest undrifted snow depth observed was 3.61m. Winds of over 80km/hr blew for 3% of the time, but more than twice that often in January.

The modern data is not always strictly comparable, but it appears that the mean annual temperature is about 2° higher than a century ago, ranging

WEATHER

A temperature inversion on the Càrn Mòr Dearg Arête. Photo: Jamie Hageman.

from an average of −2.5°C in February to 7.5°C average in July. Rainfall is also slightly higher, at 4.35m/year (up about 7%). Comparing modern data from Ben Nevis with Cairngorm the average temperature over the year is very similar, but the latter has far higher variation. Nevis is wetter and has far more days of cloud, while although the mean wind speed is marginally higher for Nevis the maximum gust recorded is 70% higher for Cairngorm.

The weather often varies hugely across the area of this guide at any given time, and even within fairly small areas there can be a marked difference. Ardgour often enjoys fine sunny days while it pours down just across Loch Linnhe in Glen Coe, for instance. Even on the same mountain good route selection can pay dividends. Garadh na Ciste is often sheltered from the worst of the Ben's winds, for example, and the East Face of Aonach Dubh on Bidean dries much faster than higher crags such as Stob Coire nam Beith. Taking into account height and aspect will often get you an enjoyable scramble during a period of unsettled weather and reduce the chances of having an epic. It's also worth bearing in mind the effects of weather on different rock types, with the rougher rhyolites keeping better friction when wet than do the granites and andesites, while quartzite becomes pretty slippery but tends to have positive holds and wet schist is just plain abominable! Obviously routes with inward-dipping holds are easier in the wet than those with outward-sloping ones – compare Alltnafeadh Buttress on Buachaille Etive Beag with Creag nan Cabar just round the corner, for instance.

WEATHER

Lower Fall of Foyers, September 2010.

Sometimes the weather can make even accessing the routes problematic. Streams can rise rapidly, especially in rocky areas such as Glen Coe or Knoydart. The Rough Bounds east of the latter contain several streams that can be uncrossable in wet weather, and people have been killed trying. It's always best to err on the side of caution when dealing with moving water, going the long way round and being late is obviously better than being swept away.

Of course the weather can produce positive effects too, with cloud seas not uncommon, especially in autumn, and scramblers on steep north facing slopes are often in the right place to see Brocken spectres or fog bows. Showery weather can mean lots of rainbows and it is not uncommon on the windy west coast to see waterfalls being blown back vertically upwards. A sudden clearing when you are high on the hill can be absolutely magical. The rapidity of change can be impressive – the north slope of the Cairngorms can go from cloud being above the summits to thick cloud covering everything above 600m in under a minute! The sheer variety and occasional ferocity of Scotland's weather means that it is worth paying close attention to both forecasts beforehand and changes during your day, but it is very rare that you can't find a worthwhile excursion to match the conditions.

Weather Forecasts

The Radio Scotland Outdoor Conditions forecast – for climbers, hillwalkers and sailors – is broadcast at 18:25 Monday–Friday, and on Saturday and Sunday during the 07:00 and 19:00 bulletins.

Many online forecasts are available, including:

<www.mwis.org.uk>
<www.bbc.co.uk/weather>
<www.metcheck.com>
<www.metvuw.com>
<www.mountain-forecast.com>
<www.xcweather.co.uk>
<www.yr.no>

MOUNTAINEERING HISTORY

The first people that bothered to record their exploits in the Scottish hills were mainly scientists looking at plants or rocks. The first recorded ascent of Ben Nevis for example was made by James Robertson, a botanist from Edinburgh, in 1771. He was followed three years later by Welsh geologist John Williams, who was looking for minerals.

Ordnance Survey parties lived on the summits of a number of mountains in the Highlands for weeks on end in the first half of the nineteenth century during the Principal Triangulation of Britain. Impressive remains of 'Colby Camps' can still be seen on Creach Bheinn, Ben Alder and Beinn Macduibh for example. Although there are no longer any signs of the Ordnance Survey's presence on Ben Nevis a party under the command of Corporal Winzer is known to have camped there from 1 August to 14 November 1846.

Perhaps one of the earliest climbs made in the area of this guide, was the ascent into Ossian's Cave by local shepherd Nicol Marquis in 1868. Getting up all alone must have been an interesting experience but getting down again in one piece without a rope was probably more impressive.

Early rock climbs were made on the Cuillin of Skye – notably the Inaccessible Pinnacle (1880) – before any were done on the north face of Ben Nevis. This was in part due to the ease of travel to Skye compared with Fort William. The arrival of the railway to Fort William in 1894 was to dramatically change the situation.

Mountaineering in Scotland developed partly as a result of the great interest in Alpine climbing in the nineteenth century. Eventually clubs started to be established to promote this interest. Though it wasn't the first to be formed in Scotland, the Scottish Mountaineering Club was set up in 1889 and soon began describing the Scottish mountains and reporting new adventures in its Journal.

The first known ascents of the routes in this guide are now listed in chronological order. These inevitably describe most of the climbs in this guide rather than the scrambles. However, it should give a flavour of the main figures involved in putting up the early routes and when they were active.

1889 Ceum na Caillich (Witch's Step), Arran (July) – T.F.S. Campbell, W.R. Lister.
1892 A' Chir Ridge (30 January) – T.F.S. Campbell, W. Douglas, J.H. Gibson, H.Fleming, R.A. Robertson & Dr Leith.
They did the traverse from south to north and all went well until they reached Le Mauvais Pas. Gibson was lowered on a rope, but couldn't get down and they went back along the ridge to the small gap. They abseiled from a peg down a loose gully on the eastern side of the ridge. They then found the route used today back up diagonally leftwards onto the crest. Finally, they descended the same route, then scaled most of the top to the north before heading homewards.
Tower Ridge, Ben Nevis (4 September) – J. Hopkinson, E. Hopkinson, B. Hopkinson, C. Hopkinson.
They made the first complete DESCENT of the ridge. The previous day (less Charles) they had climbed up from the bottom, but were defeated at the Great Tower, and retreated back down the ridge. On the second day they climbed down

from the summit, descended the west side of the Great Tower (probably in the region of Recess Route) and retraced their steps to the foot of the ridge. Two days later, on 6 September, they made the first ascent of North-East Buttress. This was an audacious visit by the Hopkinsons on a completely unknown face. Tower Ridge was eventually climbed by J.N. Collie, G.A. Solly & J. Collier in winter conditions 18 months later.

1893 Black Spout Left-hand (12 March) – J.H. Gibson & W. Douglas.
They climbed the route in winter conditions. It was not until 1 August 1926 that the route was climbed in summer by G.R. Symmers & F. King.

1894 Spearhead Arête, Beinn Narnain (May) – J. Maclay, W.W. Naismith.

1895 Castle Ridge, Ben Nevis, (12 April) – J.N. Collie, W.W. Naismith, G. Thomson, M.W. Travers.

North-East Ridge, Aonach Beag (13 April) – J. Maclay, W.W. Naismith, G. Thomson.

East Ridge, North Buttress, Stob Bàn (14 April) – W. Brown, W. Tough, L. Hinxman, W. Douglas.

A very productive few days on the SMC Easter Meet in Fort William. The routes were in winter condition.

Ledge Route, Ben Nevis (9 June) – J.S. Napier, R.G. Napier, E.W. Green.

North Buttress, Buachaille Etive Mòr (July) – W. Brown, Rose, W. Tough.

Aonach Eagach Traverse (August) – A.R. Wilson, A.W. Russell, A. Fraser.

1896 Curved Ridge, Buachaille Etive Mòr (July) – G.B. Gibbs.

1897 North-East Ridge, Stob a' Chearcaill (18 April) – J.H. Bell, W. Garden, T. Gibson, H. Raeburn, H. Barrow, W. Barrow, W. Brunskill, W. Brown.

Great Ridge, Garbh Bheinn (April) – J.H. Bell, W. Brown.

1898 The Chasm to Crowberry Traverse (10 April) – G.T. Glover, Collinson.

The Nose [Easy Route], Gearr Aonach (Easter) – W.W. Naismith, J. Maclay, H.C. Boyd.

Pinnacle Ridge, Garbh Bheinn (July) – J.H.Bell, J.S. Napier, W.W. Naismith.

1900 Crowberry Ridge Direct (May) – G.D. Abraham, A.P. Abraham, J.W. Puttrell, E.A. Baker.
This version was harder than the way described.

Eastern Traverse, Tower Ridge (6 September) – W.W. Naismith, A.E. Robertson.
Earlier parties had climbed up the (harder) western side of the Great Tower.

1901 Observatory Ridge, Ben Nevis (22 June) – H. Raeburn.
An impressive solo by Raeburn before teaming up with the Inglis Clark party. He was delighted by a snow bunting 'singing sweetly' on the summit.

1903 Inglis Clark Ridge, Creise (Summer) – W. Inglis Clark, J. Inglis Clark.

1904 Pygmy Ridge, Northern Corries (1April) – H. Raeburn, W.A. Gordon, G.H. Almond, A. Roth.

1908 Black Spout Buttress, Lochnagar (17 April) – T.E. Goodeve, W.N. Ling & H. Raeburn.

1911 Raeburn's Easy Route, Ben Nevis (28 September) – H. Raeburn, A.W. Russell.

Black Pinnacle, Coire Bhrochain (October) – J.A. Parker, H. Alexander, J.B. Millar, W.A Reid.

1928 Central Buttress, Lochnagar (26 August) – G.R. Symmers, N. Bruce.
Nesta Bruce made a formidable team with Roy Symmers and she forced the issue after they retreated from an attempt on Shallow Gully.
D Gully Buttress (by easier variation), Buachaille Etive Mòr (August) – A. Harrison, Addenbrooke, L. St C. Bartholomew.
1929 Number 4 Gully Buttress, Ben Nevis (1 January) – J.H.B. Bell, R.R. Elton.
1930 Serrated Rib, Stag Rocks (July) – J. Nimlin and party.
1931 Number 3 Buttress, Stob Coire nam Beith (May) – A. Harrison, A.J. Don
Number 1 Buttress, Stob Coire nam Beith (June) – A. Harrison, N. Allan, A.J. Don.
1933 Garadh Buttress, Ben Nevis (8 October) – G.G. Macphee, G.C. Williams, P. Ghiglione.
Piero Ghiglione made first ascents on 6 continents, including Alpine routes with Cassin, and more first ascents of Andean peaks than anyone else (still).
1934 Sron na Lairig (March) – P.D. Baird, Coulson, Allberry, Kendall, T.M. Wedderburn.
Crest Route, Creag na Tulaich (May) – G.G. Macphee, G.F. Todd, G.C. Williams, I.G.J. Jack.
1935 Restricted Crack, Beinn Narnain (May) – T. Donaldson, J.R. Hewitt.
1940 Corrour Slabs, Devil's Point (March) – Dr Hobson, W.L. Walker, W.T. Hendry.
1943 Boundary Ridge, A' Chir (4 July) – G.C. Curtis, H.J. Dunster, H.K. Moneypenny, G.H. Townend.
1943 Prospero's Prelude, Cir Mhòr (26 July) – H.K. Moneypenny, G.C. Curtis.
1944 Broomstick Ridge, Ceum na Caillich, Arran (March) – C.E. Willes-Johnson..
Cubic Ridge, Cir Mhòr (17 September) – G.H. Townend, F. Foxcroft.
1946 Old East, Cir Mhòr (August) – J.R. Jenkins, G.H. Townend.
1947 Barn Wall Route, Aonach Dubh (May) – D.B. McIntyre, T.J. Ransley, W.H. Murray.
1948 Near East Buttress, Coire Bhrochain (27 March) I.M. Brooker, A.D. Lyall, D. McConnach.
1948 Slab and Arête, Dividing Buttress (4 April) – J. Tewnion & M. Smith.
Crystal Ridge, Coire Sputan Dearg (1 September) – R. Still, E.J. Lawrence.
1949 M & B Buttress, Stob an t-Sluichd (28 May) – G. Mathieson, I.M. Brooker.
1950 Lairig Ridge, Northern Làirig Ghrù (7 July) – W.D. Brooker, T. Shaw.
1951 Dorsal Arête, Stob Coire nan Lochain (28 January) – J. Black, T. Shepherd, J. Allingham, J. Bradbury.
1952 Quartzvein Edge, Creagan a' Choire Etchachan (15 June) – K. Winram, G.C. Greig, M. Smith.
1954 Fingers Ridge, Northern Corries (September) – D. Bennet.
1955 The Escalator, Hell's Lum (30 September) – A.G. Nichol, T.W. Patey, E.M. Davidson.
1956 Afterthought Arête, Stag Rocks (September) – R.H. Sellers, M. Smith.
Final Selection, Stag Rocks (November) – R.H. Sellers, M. Smith.
1967 Broad Buttress, Barkeval (22 May) – J. Matyssek, H. Cook.
Narnia Arête, Barkeval (22 May) – H.M. Brown, A.T. Rollo.
1970 Dùn Athad Arête, Islay – D. McLeod, I. McLeod, R. Cuthbert, N. Tennent.
1971 Cannonade, Meall nan Eun (13 July) – M. Horsburgh, K. Schwartz.

ENVIRONMENT

Access

Part 1 of the Land Reform (Scotland) Act 2003 gives you the right to be on most land for recreation, providing you act responsibly. This includes climbing, hillwalking, cycling and wild camping. These access rights and responsibilities are explained in the Scottish Outdoor Access Code. The key elements are:

- Take personal responsibility for your own actions and act safely.
- Respect people's privacy and peace of mind.
- Help land managers and others to work safely and effectively.
- Care for the environment and take your litter home.
- Keep your dog under proper control.
- Take extra care if you're organising an event or running a business.

Stalking, Shooting & Lambing

Deer Stalking: The stag stalking season is from 1st July to 20th October (although few estates start at the beginning of the season): the main period is from mid September to mid October. Hinds continue to be culled until 15th February. There is no stalking on Sundays.

Grouse Shooting: The grouse shooting season is from 12 August until 10 December, although the end of the season is less used.

Lambing: It is important to avoid disturbing sheep during the lambing season, from March to May. Dogs should be kept on a lead near livestock throughout the year.

Fauna & Flora

Don't disturb nesting birds, especially the rarer species which are found on crags (such as Golden Eagle and Peregrine Falcon) between 1st February and the end of July. Wilful disturbance of nesting birds is a criminal offence. See <https://www.mountaineering.scot/campaigns/safeguarding-access/birds-and-nesting> for more information. When cleaning routes in summer take care what you remove: some of the flora may be rare.

Footpath Erosion

Part of the revenue from the sale of this and other Scottish Mountaineering Club books is granted by the Scottish Mountaineering Trust as financial assistance towards the repair and maintenance of hill paths in Scotland. However, it is our responsibility to minimise our erosive effect, for the enjoyment of future climbers.

Camping, Litter & Pollution

Responsible wild camping is permitted under the new access legislation; don't camp near houses or in cultivated fields. When camping, do not cause pollution, take a shovel and bury human waste carefully out of sight and far away from any habitation or watercourse. Avoid burying rubbish as this may also pollute the environment. Take everything home that you brought and dispose of it properly. Leave as little trace of your stay as possible.

Car & Bicycle Use

Do not drive along private roads without permission and, when parking, avoid blocking access to private roads and land or causing any hazard to other road users. The use of bicycles is covered by access legislation. Bicycles can cause severe erosion when used 'off road' on footpaths and open hillsides and are best used on vehicular or forest tracks.

Mountaineering Scotland

Mountaineering Scotland is the representative body for climbers and walkers in Scotland. One of its primary concerns is the continued free access to the hills and crags. Information about bird restrictions, stalking and general access issues can be obtained from Mountaineering Scotland.

If you encounter problems regarding access you should contact Mountaineering Scotland, whose address is:

The Old Granary, West Mill Street, Perth PHI 5QP.   Tel 01738-493942. website <www.mountaineering.scot/> email <info@mountaineering.scot>.

SAFETY

Participating

Scrambling, climbing and mountaineering are activities with a danger of personal injury or death. Participants in these activities should be aware of and accept these risks and be responsible for their own actions and involvement.

It is up to the individual climber to assess the reliability of bolts, pegs, belay stakes, slings or old nuts, which may be in place. Falls sometimes occur due to holds breaking. A number of routes in this guide have had few repeats so holds and blocks should be treated with caution, especially after a hard winter. You are responsible for your own actions and should not hold landowners liable for an accident, even if it happens while climbing over a fence or dyke.

Remember, this guide is only a guide, conditions in the mountains are constantly changing. Take a progressive approach and don't be afraid to turn back if you feel uncomfortable with the situation. Wherever possible avoid climbing directly below other scramblers.

Mountain Rescue

Phone 999, Mountain Rescue or Coastguard may be called out, depending on the location. Give concise information about the location and injuries of the casualty and any assistance available at the accident site. It is better to stay with the casualty, but in a party of two, it may be necessary to leave to summon help. Leave the casualty warm and comfortable in a sheltered, well marked place.

Weather Forecasts

Radio: The Radio Scotland Outdoor Conditions forecast – for climbers, hillwalkers and sailors – is broadcast at 18:25 Monday–Friday, and on Saturday and Sunday during the 07:00 and 19:00 bulletins.
TV: Reporting Scotland on BBC1 at 18:55 provides a good forecast for hillgoers. There is a daily forecast for the week ahead on the BBC news channel at 21.55.
Internet: There are numerous forecasts available online and people usually have their own favourites.

> Mountain forecasts are given on <www.mwis.org.uk>, <www.metoffice.gov.uk/public/weather-forecast> and <www.mountain-forecast.com>.
> Maps at six hourly intervals are given on <www.metvuw.com/ forecast> making it easy to see how the weather is expected to develop.
> Weather at hourly intervals is given on <www.yr.no>.
> Other sites include <www.bbc.co.uk/weather> and <www.metcheck.com/uk>.

Tides

Tide details can be found on a number of websites.
> <www.bbc.co.uk/weather/coast>, <www.sea/tide_tables> and <www.tidetimes.org.uk>.

Midges & Ticks

Midges can be plentiful in the summer months, so try to keep to areas that are exposed to wind and sun and avoid damp sheltered, vegetated places. Midges are at the worst from evening to morning, so only the hardy will camp in the west in mid-summer. Be prepared with repellent and midge net for belayers. Ticks may carry Lyme disease. It is worth wearing long trousers with elasticated ankles to stop ticks, or apply insect repellent. Check for ticks at the end of the day and remove any found. An early indication of Lyme disease is a circular outwardly expanding skin rash round the site of the bite. If you see this, or feel unwell after a tick bite, go to a doctor as soon as possible.

TECHNICAL

Classification of Routes

This guide includes both scrambles and easy climbs. The climbs have mainly been chosen because they are not sustained at their grade and usually include lengthy sections of scrambling. In order to make it obvious which type of outing is involved, a logo is shown at the start of each route description. The scrambles and climbs are each further sub-divided into three levels of difficulty. **All the routes are graded for dry, summer conditions. They will become much harder when it is damp or snowy.** In winter they are much more serious undertakings, and appropriate winter mountaineering skills and equipment will be required.

SCRAMBLES

At some point on a scramble the hands will need to be used for progress. A simple numerical grading system (1–3) is used to indicate the difficulty of a scramble. For those unfamiliar with scrambling, a rough guide might be to say that most hillwalkers should be fairly happy to tackle Grade 1 scrambles. However, those without climbing experience may well find that Grade 3 scrambles are too difficult or too frightening for them.

Grade 1
Most hillwalkers should find scrambles of this grade reasonably straight-forward. The hands will occasionally be required for progress, but the holds will normally be large, so the moves themselves will not be difficult. There may be some exposure, but usually it will not be too daunting.

Grade 2
Routes of this grade will normally require the hands to be used for more sustained sections. There may be considerable exposure. Some routes may have short technically difficult sections, while others may be easier but hard to escape from. Retreat may be quite difficult.

Grade 3
This grade of scramble may involve making thought-provoking moves on steep rock in exposed situations. All but experienced climbers might prefer the reassurance of a rope in some places. In which case, a few slings, nuts and karabiners may prove useful for setting up belays. The route might be hard to escape from, and the ability to abseil could be useful if a retreat has to be made.

ROCK CLIMBS

The rock climbs described in this guide are graded according to the standard adjectival system for summer climbs. Only routes in the three lowest grades are described. (The Easy grade is not recognised here.) Climbs are graded for their hardest move irrespective of length. Such routes will normally be climbed using standard rock climbing equipment.

Moderate
Climbs of this grade will normally make use of fairly obvious holds. However, there may be tricky moves in exposed positions. The route could be serious or sustained (but probably not both at the same time).

Difficult
Technical climbing skills are required here. There could be long exposed sections and hard moves in airy and serious situations. Most will want a rope and retreat could be tricky.

Very Difficult
Routes of this grade call for a fairly high level of climbing skill. They may have quite small holds and be extremely exposed. Only a small number of outings of this grade are included in this guide.

Use of the rope

It goes without saying that a rope will only increase safety if at least one member of the party knows how to use it properly, and if it is put to use as soon as anybody needs it. Many parties will also decide to carry harnesses and a rack of gear for Difficult and Very Difficult climbs.

Left and Right

The terms left and right are used when facing the direction being described, i.e. facing a crag in ascent, and facing out in descent.

Diagrams

Most of the routes are shown on diagrams close to the relevant text. The route numbers in the text correspond to the route numbers shown on the diagrams. Scrambles are marked as **red dashed** lines – – – , whilst climbs are shown by **blue dotted** lines · · · · · . Some approaches or linking sections of walking are shown by a white dashed line.

Descent Routes

Advice on descent routes is not generally given, so some thought may need to be given to the best way off. Many routes finish on high mountain summits and the subsequent descent may entail difficult navigation in bad visibility.

Recommended Routes

A three star system has been used to indicate the 'quality' of a route. The stars generally refer to the quality of the activity itself. Various aspects of the route may also contribute to the overall quality rating. These include soundness of the rock, the situation, how sustained a route is and how natural a line it follows.

***	The best routes of their grade in Scotland.
**	A good route, but lacking one or more of the features that make it top class.
*	A worthy outing which may lack line, situation, or balance.

Even routes with no stars can make very enjoyable outings. They may be in wild and beautiful country.

Maps

Various symbols are used on the sketch maps in this guide to indicate different categories of summit.

- ▲ Munro
- △ Munro Top
- ● Corbett
- ○ Corbett Top
- ◆ Graham
- ◇ Graham Top
- ⊗ Other peak

Munros are 3000ft high and above.

Corbetts are 2500–2999ft high.

Grahams are 2000–2499ft high.

There are different criteria (or not!) for the various tops.

Two main sources of map are available for the different areas in this guide.

Ordnance Survey maps cover the whole country and are available at both 1:50,000 scale (Landranger) and 1:25,000 scale (Explorer).

Harvey maps are available for all the more popular areas. They are also available in a variety of scales.
Waterproof British Mountain Maps at 1:40,000 scale are available for Ben Nevis & Glen Coe, Cairngorms & Lochnagar, Knoydart & Kintail and Southern Highlands.
Superwalker™ maps at 1:25,000 scale are available for Arran, Arrochar, Ben Alder, Ben Nevis, Cairn Gorm & Ben Avon, Glen Coe Glen Etive & Black Mount, Knoydart, Lochagar and Rum.
Summit Maps are available at 1:12,500 scale for Aonach Mòr, Ben Nevis, Buachaille Etive Mòr and Creag Meagaidh.

Books

Hostile Habitats is a very informative book on Scotland's mountain environment.

A list of guidebooks produced by SMC/SMT is shown at the end of the guide.

AMENITIES

Travel
The Traveline Scotland website <www.travelinescotland.com/>, among others, gives general information about travel in Scotland.
Information about current incidents and roadworks can be found on the Traffic Scotland website <https://trafficscotland.org/>.

Trains
Scotrail (<www.scotrail.co.uk> 08456 015929) operates a rail service from Glasgow and Edinburgh up to Inverness via Aviemore and to Mallaig via Fort William. Trains can be used to access the northern Cairngorms, the Cobbler and some of the Lochaber hills. Corrour and Dalwhinnie stations are also often used as jumping off points for Ben Alder, with the through trip between them a challenge for the energetic.

Coaches
Citylink Coaches (<www.citylink.co.uk> 08712 663333) run from Glasgow to Fort William and on to Mallaig or Kyle of Lochalsh, Glasgow to Oban via Tyndrum, Glasgow to Kennacraig via Arrochar and to Aviemore and Inverness from both Glasgow and Edinburgh. The Eastern Cairngorms and Lochnagar are harder to get to without a car, requiring long walk ins from Braemar or Ballater after buses from Aberdeen. In Galloway too the bus routes don't approach the hills closely and require either a car or a long walk.

Ferries
Ferries to Rum from Mallaig; Mull from Oban, Lochaline and Kilchoan; Islay and Colonsay from Kennacraig and Arran from Ardrossan are operated by Caledonian MacBrayne (<www.calmac.co.uk>, 0800 066 5000). Rum also has ferries from Arisaig via the Shearwater (<info@arisaig.co.uk> 01687 450224).
Ferries to Knoydart from Mallaig are operated by Knoydart Seabridge Ferry (<www.knoydartferry.com> 01687 462916), several times a day all year. Western Isles Cruises (<info@westernislescruises.co.uk> 01687 462233) also run from Mallaig to Knoydart, Monday to Friday from April to October. They also call at Tarbet further up Loch Nevis.

Road
Roads in the Highlands have vastly improved since the single track days of the 1970s and '80s, with a fast A9 up to Inverness and a largely improved A830 to Mallaig. The A82 up the west and through the Great Glen can still be a slow crawl in places at times, but much of this is now a fast road too. A flavour of the older roads can still be found on Mull and in places like Glen Garry and Glen Etive, while the road up Loch Arkaig side deserves special

mention – allow at least an hour for the 30km. There are no tarmac roads on Rum.

There are convenient petrol stations at Invergarry, Mallaig, Strontian, Fort William, Ballater, Braemar, Grantown, Aviemore, Newtonmore, Dalwhinnie, North Ballachulish, Glencoe village, Tyndrum, Arrochar and Newton Stewart. On the islands petrol is available at Craignure on Mull, Bowmore on Islay and Brodick on Arran.

Accommodation

Most of the areas covered here are well supplied with hotels and B&Bs, the exceptions being Rum, Knoydart and Colonsay, where the choice is much more limited.

Booking accommodation ahead can be done through Visit Scotland 0845 2255121 (8 a.m. to 8 p.m.) or <www.visitscotland.com/accommodation/> as well as through local Tourist Offices.

Youth Hostels
There are SYHA Hostels at Aviemore, Braemar, Crianlarich, Glen Nevis, Glencoe, Loch Ossian, Lochranza, Newton Stewart, Oban, Port Charlotte (Islay) and Tobermory.

Bunkhouses
Bunkhouses are numerous. See <www.hostel-scotland.co.uk> and <independenthostels.co.uk>.
The following are usefully situated:
a) Mainland
Barisdale, Knoydart. <www.barisdale.com>
Glenfinnan Sleeping Car. <enquiry@glenfinnanstationmuseum.co.uk>
    01397 722295
Ariundle Centre(Strontian). <www.ariundlecentre.co.uk>
    <ariundle@aol.com> 01967 402279
Craignure Bunkhouse(Mull). <info@craignure-bunkhouse.co.uk>
    01680 812043
The Smiddy, Corpach (Fort William).
    <www.highland-mountain-guides.co.uk> 01397 772467
Fort William Backpackers. <www.fortwilliambackpackers.com>
    01397 700711
Grey Corries Lodge (Roy Bridge). <www.roybridgehottel.co.uk>
    01397 712236
Aite Cruinnichidh (Roy Bridge). <gavin@highland-hostel.co.uk>
    01397 712315
Habitat, Ballater. <www.habitat-at-ballater.com> 01339 753752
Braemar Lodge. <www.braemarlodge.co.uk>
Aviemore Bunkhouse. <www.aviemore-bunkhouse.com> 01479 811181

AMENITIES

Insh Lodge, Kincraig. <www.lochinsh.com> 01540 651272
Tipsy Laird, Kingussie. <www.thetipsylaird.co.uk>
　<thetipsylaird@outlook.com> 01540 661708
Newtonmore Hostel. <sue.ali@highlandhostel.co.uk> 01540 673360
Strathspey Mountain Hostel. <www.strathspeymountainhostel.com>
　<strathspey@newtonmore.com> 01540 673694, 07799 058540
Glencoe Independent Hostel. <info@glencoehostel.co.uk>
　01855 811906
Inchree (near the Corran Ferry). <stay@inchree.co.uk>
　01855 821287
Corran Bunkhouse. <www.corranbunkhouse.co.uk>
　<corranbunkhouse@btconnect.com> 01855 821000
Blackwater Hostel, Kinlochleven. <www.blackwaterhostel.co.uk>
By The Way, Tyndrum.< info@tyndrumbytheway.com> 01838 400333

b) Islands
Rum Bunkhouse. <bunkhouse@isleofrum.com> 01687 460318
Craignure Bunkhouse (Mull). <www.craignure-bunkhouse.co.uk>
　01680 692973
Arle (north of Salen, Mull). <www.arlelodge.co.uk>
　01680 300299
Colonsay Backpackers Lodge. <www.colonsayholidays.co.uk>
　01951 200211
Corrie Croft (Arran). <www.corriecroftbunkhouse.co.uk>
　07580 359500

Mountaineering Club Huts
Mountaineering Scotland maintain a list of club huts bookable by individual MS members and members of clubs affiliated to either MS or the BMC. <www.mountaineering.scot/huts> 01738 493942.

Camping
The following campsites are convenient:
a) Mainland
Barisdale (Knoydart). <www.barisdale.com>
Invergarry. <www.faichemard-caravancamping.co.uk>
　01809 501314
Strontian. <www.sunartcamping.co.uk> 01967 402080
Kilchoan. <www.ardnamurchanstudycentre.co.uk> 01972 510766
Ballater. <www.ballatercaravanpark.com> 01339 755727
Braemar. <www.braemarcaravanpark.co.uk> 01339 741373
Glenmore. <www.campingintheforest.co.uk> 02477 986991
Roybridge. <www.bunroy.co.uk> 01397 712332
Glen Nevis. <www.glen-nevis.co.uk> 01397 702191

Glencoe. <https://redsquirrelcampsite.co.uk/>
  <office@redsquirrelcampsite.co.uk
  and <www.campingandcaravanningclub.co.uk> 01855 811397
Tyndrum. <www.tyndrumbytheway.com> 01838 400333
Glen Trool (Galloway). <www.glentroolcampingandcaravansite.co.uk>
  01671 840280

b) Islands
Rum:
  There is a basic campsite at Kinloch (no prebooking)
  and also camping cabins which take up to 4 people
  <RumKabins@gmail.com>
Mull:
  Tobermory. <www.tobermory-campsite.co.uk> 01688 302624
  Craignure. <www.shielingholidays.co.uk> 01680 812496
  Killiechronan at the head of Loch na Keal. 01680 300403
Colonsay:
  Camping is not allowed on Colonsay.
Arran:
  Lamlash. <www.middletonscamping.com>
  Lochranza. <www.arran-campsite.com> 01770 830273
  Basic site at the foot of Glen Rosa. 01770 302380

Other Amenities

Most of the small villages have a shop and there are large supermarkets in Fort William, Inverness, and Aviemore.

There are several climbing shops in the same three towns, and also in Braemar, while items such as maps, fuel or outdoor clothing can be obtained in many smaller places, Mallaig, Kingussie, Tyndrum, Arrochar and Brodick, for example.

Good venues for apres-hill refreshment include the Old Forge in Inverie, the Glenaden in Ballater, the Old Bridge in Aviemore, Roybridge Hotel, Ben Nevis Inn in Glen Nevis, the Clachaig and Kingshouse in Glen Coe, the Creagan in Appin, the Village Inn in Arrochar, the Ormidale in Brodick and House o'Hill in Glen Trool.

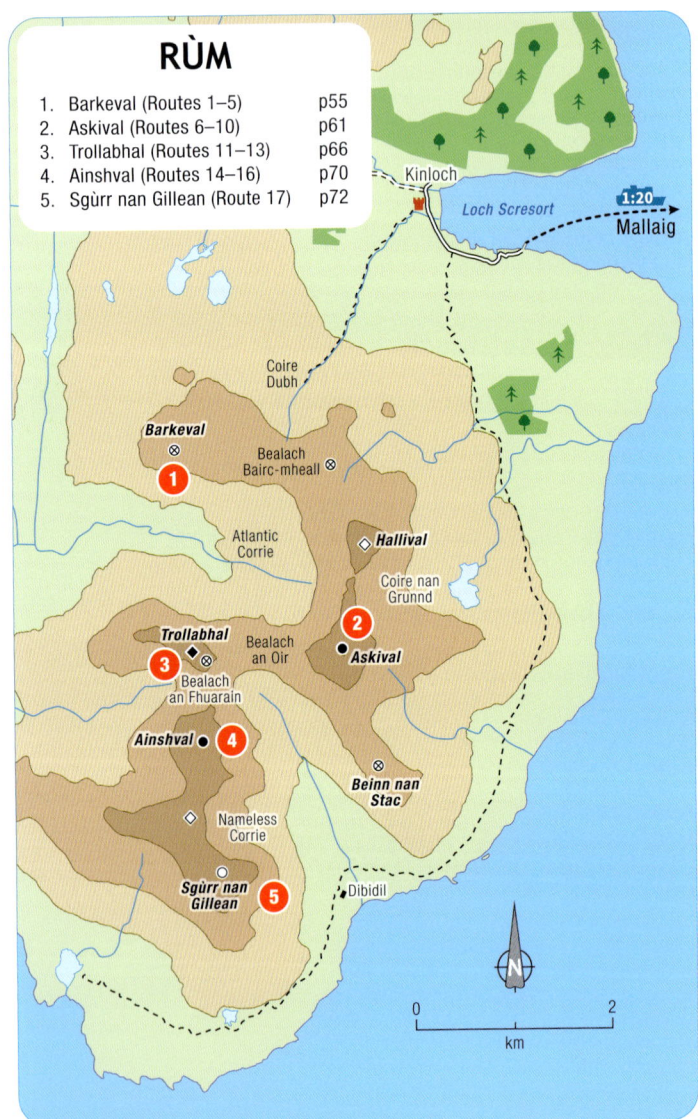

RÙM

Rùm has the largest complex of gabbro outside Skye, and the traverse of its main ridge is one of the great days out. As well as the one-pop big day there are several excellent scrambles on the subsidiary ridges and faces. The trio of routes on the south flank of Barkeval are particularly good, on delightfully rough peridotite. The island is worth a visit for the wildlife alone, with both Golden and Sea Eagles and Britain's biggest colony of Manx Shearwaters. The bizarre legacy of the Bullough family in the extravagant Kinloch Castle and the Harris Mausoleum adds another layer to the island's attractions.

Kinloch has both a bunkhouse and a basic campsite, and there are bothies at Dibidil and Guirdil, the former handy for the southern part of the Rum Cuillin. All of these can be booked through
<www.isleofrum.com/placestostay.php>.

BARKEVAL 591m

(NM 375 972)   OS Explorer 397   Map p54

This often neglected summit is the true start to the main ridge traverse and has the best scrambling on Rùm on its south face. The peridotite of which it is composed has some of the juggiest and roughest holds you could desire.

Please note there are nesting raptors on Barkeval, so be sure to check for access restrictions on the Mountaineering Scotland website before visiting. <https://www.mountaineering.scot/campaigns/safeguarding-access/birds-and-nesting>.

 1 North-West Flank   Grade 1 or 2
Alt 450m   Ht Gain +140m   (NM 375 975)   Map p54
Quite broken but very rough slabs, with avoidable steeper parts.

Approach
Take the path south of the castle (signed 'Rum Cuillin') and turn left over the bridge. Follow this path up into Coire Dubh. Once into the corrie take a smaller path slanting up right, not obvious at first, to cross the col south of Meall Breac. Carry on in the same line to a small lochan at 377 978, then cross the shallow corrie to the south to reach walking angle slabs facing down towards Kilmory.

The Route
Ascend the slabs and go up left to climb a cracked slab with steeper rock to its right. More slabs lead up right, with a steeper square tower climbed right to left (Grade 2 direct). Reach a wide grassy rake and walk up right to slabby outcrops on the skyline. These lead up to the summit, often only walking but finishing with a lovely 'crazy paving' wall just below the top.

Broad Buttress, Barkeval (Route 2, Moderate).
Climber: Jo Roberts.   Photo: Noel Williams.

Narnia Arête, Barkeval (Route 3, Moderate).
Climber: Davie Austin. Photo: Noel Williams.

BARKEVAL

RÙM

2 Broad Buttress   Grade 3 or Moderate   ★★★
Alt 300m   Ht Gain +280m   (NM 374 969)   Map p54   Diag p56

Stepped tiers to reach a half-height easing, then a more sustained steep headwall with superb holds.

Approach
The route is the left-hand of the two right slanting ribs that make up the right half of the face, Descent Spur being the right-hand one. It is most easily approached by descending the latter (see Route 5), but alternatively slant down from Bealach Barkeval for about 1km. Cross the gully beyond Descent Spur and keep slanting down westward until there is no more rock beyond.

The Route
Start up a steep knobbly wall, then several more short walls lead to a bigger face. Climb a cracked rib near its left end on excellent holds (sustained and airy but avoidable on the left). Where it eases move right across a minor gully, where more outcrops lead up right towards the steeper headwall (the biggest outcrop has a lovely central juggy crack).

Arrive at the headwall just left of a minor scree gully, with Honeycomb and Narnia Arêtes starting just off to the right. Climb a juggy rib left of the gully and where this merges into the steeper ground climb direct on huge holds. A nearly vertical rib on the right skyline provides an exposed variation (Moderate), but beware the wobbly block halfway up. This section is easily and more logically bypassed on the left, then the ground eases as you approach the summit.

3 Narnia Arête   Moderate   ★★★
Alt 500m   Ht Gain +100m   (NM 375 971)   Map p54   Diag p56

The left-hand and sharper of the two arêtes starting from halfway up Broad Buttress. One of the best easy climbs in the country, sustained and exposed but on amazing holds.

Approach
Start by climbing Broad Buttress (Route 2) as far as the foot of the headwall, then move right across the minor gully to the foot of the left-hand ridge.

The Route
Climb the exact crest on some of the best holds you could ever hope to find. Try to refrain from whooping too much! If you haven't had enough at the top a short tower off left gives a steep finish on yet more jugs.

4 Honeycomb Arête   Grade 2   ★★
Alt 500m   Ht Gain +100m   (NM 375 971)   Map p54   Diag p56

The right-hand of two arêtes starting from halfway up Broad Buttress, with a distinctive honeycomb effect on its left flank.

Approach
Start by climbing Broad Buttress (Route 2) as far as the foot of the headwall, then move right across the minor gully to the foot of the right-hand ridge.

Honeycomb Arête, Barkeval (Route 4, Grade 2).
Scrambler: Jo Roberts.   Photo: Noel Williams.

ASKIVAL

The Route
Use a combination of the crest and the left flank, sustained but on excellent holds. Finishes all too soon. Sometimes descended by confident climbers, allowing all five Barkeval routes to be linked in one go (NW-Descent-Broad-Honeycomb-Narnia).

5 Descent Spur   Grade 1, 2 or 3   *
Alt 300m   Ht Gain +280m   (NM 375 969)   Map p54   Diag p56

Descending this from the summit is a good way of reaching the harder routes on the face, but it makes an enjoyable route in its own right.

Approach
The route is the rightmost buttress on the face, slanting up rightwards with very steep rock on its right flank. Approach as for Route 1 into Coire Dubh but continue straight ahead over Bealach Barkeval and slant down right to the foot of the buttress, about 1km beyond the bealach and 150m lower. The steep right flank mentioned above is a good landmark.

The Route
Start in the gully left of the spur. The superb rough groove up the front is Grade 3, with an easier line just right. Above this the best rock is on the left at first. Zigzag up (or go direct at Grade 2) to where the buttress eases. Dodge stepped overlaps on their left and continue up the crest above, never difficult but occasionally exposed.

In Descent
About 200m east of the 591m summit of Barkeval a minor top projects southwards. This is the top of Descent Spur. It is in line with Hallival from the summit cairn. Descend the crest, zigzagging in places, then keep right (facing out) in the lower section to finish in the gully.

ASKIVAL 812m

(NM 394 952)   OS Explorer 397   Map p54

A dramatic pointy peak of mostly excellent gabbro with four good ridges perched high above the sea. A tremendous viewpoint.

6 North Ridge via Askival Pinnacle   Moderate   **
Alt 700m   Ht Gain +120m   (NM 394 955)   Map p54   Diag p62

Quite grassy in places but the positions are superb. The main section is serious and inescapable.

Approach
From Kinloch follow the path up into Coire Dubh as for Barkeval, then continue more steeply up to the Bealach Barkeval. Head SE up the broad shoulder and either clamber over Hallival with minor scrambling or traverse round it on the west. From the col between Hallival and Askival a narrow grassy ridge leads towards the latter, then at the first rocks the path goes left.

ASKIVAL - North Ridge

6. North Ridge via Askival Pinnacle — Moderate **
7. North Ridge Easy Route — Grade 1
8. East Ridge — Grade 2 *
10. West Ridge — Grade 1

ASKIVAL

The Route
The minor pinnacle at the foot of the ridge can be climbed direct, but it is quite loose and harder than it looks. It is easily avoided on either side (most go left), returning to the crest at a small col beyond it. Clamber over a minor spike to another small notch, then step up right off a block to a slab on the right flank. Traverse right a few metres on a grass ledge then climb the main slab on good but spaced holds – definitely the crux. A short arête leads to an awkward step up, then traverse left and up two short steps before regaining the crest. Pass left of a big pinnacle then the crest becomes easy. After a short descent bypass a steep wall by a bouldery groove on the left, then more crest leads to a broad gravel area. From here to the top is easy.

7 North Ridge Easy Route   Grade 1
Alt 700m   Ht Gain +120m   (NM 394 955)   Map p54   Diag p62
Not great scrambling but the easiest way up the highest peak on the island from Kinloch.

Approach
As for Route 6 to the first rocks.

The Route
Follow the path leftwards, gradually rising but staying below the cliffs. Zigzag up just before reaching a short steep black wall with a slanting overhang on its right. Keep left under another short black wall, then as you approach the East Ridge head steeply up right. Cut back left towards a prominent hole in the crest of the East Ridge, but before reaching it go up right then left and grovel onto a block on the ridge about 20m right of the hole. The gravel area at the top of the North Ridge is just to the right and the summit is easily reached from here.

8 East Ridge   Grade 2   *
Alt 650m   Ht Gain +150m   (NM 395 953)   Map p54   Diag p62
Steep and quite fierce scrambling on a blunt ridge. The closeness of the sea gives it more of an 'up in the sky' feel than the other ridges.

Approach
From Kinloch take the back road towards the pier, turning right onto the Dibidil Track after a few hundred metres. Follow this for about 5km to its high point above Lochan Dubh. Head up right to go steeply up the prow south of Coire nan Grunnd, then from the col beyond walk steeply up to the first rocks of the ridge. This point is also easily reached by traversing south (and slightly down) from the first rocks of the North Ridge.

The Route
The rock starts with an overhanging prow. Pull onto this from the left, then ascend blocks on the crest, some of them lovely knobbly peridotite. Climb a squareish groove left of the crest, then continue in the same line to reach grassy walking. The top tier is steep and intimidating, but can be sneaked up

indirectly. Clamber up cracked blocks right of centre, then move up right behind a big pointed block. Go up a damp grassy groove to a platform, then climb an easy stepped arête. As the angle eases make an airy step across a jammed block over a prominent hole. This is avoidable but most scramblers will find it irresistible. A short distance further is the gravel area at the top of the North Ridge, with the summit an easy step away.

9 South Ridge   Grade 3   **
Alt 650m   Ht Gain +150m   (NM 394 949)   Map p54

Better scrambling than the well known North Ridge but not quite as well positioned. Only Grade 2 if the three grooves and the vertical wall are avoided, but this is less good.

Approach
The obvious approach is from the coast path east of Dibidil Bothy, from where pathless walking leads up to the summit of Beinn nan Stac. The descent from this is an unpleasantly loose scramble at first, then more walking takes you down to the saddle and up the easy ridge ahead to the first rocks. A path goes off left here to avoid all difficulties.

The Route
Climb the first step on the left, then go right to the crest and up boulders. Ahead is a steep block with a pinnacle on its right. Climb a groove in the left side of the block (escaping left at half height is Grade 2). Follow the continuation groove and its left arête to a platform, where a convenient jug allows the vertical wall ahead to be surmounted from a block halfway along. This is strenuous but easily avoided on the left. The ridge now eases to walking, then a fine long easy scramble up a blocky spur. About 50m below the summit this breaks up into outcrops, which are fun if tackled direct, a left slanting V Groove making an excellent finish.

10 West Ridge   Grade 1
Alt 700m   Ht Gain +100m   (NM 392 952)   Map p54   Diag p62

Most often followed in descent during a traverse of the main ridge, with any difficulties generally avoided, but a pleasant easy scramble if tackled direct.

Approach
Most people reach the Bealach an Oir by climbing something else first, but it can be reached from Kinloch by crossing the Bealach Barkeval, losing about 100m then traversing round the head of Atlantic Corrie (traces of path).

The Route
From Bealach an Oir (385 952) take the path up eastwards, avoiding the lowest shattered rocks, then steep walking leads to higher rocks. Where the path goes right keep ahead up blocks and steps on the crest, finishing right at the summit.

In descent it is easiest to keep left (looking out) on a well used route, but a direct line is still quite reasonable.

TROLLABHAL 702m

(NM 377 952)   OS Explorer 397   Map p54

This very fine hill has twin summit peaks, and is the only Graham on Rùm. The western top, which is the main summit, is normally reached from the broader eastern top along an airy ridge with steep drops on its southern flank.

11 East Ridge   Grade 1
Alt 600m   Ht Gain +100m   (NM 380 952)   Map p54   Diag p65

Walking at first, then enjoyable easy clambering to a superb sharp summit.

Approach
From Bealach an Oir (385 952) go up the grassy spur to reach the rocks.

The Route
Clamber up blocks and short steps on the crest, all easily avoided if desired, usually on the right. Cross the East Top and follow the sharp arête to the higher West Top.

12 South Flank   Grade 1 or 3   **
Alt 550m   Ht Gain +120m   (NM 378 950)   Map p54   Diag p65

This is on the main route between Trollabhal and Ainshval. Off left some superb rough slabs with the odd steeper section, offer a harder but enjoyable alternative in ascent.

Approach
Bealach an Fhuarain (378 948) can be reached either up Glen Dibidil, over Gillean and Ainshval or by traversing across south-west from Bealach an Oir.

The Route
a) South Flank Grade 1
From Bealach an Fhuarain go right of the first outcrop and up scree. Zigzag left then right through a broken rock band, then go up right of a steeper spur (which is Grade 2) to reach easy ground below the East Top. Follow the narrow arête to the higher West Top.

In descent
This is used in descent on the usual version of the Main Ridge Traverse. From the East Top keep well left (looking out) until past the steep spur, then slant right down grass and rubble and zigzag through broken ground to a levelling (bits of path). Avoid the lowest outcrop down a gully on the left.

b) South Slabs Grade 3 **
From Bealach an Fhuarain go up the first minor outcrop direct to an easing. Walk a fair way left below steep slabs and pass under an overhanging prow. Go up left towards another steep wall and surmount it by a right to left ramp. Climb slabs above, heading for a vertical square tower. Dodge this on the right then work right up excellent cracked slabs to an airy step up on the right

TROLLABHAL

*Topping out on South Flank, Trollabhal, (Route 12a, Grade 1).
Scrambler: Pete McLeod. Photo: Noel Williams.*

*Looking towards the main summit of Trollabhal, from the broader east top.
Photo: Noel Williams.*

skyline. Keep ahead to finish up a superbly positioned cracked slab. Easy ground and a minor craglet lead to the East Top.

13 West Ridge   Grade 1   **
Alt 650m   (NM 374 954)   Map p54   Diag p65

This lovely narrow ridge on excellent gabbro deserves more popularity, but because it's a long way from anywhere it gets few suitors. The good section is easily included as an out-and-back from the summit.

Approach
From Harris cross the bridge at NM 345 955 and head eastwards up pathless ground. This is grassy at first but becomes bouldery as it steepens. Carry on up the shoulder until it flattens out at about 600m. Soon after this it narrows into a fine arête.

The Route
Follow the crest direct, over several small pinnacles, as avoiding them is no easier. The fun continues all the way to the West Top, which is the true summit.

AINSHVAL 781m

(NM 378 944)   OS Explorer 397   Map p54

A grassy summit ridge, but with lots of steep rock on the north and east flanks. The rock is not as good as the gabbro of the peaks further north and east.

14 Forgotten Ridge   Grade 2   *
Alt 370m   Ht Gain +400m   (NM 385 944)   Map p54   Diag p69 & 71

Ainshval's east ridge is a good line with excellent slabs to start. Higher up the ridge gets nice and sharp but is mainly walking.

Approach
Easily reached from the Bealach an Oir (385 952) by heading southwards across the head of Glen Dibidil. The right-hand side of the foot of the ridge has two ribs with clean slabby right flanks.

The Route
Start up the left rib, following the angle of crest and slab to reach grass. Climb a spiky arête, then when a smooth clean slab appears off left cross below it and up another arête (crux). Link up slabby outcrops to reach the narrow ridge. This is a bit loose in places but easy and enjoyably airy. It steepens slightly before finishing suddenly right at the summit cairn.

15 North Ridge   Grade 2 or 3
Alt 550m   Ht Gain +230m   (NM 379 948)   Map p54   Diag p69 & 71

A route in two sections, the first quite hard, the second easier. Both are easily bypassed, and many of the Main Ridge aspirants miss out the lower buttress by scree to the right. In the wet this is a very sensible plan.

Approach
The lower buttress starts just above the Bealach an Fhuarain (378 948).

The Route
The buttress has a steep wall at the bottom. Follow a ramp up left below this and round onto the left face. Go up a grassy groove and the slab on its right to reach the crest. Move left up slabs and bypass the vertical rock band by a steep grassy groove on the left. Easy rock leads to a large overhang, passed on the left, then the ground gradually eases to walking.

There are several harder alternatives to this on the slabs to the right, all at least Moderate when dry and a very bad idea in the wet.

Walk up to the upper spur, which the path bypasses on the left. Tackled direct just right of centre this is a delicate and exposed Grade 3, but it is much easier to go up a short gully round to the left. Follow the airy crest above or an easier line to the right, not great rock but nice positions, to reach grass fairly close to the summit.

16 Harris Face Moderate
Alt 450m   Ht Gain +200m   (NM 375 947)   Map p54   Diag p71

Lovely rock lower down, less so higher up. Unfortunately the crux is on the poorer rock.

Approach

This can be reached up Coire Fiachinis from Harris, but as few people base themselves there most will arrive by traversing westwards from the Bealach an Fhuarain. The quickest route slants upwards across unpleasant scree to reach a grassy saddle at the top of a stubby spur then descends the far side. It is much nicer but longer to descend the upper corrie to about the 400m contour then bear left along the foot of the slope until right of a scree shoot. The lower tier of the face is steep and shattered, but well right is a rib of rough gabbro. From the top of this walk left along the shelf below the main face until just short of a stubby projecting spur with a grassy saddle at its top.

The Route

Climb the lowest rib, the rightmost of three, then use a dyke to break through a steeper band. Go up left then ascend a slab on the right. Climb another steep band delicately by a right to left diagonal. The spur now eases, heading for a steep tower right of a deep gully. This is the crux. Climb the left edge of the tower past a sharp pinnacle (an unlikely looking escape is possible from its top). Continue up the edge above the pinnacle until an airy traverse is possible to the crest. Breathe a sigh of relief and romp up the now much easier spur over a small pinnacle and up slabs until they peter out into the hillside. Moving left gains a few more outcrops and joins the North Ridge near its top, much better than slogging straight up the slope.

SGÙRR NAN GILLEAN 764m

(NM 380 930)   OS Explorer 397   Map p54

The ridge is a pleasant upland stroll above a steep east flank. There are also some enjoyable easy slabs low down on the south flank if coming up this way.

17 Dibidil Face   Grade 2
Alt 450m   Ht Gain +100m   (NM 385 930)   Map p54   Diag p73

Nice scrambling but a masochistic approach. The start is harder than it looks but it soon eases.

Approach

Directly above Dibidil Bothy a minor gully is central on the face, slanting up right directly below the apparent summit and well up left from the much larger dark gully lower down. Slog up to the upper gully, easiest further left. Right of the scree emerging from the gully are three ribs, the central of which has a slab topped with a vertical wall 10m up.

SGÙRR NAN GILLEAN

17. Dibidil Face — Grade 2

Slab Approach, South Ridge, Sgùrr nan Gillean.
Scramblers: George Archibald & George Sawicki. Photo: Noel Williams.

The Route
Scramble up to and climb the slab, then avoid the vertical wall on the right. Follow a rib up right to a grassy gully with steep broken rock up left and a clean rib on the right skyline. Climb the rib then go up left until you can string together outcrops to the top of the shoulder. Where this merges into the main mountain short easy rock steps lead to the summit ridge just south-east of the cairn.

Traverse of the Rum Cuillin

The classic one day traverse of the island's main peaks will be many people's primary objective on a trip to Rùm. At around 22km and with nearly 2000m of ascent it is comparable to the Cuillin Ridge in terms of effort, although considerably easier in technical difficulty. Barkeval is usually omitted but can easily be added in via its north-west flank or as a detour from the Bealach Bairc-mheall.

The traverse is usually done north to south as this gives a less steep approach and means that you are going upwards at the Askival Pinnacle and the North Ridge of Ainshval, the hardest parts of the traverse. The trail back from Dibidil can seem a long drag at the end of the day though, and going the other way round gets this out of the way early. This would let you include Trollabhal South Slabs but most would probably descend the easier route avoiding the Askival Pinnacle.

18 Main Ridge Traverse   Grade 1 to Moderate ***
22km   Map p54

For the usual north-south traverse follow Route 1 into Coire Dubh, then either continue direct up to Bealach Bairc-mheall or slant up left before this (small path) to the small col behind Cnapan Breaca. Then continue slanting up to reach the ridge at the stony area just before it rises to Halllival.

Carry on over Hallival and down its South Ridge, with some minor scrambling. Climb the North Ridge of Askival by either Route 6 (Moderate) or Route 7 (Grade 1), then descend the West Ridge by either Route 10 (Grade 1) or the path to its left.

From Bealach an Oir climb Trollabhal by its East Ridge, Route 11 (Grade 1), then from the West Summit return across the East Summit and descend the South Flank by the easier version (Grade 1) to Bealach an Fhuarain. Climb the North Ridge of Ainshval by Route 15, most people avoiding the lower buttress (Grade 3) by the scree to its right, and the upper section (Grade 3) by a gully to the left. An easy ridge leads to Sgùrr nan Gillean, with a brief easy scramble over a minor summit on the way.

Descend well southwards, veering left once the angle eases to reach the bothy at Dibidil. A good but occasionally boggy path leads back to Kinloch in about 8km, gaining around 250m along the way, which inevitably seems quite a lot at the end of the day.

KNOYDART TO THE GREAT GLEN

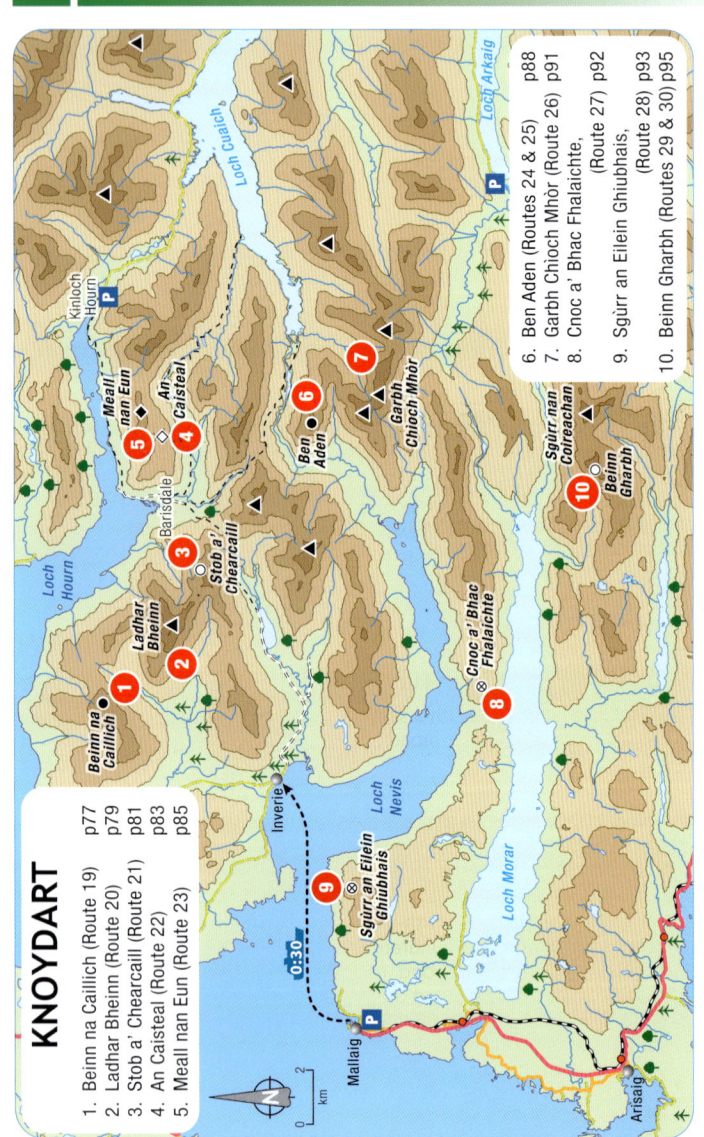

KNOYDART

1. Beinn na Caillich (Route 19) p77
2. Ladhar Bheinn (Route 20) p79
3. Stob a' Chearcaill (Route 21) p81
4. An Caisteal (Route 22) p83
5. Meall nan Eun (Route 23) p85
6. Ben Aden (Routes 24 & 25) p88
7. Garbh Chioch Mhòr (Route 26) p91
8. Cnoc a' Bhac Fhalaichte, (Route 27) p92
9. Sgùrr an Eilein Ghiubhais, (Route 28) p93
10. Beinn Gharbh (Routes 29 & 30) p95

KNOYDART TO THE GREAT GLEN

The area north of the Mallaig railway is dominated by east-west chains of rugged peaks, with the Rough Bounds of Knoydart in particular being amongst the craggiest areas of the Highlands. Despite this continuous rock lines are few, with most of the scrambles here made up of a succession of outcrops, but some are fine scrambles nonetheless. Some of the routes are accessible in a day from the Fort William to Mallaig road or the minor roads up Loch Arkaig and Glen Garry but many require a longer trip. There is a regular boat service from Mallaig to the village of Inverie and this provides a good base for those in Knoydart proper.

Also included here is the compact group of hills overlooking Loch Lochy, where two very accessible Munros have long but quite vegetated scrambles on their south-east flanks.

Knoydart

Although Knoydart is on the Scottish mainland it is only reachable either by ferry or a long walk, and many of these routes are best enjoyed as part of a multi day expedition, using either bothies or a tent. The first two routes are usually climbed from Inverie, the next three from Barrisdale, which is usually reached by a delightful coastal walk from the end of the remote minor road at Kinloch Hourn. Allow nearly an hour for the drive from the main road and plenty of time for the coastal walk, which is hillier than many expect.

BEINN NA CAILLICH 785m

(NG 796 067)   OS Explorer 413   Map p76

A remote and rugged hill with a sense of being poised above the ocean, this is quite a complex sprawl of broad ridges and hidden corries.

19 South-East Slabs   Grade 3   **
Alt 300m   Ht Gain +250m   (NG 801 061)   Map p76   Diag p78

A long route up tiers of slabs with lots of possibilities, both hard and easy. Open and sunny in aspect and quick to dry, but not a good choice in the wet.

Approach
From Inverie take the track north-west over Mam Uidhe to the forestry just beyond the saddle. A few hundred metres after reaching this, take a right fork and go through the wood for 1.5km to join the Abhainn Inbhir Ghuiserein. About 1 km beyond the forest cross the river and take a smaller path alongside the Abhainn Bheag. In a little under 3km the slabs are obvious, up to the left. They slant up leftwards, bounded by a stony gully to their left, and are quite steep in the middle. At the lower right-hand end there are prominent twin cracks with a birch tree up right and a mossy tier below.

BEINN NA CAILLICH
South-East Face

19. South-East Slabs — Grade 3 **

LADHAR BHEINN

The Route
The mossy tier is feasible if dry, then climb the slab left of the twin cracks and a smaller slab above by a knobbly crack. Walk left up a rock ramp until more slabs lead up to easy ground. Climb a small clean slab, then broken ground to two more slabs, the second climbed with relish using the left hand of two diverging cracks. More easy craglets run up to a thin boulder field angling up left.

The outcrops above are steeper, so move 50m left and go up a pink rib above a small pointed pinnacle (the spike on the right is loose). Up left is a larger crag, where several possibilities converge past a big rock crevasse to finish up a steep wide crack (avoidable on the right). Two small outcrops lead up to another large crag, climbed on big blocks near its right edge, weaving about a bit. The general angle now starts to lean back at a heathery section, but there are still several fun outcrops above, starting with a steep crack on jammed flakes. The craglets finally peter out about 100m below the summit.

Beinn na Caillich has lots of other scrambly outcrops to play on, the slabs on the west side of the north top (Point 666m) being particularly good, although short.

LADHAR BHEINN 1020m

(NG 825 040)   OS Explorer 413   Map p76

Knoydart's highest peak is some people's candidate for the finest hill in Scotland. Certainly the tremendous Coire Dhorrcaill on the north-east side of the summit is a dramatic sight, especially in winter. The scrambles on this side are very vegetated though and win no prizes despite their situation. The North-East Ridge of Stob Dhorrcaill, though prominent, is mainly steep grass. By far the best scramble on the hill is on the remote and much less impressive western spur, An Dìollaid.

 20 An Dìollaid   Grade 3   **
Alt 300m   Ht Gain +350m   (NG 801 047)   Map p76   Diag p80
Another long route, linking together steep slabs of excellent rock, where inward dipping holds allow quite steep rock to be climbed in comfort. Many of the outcrops are quite sustained (although not hard) and slightly taller than you would prefer, making this very much a route for those happy with exposure.

Approach
As for Route 19 as far as the Abhainn Bheag, then about 1.5km beyond the crossing of the Guiserein you reach a large cairn-like shattered boulder just above the path. From here the crag is obvious up right. The centre of the face is steeper and quite mossy, so the route follows the cleaner right-hand side, before moving left as the angle eases (slightly!).

STOB A' CHEARCAILL   81

The Route
Start up purplish clean slabs on the right-hand side of the face, fairly continuous but little more than walking. Follow small outcrops above until they run out, with bigger steeper cliffs off left. Walk over to these. The toe is steep and easily avoided, but small sharp holds make it much easier than it looks. Above this much easier slabs lead up to a large clean slab with more good holds. After a broad slab the ground becomes grassier, but still with small scrambly craglets which run up to a wide shelf below the upper face.

Climb the first outcrop above the shelf, then traverse horizontally left to the first crag on the far side of a small stream/gully. Starting this direct is Moderate, but by coming in from the left big holds allow you to climb the rest of the rib direct. Continue up left on excellent rock to boulder slopes. Just left is an irresistible steep pink slab above a small pool, climbed direct on superb holds. These continue on easier rock, although getting mossier, to the top of the main face. Off left is a steep square outcrop – reach over the biggest bit of the overhang to get a nice surprise! Easy pink rock continues past perched boulders to the top of the tier. Several more short walls provide more fun with fantastic sharp holds before the 650m shoulder arrives all too soon.

KNOYDART

STOB A' CHEARCAILL 840m

(NG 456 641)   OS Explorer 413   Map p76

This is the jutting rock peak that forms the southern flank of Ladhar Bheinn's Coire Dhorrcaill, included in the classic horseshoe from Barrisdale. The huge north-west face carries several classic winter climbs but is too vegetated for summer climbing.

21 North-East Ridge   Grade 1
Alt 700m   Ht Gain +100m   (NG 847 031)   Map p76

The rearing prow is impressive from below, but it turns out to be fairly grassy, giving a rather wandering scramble.

Approach
This will almost always be climbed from Barrisdale, taking the path into Coire Dhorrcaill and leaving it as it contours round the foot of the ridge to follow the crest up over Creag Bheithe.

The Route
The nose of Stob a' Chearcaill looms up intimidatingly, and direct routes are as unpleasant as they look. It is better and much easier to go round left and up well-trodden steps in a steep gully. On regaining the crest go up a left slanting ramplet and zigzag up grass until the ground gets steeper and rockier. Go up the first step, then traverse horizontally right to a jammed flake. Squeeze up behind this, exit right and go up a steeper groove on good holds. Zigzag up more grass steps, then climb an awkward left-slanting weakness.

Approaching the North-East Ridge of Stob a' Chearcaill (Route 21, Grade 1). Photo: Chris Eilbeck.

Everything above is much easier. The route is sometimes descended, but this is considerably more awkward, both technically and in terms of route finding.

AN CAISTEAL 522m

(NM 894 044)   OS Explorer 413   Map p76

A very rocky hill with steep slabs on its north face giving climbing at around VS and a steep but broken South Face which makes an excellent scramble.

   22 South Face   Grade 3   **
Alt 50m   Ht Gain +500m   (NM 898 035)   Map p76   Diag p84

Nearly 550m of scrambling, mainly on steepish slabs with sharp holds and good friction. Quite tricky in places but not sustained. This route will mainly be of interest to those staying at Barrisdale, either camping or in the bothy, but it can be done as a day trip from Kinlochhourn by following the coast path to Barrisdale and returning by slanting down from Meall nan Eun to meet the track at the col west of Skiary.

Approach
From Barrisdale follow the track up Glen Barrisdale for 3km to the foot of a knoll just beyond a small stream running down south-east from the col between Meall Bhuidhe and An Caisteal. At the foot of the knoll there is a small steep slab just beside the path, which returns to the main river about 100m further on.

The Route
Climb the small slab then easier slabs to pass left of a steep wall with an obvious quartz vein and continue to the top of the knoll. From the col beyond dodge two steep walls, the first on the left, the second on the right. Go up to a pointed boulder and climb the rock behind just right of a small birch tree. Easy slabs then lead up to a group of trees below a long steep wall.

  Walk left up a wide bouldery ramp, occasionally using slabs on its outside edge. Just before the ramp ends, about 10m right of small trees, go right onto a ledge with small boulders, then bear left up delicate slabs (easier on the right) to the top of the tier. Stepped slabs then lead to a larger slabby wall. Walk right below this and climb its delicate right edge bearing left (easier the further right you go). Go up to reach the next rock band just right of a wet area. Climb a stepped weakness up right to the broad crest and go up a left-slanting ramp. This leads easily to the crest, but a more exciting finish quits the ramp after 10m and goes right up flakes, finishing up exposed slabs on positive holds.

  A short distance higher is a bigger buttress with a long steep wall at its foot. Climb a juggy staircase on the extreme left end of the wall, then traverse horizontally right onto the buttress proper and take either of two lines slanting up right onto the front (the lower one is easier). Climb a right slanting groove to heather, go up left to a niche and traverse right onto a slab above its

KNOYDART

AN CAISTEAL

Glen Barrisdale

22. South Face — Grade 3 **

MEALL NAN EUN

smooth start. Climb this to easy ground. Small outcrops now lead up to a large terrace below the upper face.

Head up right to more clean slabs and trend up right past a perched block, delicate at first. Either carry on in the same line or take a harder direct finish up slabs with sharp rippled holds. Walk up right below one outcrop to reach a larger face with a left-slanting vein of pink pegmatite. Climb the easy first part of the vein to a grass ledge, then a more sustained section to a niche. Pull steeply out of this, then step left to a ledge and finish up a thinner quartz vein. An easier version moves right from the grass ledge then up directly. Climb easy slabs past quartz, then a couple of steeper outcrops, after which more short walls and slabs lead to the summit ridge. The actual summit is a few hundred metres up left, the western top being the highest.

MEALL NAN EUN 623m

(NM 903 052)   OS Explorer 413   Map p76

The twin hill to An Caisteal has a broad knobbly ridge with great views out over Loch Hourn. The west face has four buttresses with clean rock climbs in the lower grades. The right-hand, biggest and steepest is Severe; the middle two are slabby, set back a little and around V Diff, while the left hand and longest gives two easy angled Diffs, of which the following is the better.

23 Cannonade   Difficult, Moderate or Grade 3   **
Alt 410m   Ht Gain + 120m   (NG 894 049)   Map p76   Diag p86

A clean slabby rib, mostly Grade 3, with harder variations on the top slab. It makes a good follow on from Route 22.

Approach
From the top of the scramble on An Caisteal (i.e. well right of the two summits) descend northwards fairly steeply, cross a sluggish stream then slant left up a ramp below a steep wall (nice bouldering). Drop down the other side of the spur to the outlet of the lochan, then bear left before slanting down rightwards below the middle two buttresses to reach the foot of the left-hand one. The foot of the buttress breaks into two ribs and Cannonade starts up the right-hand one.

The Route
Climb the groove up the front of the rib to easier rock. At the top of this climb the clean slabby left side of the rib (or the easier crest). Climb a slightly steeper section by a left-slanting grove, then go right to the arête and up to easy rock. Swing up left steeply onto the crest of the next rib and go up it to grass. Up left is a larger clean slab, the crux. Climbing the right edge of this direct is Difficult, whilst meandering around a bit following the lines of weakness brings the grade down to Moderate. The groove on the right avoids it altogether at Grade 3. Less sustained slabs above lead to easier ground, then more scattered outcrops continue almost to the west summit, often with

KNOYDART

MEALL NAN EUN
West Face

23. Cannonade — Difficult **

*Immaculate rock on Cannonade (Route 23, Difficult **).
Climber: Nicky Gear. Photo: Iain Thow.*

surprising holds just where you need them. The central summit is a metre higher but the west top has by far the finer view.

The Rough Bounds

Knoydart proper is fringed by some of the roughest ground in Scotland, jaggy peaks with many rock outcrops (although few natural lines). The scrambles here will mainly be done as part of a backpacking trip, but can be reached in a day using the winding road up Loch Arkaig or by some radical up and down from the A830 near Glenfinnan. For the adventurous, an interesting approach to the routes on Beinn Gharbh is to kayak up Loch Morar to the bothy at Oban (NM 863 899).

BEINN AN AODAINN (BEN ADEN) 887m

(NM 899 986)   OS Explorer 413   Map p76

Hidden away in the wild heart of the Rough Bounds, this rather squat-shaped but very rocky peak is one of the remotest hills in this guide.

**24 East-North-East Ridge   Grade 1 or 2   ** *
Alt 250m   Ht Gain +600m   (NM 921 994)   Map p76

A long slabby ridge of excellent rock, mainly walking but with some good steeper bits.

Approach
The only feasible day trip version of this route from a road is to come in via the head of Loch Quoich, a 30km outing, while a more reasonable day involves using Barrisdale as a base, around 22km but involving two crossings of the 500m Mam Unndalain. For the former start at the two bar 'bridge' at 985 036 and head east across either pathless bog or mudflats depending on the height of the reservoir. The remains of an old road help you round to the shore of the main loch, then a rougher path takes you to the mouth of Gleann Cosaidh. The river here can be difficult or even impossible to cross after wet weather. Continue along the rough lochshore for 1km until the remains of a construction road appear a little above the shoreline. Follow this to the head of the loch, cross both dams and stay on the track for another 200m or so. A smaller path now heads off right over a minor col and descends to the head of Lochan nam Breac. At the stony saddle 300m before this the Allt Coire na Cruaiche comes in from the left. The two approaches join here.

For the Barrisdale route cross the bridge by the bothy and take the path up over Mam Unndalain. On the other side a good path slants down to the head of Lochan nam Breac, and another stream that can be hard to cross after heavy rain (not an uncommon event in Knoydart). Cross the beach and take the path up eastwards for 300m to the foot of the Allt Coire na Cruaiche.

The Route
Ascend the west bank of the Allt Coire na Cruaiche until it opens out, then go right up slabs (mostly walking angle) to reach the crest overlooking Lochan nam Breac. Continue south-west up more easy slabs with optional steeper bits (usually mossy) to reach the main east-north-east crest at around 450m. Follow this up on delightfully rough rock, mostly easy but with the odd harder section. A steep quartzy slab on the right side of the ridge is a highlight (Grade 2). Above a prominent step the ridge bends left and narrows, before reaching a large rock platform. The cracked prow above is Grade 2 by the left hand crack, or avoid it on the left. A narrow but easy ridge now leads over a minor top to a grassy col with a big pointed flake. The flake is Moderate, but beware the wobbly jug, and of course it must be reversed. More sensibly, go up slabs right of the flake and over another minor top, then an easy broad ridge leads to the summit.

25 South Face   Grade 2
Alt 400m   Ht Gain +350m   (NM 899 980)   Map p76   Diag p89

A long run of slabby outcrops of good but often lichenous rock following the right-hand side of the face. Not particularly good scrambling but in an impressive setting.

Approach
By far the best base for this route is Sourlies Bothy (NM 869 950) or a wild camp nearby (the quite small bothy can get very busy). From the bothy go round west into the Carnoch valley and follow the south-east bank of the river up to the Allt Achadh a' Ghlinne. Go up the south bank of this (sketchy path) until above a small gorge and beyond the spur projecting from the South Face of Beinn an Aodainn which forms the start of the route. Cross the stream at around NM 900 978 to reach the right-hand side of the spur, just left of a steep stream.

The Route
Go up steep grass to gain the spur at a flattening above its steep initial section. Mossy ribs and more steep grass then lead up for 100m or so to a small col. Climb a pinkish rib to another small col, then walk up to a third one. A large grey slab off right is unfortunately too hard so climb the mossier rib and pink slab directly ahead, left of the stream. Above is a spill of gigantic boulders with a vertical 'Cenotaph Corner' rock face to their left. Go right up easy slabs past the boulders, then up grass to a clean rock band right of a black wet wall. Zigzag up ledges about 30m right of the black wall, then climb a harder slab by a left to right line of small flakes, delicate to start. Go left up a grass runnel, then easy rough slabs lead up to a big terrace, with the skyline of the East-North-East Ridge up left. This is easily gained up steep grass, then followed to the summit, but the bouldery landslip on the left is worth investigating on the way – it has some quite impressive holes in it!

GARBH CHÌOCH MHÒR 1013m

(NM 909 961)   OS Explorer 413   Map p76

The twin Munro to the more famous Sgùrr na Cìche, is just as rocky as its neighbour but not as distinctive a shape. It is notable for the example of extreme wall building that follows the ridge crest. There is a short steep buttress below the main summit on its north side, but by far the best scrambling is on the huge triangle of slabs below Garbh Chìoch Bheag.

26 Coire nan Gall Slabs   Grade 2   *
Alt 450m   Ht Gain +300m   (NM 928 965)   Map p76   Diag p91

A vast acreage of slabs, mostly easy angled but with some overlaps and steeper sections. It is unlikely that any two people would follow the same route so only the general line is described.

Approach
From the head of Loch Arkaig follow the track up the north side of Glen Dessarry past the lodge, then the rougher path up to and along the top side of the forest. Cross the Allt Coire nan Uth and turn right up the next stream to go up steeply to the col between Sgùrr nan Coireachan and Garbh Chìoch Bheag. Descend the other side into the east branch of Coire nan Gall. You can either drop down to the 450m contour and start up a narrow slab just right of a stream or traverse in higher up below a line of steeper outcrops.

The Route
From the narrow slab more slabs lead up to a large grass terrace where the traverse comes in. Above this steeper slabs or easier ground on the right lead to broad slabs with overlaps, which gradually ease in angle to walking. These take you to the main ridge a little east of the summit. A slightly steeper finish can be found by moving left to arrive on the ridge at a subsidiary top.

If continuing over Garbh Chìoch Mhòr to Sgùrr na Cìche there are outcrops on the east shoulder of the latter that are easily gained by going up right from the col between the two. These are rather discontinuous but can be made fairly hard if required.

Morar

This range of mostly small but very rocky peaklets on the south side of Loch Nevis runs up into bigger steeper hills around the head of Glen Finnan.

CNOC A' BHAC FHALAICHTE 388m

(NM 801 921)   OS Explorer 413   Map p76

Only a minor summit, but a splendid viewpoint, with a steep slabby west face which dominates the tiny settlement at Tarbet.

SGÙRR AN EILEIN GHIUBHAIS

KNOYDART

27 Tarbet Slabs   Grade 3 or Moderate
Alt 300m   Ht Gain +250m   (NM 797 919)   Map p76

Not as impressive as it looks from a distance but well worthwhile, with good flaky slabs after a scrappy start. Sadly some of the best slabs are too hard to be called scrambling, forcing detours onto grass ledges and cracks.

Approach
Tarbet can be reached by boat from Mallaig (Western Isles Cruises, arriving at around 3.30 p.m. Pick up is also available, same time, Mondays to Fridays from April to October). Alternatively take the beautiful path along the north shore of Loch Morar, one of the best easy walks in the country. Looking east from the cairn which marks the top of the pass south of Tarbet you can see a big vertical crag off left and a smaller vertical crag well right, with broken rocky ground between (lots of bracken later in the season).

The Route
Start up the left hand edge of the broken area, left of birch scrub. Short steep outcrops lead to bracken and grass. Go up past a split boulder to more juggy shattered craglets, then steep broken ground becomes slabs leading to the top of the first tier. The deer fence above has no stile and is best crossed using an old straining post a little left of the obvious arrival point. Above this a short juggy wall leads to a big grass shelf.

Walk right along the shelf, almost to a minor summit, to where a pyramidal boulder lies below the cliff ahead. The slab behind the boulder followed by a grassy groove is the best of several options. Climb a steep crack with a small holly, then rough slabs to another shelf below a steep rock band. Traverse left below this until past an easy square-cut gully. Climb the left edge of the rib left of this (the rib direct is Moderate), then continue up to a minor top.

Across the saddle ahead are three slabby ribs. Climb the right-hand one, starting steeply on big sharp holds and finishing up a flaky groove. Cross another minor summit and a boggy col. Now climb a slab behind two boulders, going up left to a right-slanting rib and finishing up a groove. The next slab is easy, then a final tier has either twin cracks on sharp holds or easier slabs to the right.

If carrying on to Sgùrr Mòr then many more outcrops can be found in the rough backlands.

SGÙRR AN EILEIN GHIUBHAIS 522m

(NM 727 973)   OS Explorer 413   Map p76

A very rocky hill with a steep north face and a tremendous view out over Loch Nevis.

28 Right-hand Rib   Grade 3
Alt 150m   Ht Gain +300m   (NM 726 977)   Map p76   Diag p94

The central rib on the face looks terrific from a boat but is too hard for

SGÙRR AN EILEIN GHIUBHAIS
North Face

28. Right-hand Rib — Grade 3

scrambling. The easier-angled right-hand rib, however, has some excellent rock sections despite the copious heather.

Approach
From the end of the minor road running east from Mallaig (very limited parking) take the track round to Mallaigmore. Before reaching the cottages traverse right across the stream to a ruin. The coast from here can be followed but is extremely rough, so it is easier (and probably quicker) to go up eastwards to the top of the steep slope at around 350m, traverse along to the top of Coire Liath at NM 719 972 then descend its west side. This does mean dropping back down to about 50m to pass below the lowest cliffs on the north-west shoulder of the peak.

If coming in via the coast go up slightly from the ruin to pass over the first hump, then slant down to sea level. Go up steeply to pass over the top of Sròn Raineach at around 70m ('Bracken Nose' – a good reason to go high later in the season). Descend a steep narrow gully to sea level again and go along for about 1km before gaining about 60m to pick up a rough deer path through the heather round into the foot of Coire Liath, where the two approaches join.

Below the main face a wide heathery ramp slants up left and some short steep slabs can be found on this, providing quite tricky scrambling on superb rough rock. Looking up, the face has a steep blunt central spur rising from a heathery bay, with less defined but quite steep rock to the left and an easier angled spur to the right. The latter is the described route, curving up right from the foot of the heather bay, with very steep heathery ground to its right.

The Route
From the left edge of the lowest rock on the spur go up a clean slabby rib to heather (harder than it looks). Continue up right on rock steps and more heather, awkward in places but with the steps generally climbable fairly directly. The rib soon opens out to more heather with some easy slabs. When the ground steepens again go right to the skyline and climb this, crossing a distinctive oblique trench. Climb a short steep wall, either by its reachy left edge or more easily right to left, then gentler slabs lead up to the top of the main steep section. The ground soon eases to walking, where you can either slant up left and string together minor outcrops all the way to the summit or walk up and right for some distance to gain shorter but more sustained slabs.

From the higher approach, if you can't face losing all the height then nice slabs on the east flank of Coire Liath (NM 723 973) are also good fun.

BEINN GHARBH 896m

(NM 883 877)   OS Explorer 413   Map p76

Considered a subsidiary top of Sgùrr nan Coireachan, but actually quite an independent hill (with another three metre of drop it would be a Corbett) with a fine summit and a rocky north-west face of steep slabs. The minor tops

along its south-west ridge have plenty of rock too, with the north flank of the top west of Sgùrr an Ursainn providing the best scramble.

29 Ursainn Slabs   Grade 2 or 3   *
Alt 550m   Ht Gain +120m   (NM 865 872)   Map p76   Diag p96

An excellent main slab of rough gneiss with easy slabs below and outcrops above. A long walk in by any route.

Approach
The quickest way in is from the road 2.5km west of Glenfinnan (876 818). Take the forest road north for a kilometre until it forks. Take the left track until it bends left, then take an indistinct boggy path to cross a broad col and descend to the stream junction just east of Kinlochbeoraid. Cross both streams, the second of which can be tricky. In this case there is a large boulder jammed in the gorge 100m upstream which provides an exposed crossing.

Go up steeply to the saddle west of Sgùrr an Ursainn (866 867). Descend a grassy stream/ramp northwards until lower than the slabs on the left. Traverse left (west) to reach a rock terrace below a two-tiered steep wall. There are easy slabs below this to provide a longer start.

The Route
At the right end of the steep wall a tongue of slab descends from the upper tier to reach the terrace. Climb this (the only bit of Grade 3 on the route, avoidable by grass on the right) to reach a huge slab. Go leftwards up this then rightwards to its apex, almost walking for the confident. Smaller but steeper outcrops lead up to the summit, finishing with another delicate slab. There is a beautifully perched paddling pool just east of the summit.

To reach the North-West Face of Beinn Gharbh go back down the approach rake then traverse north-east to the col with An Stac. There are several short slabs of superb rock just below and west of the col, all around Moderate.

30 North-West Face   Grade 2/3
Alt 550m   Ht Gain +250m   (NM 883 883)   Map p76

300m of slabby rock, much of it excellent, but there are no strong lines, and sadly most of the slabs are too steep to be called scrambling so the end result is disappointing. Anyone happy soloing at around 4c would have a field day here. The ramps between the slabs make a good winter grade II.

Approach
The route fits in well after Ursainn Slab as described above, but an alternative is to come up Glen Pean from the head of Loch Arkaig. Go through a huge landslip (an amazing place) and turn left up a stalkers' path at 889 895. At the 350m contour slant right up a grass shelf to reach the col below the cliff. Using Glen Pean bothy markedly shortens this approach.

The Route
The nature of the face produces lots of route choice, so the following is just

a suggestion. At the bottom left of the face is a steep buttress with a prominent boulder on its top. Reach this from the right, then find a way through the steep slabs above, probably using the grassy grooves between them. A grassy ramp now runs up right, follow its rocky outside edge. Near the top of this cross the rake to the right edge of a steep slab which provides a continuation (exposed but easy). Above this are lots more slabs at a more amenable angle leading to the ridge about 300m north-east of the summit.

Other possibilities nearby

The south flank of Sgùrr Sgeithe (NM 857 983) has tiers of quite technical slabs, reached by slanting up right from Mam Meadail. The north face of Beinn an Aodainn (NM 899 986) looks promising, but steeper slabs mostly push you out onto grassy ramps. The towers on the east ridge of Sgùrr a' Choire Bheithe (NM 895 015) look intimidating but turn out to be easy (but enjoyably airy). The upper parts of An Stac (NM 866 889) have lots of fun short outcrops but no lines and the north-east ridge of Meith Bheinn (NM 822 882) has many short easy slabs of excellent rock. The north-east flank of Sgùrr a' Mhuidhe (562m) has a very accessible crag at NM 864 826 (not shown on the Landranger map, stay low on the approach until below the cliff). The left flank of this gives 100m of lovely Grade 2 slabs, with more outcrops above leading almost to the summit. There is also an irresistible pinnacle at NM 868 819.

Sgùrr a' Mhuidhe, North-East Flank (Grade 2).

Scrambler: Jamie Hageman. Photo: Iain Thow.

LOCH LOCHY HILLS

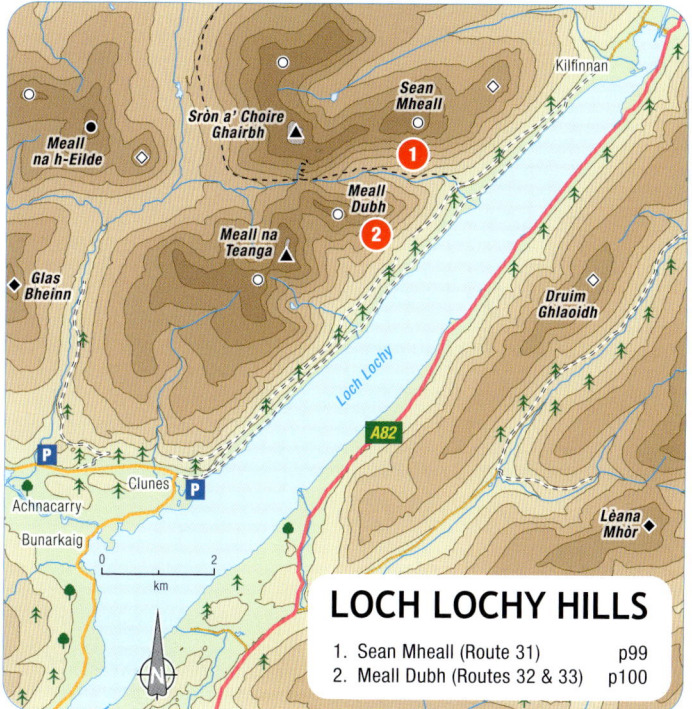

LOCH LOCHY HILLS
1. Sean Mheall (Route 31) p99
2. Meall Dubh (Routes 32 & 33) p100

The Loch Lochy Hills

Sròn a' Choire Ghairbh and Meall na Teanga are a popular round from either Kilfinnan at the north end of Loch Lochy or Clunes to the south. They give easy though quite steep walking on good paths with tremendous views out over the Great Glen and west to Knoydart and Kintail.

SRÒN A' CHOIRE GHAIRBH 935m

(NN 223 945)   OS Explorer 413   Map p99

Steep sided and flat topped, this Munro is easily combined with its neighbour on good paths. The south face has plenty of rock, but it is well guarded by purgatorial grass and heather. The scramble is on the south face of Sean Mheall (887m) a subsidiary top 2km east of the main summit.

31 Sean Mheall, South Face Grade 2 or 3
Alt 250m   Ht Gain +500m   (NN 244 937)   Map p99

A good finish spoiled by a scrappy middle. Starts up a stream gully then, when this forks, follows the buttress between the gullies.

Approach
This route is most easily approached from Kilfinnan to the north but it can also be done after one of the next two routes by dropping down the east ridge of Meall Dubh to the forest edge. From the road end at Kilfinnan follow the forest road south-west, keeping on the higher track when the Great Glen Way drops down left. After about 3km take a well-used but smaller path up right into the forest. Cross the stream at the forest edge, then in 300m reach another stream (at 244 937), which is the start of the route.

The Route
Go up boulders and short falls, quite lichenous in places. Eventually you are forced out of the gully bed by a slimy slabby fall. Go up the right bank and up steep grass and heather until the stream forks. Descend into the right fork above its first pitch, then go out left onto the heathery buttress between the two branches of the stream. From two small birches zigzag up heather, with traces of path. Where these start to peter out, mossy cascades in the stream bed on the right are a better option. Follow these until better rock starts to appear on both banks. Go left back onto the buttress and things improve.

After an easy start climb slabs left of centre (Grade 3, easier to the right), then a central rib. Go left into a mossy niche and pull out steeply leftwards on big flakes. After an easier ridge go up between two big boulders to easy ground. The next step can be climbed by a steep juggy pillar on its right or avoided further right. Then you have the options of an easy finish or harder slabs both left and right.

MEALL NA TEANGA 917m

(NN 220 924)   OS Explorer 413   Map p99

This mountain has a trio of tops linked by pleasant grassy ridges. The highest top just scrapes Munro status. The scrambles are on the south face of Meall Dubh (837m), a subsidiary top 1km to the north-east of the main summit. With a little cunning it is possible to combine Meall na Teanga with its Munro neighbour, Sròn a' Choire Ghairbh, via scrambles on both mountains.

32 Meall Dubh, Central Buttress Grade 2 or 3
Alt 450m   Ht Gain +200m   (NN 236 927)   Map p99   Diag p101

A very steep and indirect approach, but the scrambling is quite good once it gets going.

Approach
From the bend in the road at Clunes (NN 201 886) take the forest road

102 LOCH LOCHY HILLS

*Meall Dubh, Central Buttress (Route 32, Grade 3).
Scrambler: George Archibald. Photo: Noel Williams.*

towards Loch Lochy, taking the upper fork after a few hundred metres. Some 6km later the track ends just before a prominent stream, the Dearg Allt. Go steeply up the south bank of this stream, and once above the forest carry on up the spur, with excellent views of the scrambles, to reach a small col at 530m. Take a deer track slanting down right onto the main face. This passes 10m below a prominent small pine and then crosses a deep gully with a small stream. The next buttress is guarded by a bluff which is split by a faint gully/groove just left of centre. There is a bigger pine tree on its right-hand side.

The Route
The top of this bluff can be reached either by ascending the central gully/groove on heather and then slanting right or by heading rightwards towards the pine tree, climbing a tiny slab 3m to the right of it and pulling up on heather before moving back left. Either way, gain the crest of the buttress, where the scrambling proper begins. More rock gradually appears and things get much more pleasant. At a steep slabby buttress go left and climb a heathery recess before rejoining the crest. At twin buttresses above this either climb the right-hand one on small sharp holds (Grade 3) or more broken rock on the left side of the left-hand buttress. Easier rock leads to the top.

33 Meall Dubh Right-hand Buttress   Grade 3
Alt 450m   Ht Gain +200m   (NN 237 927)   Map p99   Diag p101
More broken than the previous route but the scrambling parts are better.

Approach
As for the previous route follow the deer track to the stream beyond the small pine. Continue along the deer path and go across Central Buttress to another wet gully and so reach the buttress beyond.

The Route
Grovel up steep heather on the left-hand angle of the buttress, with traces of path and occasional rock. Arrive at much steeper rock, split into two buttresses by a chimney groove. Climb steeply up the right edge of this on good holds (a little extra rock can be found rather artificially by starting a little further right, going up to a steep slab and traversing left across the lower part of this to reach the right edge of the groove). The groove itself is less exposed but not much easier. Either way reaches a heathery area with steep rock above. From the top left of the heather pull awkwardly up left to reach another heather slope and go right across the bottom of this to the rib beyond it. Climb the rib on positive holds (some loose), first left then right to finish up the skyline. A little higher are twin buttresses. Climb the left arête of the left one airily on excellent holds. The right arête is only slightly harder if you use the heather on the right just below the top. Now walk up a nice narrow arête with occasional rock to climb an enjoyable final buttress by the left hand of two spurs on good small holds.

ARDGOUR & ARDNAMURCHAN

West of Fort William and south of the railway to Mallaig the landscape is fretted by sea lochs and dissected by deep glens, with glacial scouring having left lots of exposed rock. Climbers and scramblers will home in on the gneiss of Garbh Bheinn, which boasts fine examples in both categories, with the Great Ridge the obvious classic. Many of the nearby hills are also extremely rocky, but finding consistent lines is another matter and most of the routes here involve stringing together isolated outcrops. The excellence of the rock, however, often makes up for a certain amount of disjointedness. Out on its own at the far end of the Ardnamurchan peninsula the ring of gabbro crags offers a few short but excellent routes, as well as superlative single pitch rock climbing.

Ardgour

The main grain of this rugged area runs east to west, and the deep glens between the ridges provide the access for most routes here, usually from either Glen Tarbet on Loch Linnhe or Strontian further west. However, the first two routes are accessed by the forestry road down Loch Shiel from Glenfinnan.

SGÒRR CRAOBH A' CHAORAINN 775m

(NM 895 758)   Map p105

This Corbett is situated on the south side of Loch Shiel. It is usually ascended along with its higher neighbour, Sgùrr Ghiubhsachain. Its northern ridge is a switchback of smaller summits, the northernmost of which is Meall na h-Airigh (443m). This has a fun, if rather heathery route up the west ridge of its west summit, Sgòrr Chòinnich (not named on the OS 1:50k map).

 34 Meall na h-Airigh, West Ridge   Grade 2/3   *
Alt 150m   Ht Gain +200m   (NM 898 789)   Map p105   Diag p106

Steep heather leads to a series of outcrops with a dramatic finish.

Approach
Follow the path from Glenfinnan visitor centre south-east and over a bridge to meet the forest road down the east side of Loch Shiel. Follow this to 895 790, about 1km down the loch, where the steep slopes on the left open out, at the first stream beyond the forest, roughly opposite the far end of the fish farm. Go up either bank of the stream (right easier) to the mouth of a gorge.

The Route
Go up heather left of the gorge, with a path appearing as the ground steepens. Climb occasional slabs and more heather to reach boulders at an easing of angle below a steep buttress. Traverse well right here above the

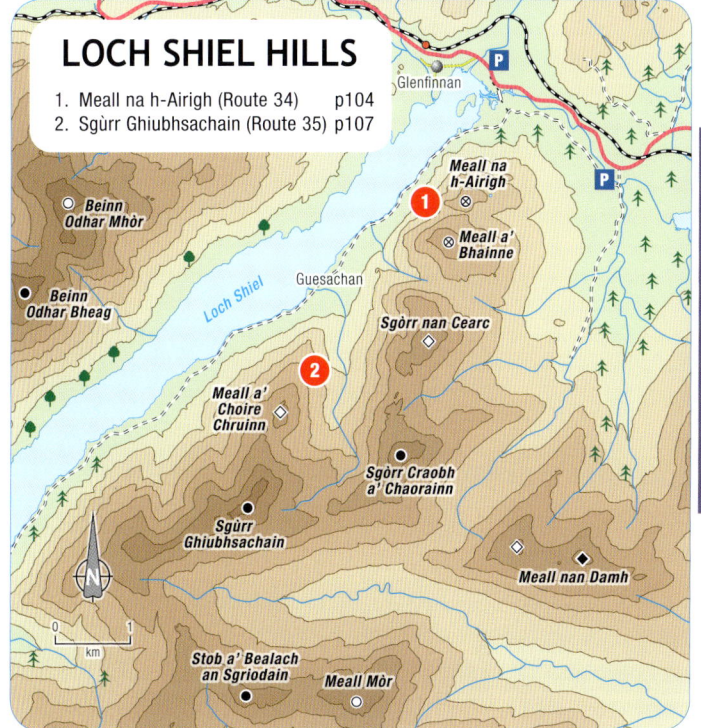

gully, to reach two rock ribs. Either of these is good, the left one steep but positive, the right one easier. Go up a slab, then up left to a steeper rib. Start up this direct on surprisingly good holds (or avoid the start on the left). Carry on up the ridge on superb rock and at the final steep step either climb it direct on positive holds (Grade 3) or avoid it on the left. The summit of Sgòrr Chòinnich is just beyond.

Nearby, the south flank of Meall a' Bhainne has a line of Grade 3 outcrops running up leftwards from just left of the col and a Grade 1 rib in the centre of the face. South again, the east-facing slab on the north-east flank of Sgòrr nan Cearc at NM 903 777 is a good but short Grade 2. Climb the lower slab centrally then move left to a steeper slab, gradually petering out as you approach the ridge.

34. West Ridge — Grade 2/3 *

SGÙRR GHIUBHSACHAIN 849m

(NM 875 751)   Map p105

Most recognisable as the pointed peak on the left in the classic view of the Glenfinnan monument, this steep-sided summit would be very popular if it was 70 metres higher. All three ridges are worthwhile, with the North Ridge incorporating some excellent scrambling.

 35 North Ridge   Grade 3 or easier   **
Alt 300m   Ht Gain+600m   (NM 884 769)   Map p105

Slabs and outcrops link together logically into a good long scramble up a nicely poised ridge. The route described is Grade 3, but very escapable, so could be made much easier, or even reduced to walking.

Approach
As for the previous route but carry on along the forest road to Guesachan. Go up the west side of the stream past a new hydro intake to about 200m, then head up right to the largest slab above, with a steep right-hand side and three perched blocks 10m up on the left. There are many more slabs further up left, some quite steep and smooth.

The Route
Climb a crack 10m right of the blocks, then move left and up much easier slabs to reach the ridge. Outcrops and walking lead over a minor summit and up to another steepening. After the first outcrop go left and up a quartzy rib to easy ground and a small pool. At the next rise go left and up the left side of a vertical face, then slabby ribs lead to the summit of Meall a' Choire Chruinn.

At the col beyond go left below a huge detached block and climb lovely knobbly slabs. As the ground steepens beyond another pool go up an easy angled right slanting rib. At its top go left up bouldery outcrops to arrive at the right side of a bigger cliff. A big slab curves up left, with a narrow start below a corner. Make an awkward move onto the slab then take cracks up left to climb the skyline, soon easing. There are easier slabs further right and the cliff can be tackled direct from further down to the left at Moderate. Minor outcrops lead up to the north top, then on to the higher south top.

The next two hills are more remote. They are usually approached from the single-track road which runs over the hill from Strontian to Polloch.

CÀRN NA NATHRACH 786m

(NM 886 699)   Map p108

A long ridge, steep and rocky on both sides and in the heart of some fabulously wild country (having no peaks over 3000 feet definitely makes the area quieter!).

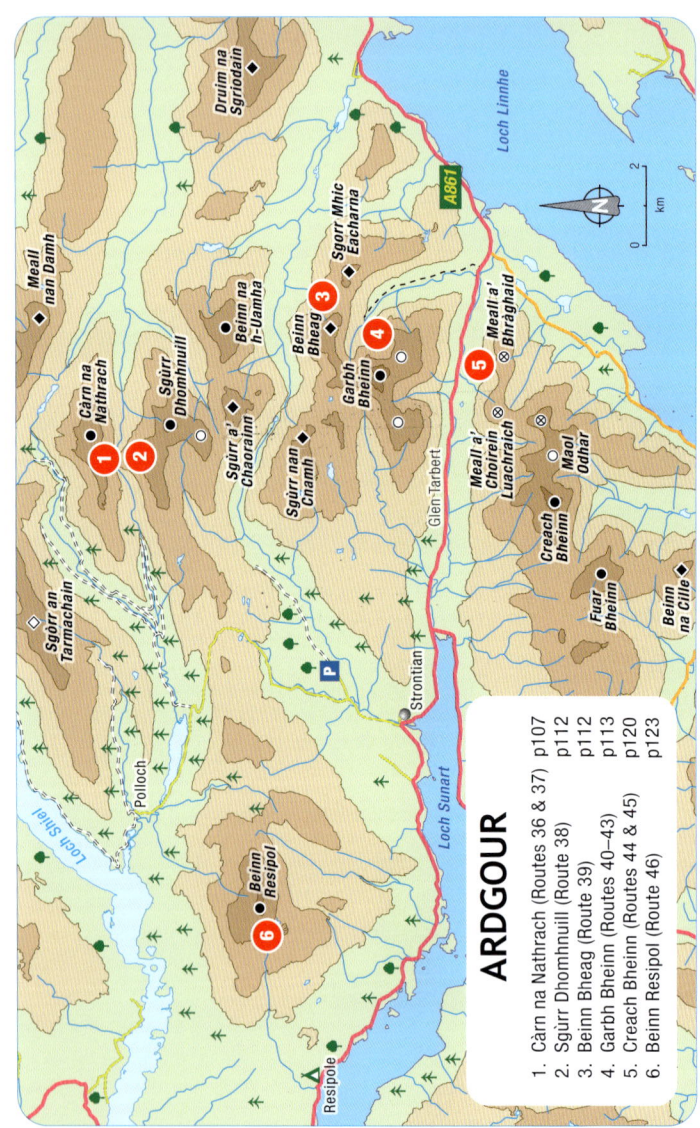

36 Left Spur   Grade 2
Alt 450m   Ht Gain + 120m   (NM 888 694)   Map p108   Diag p109

Nothing special but much more enjoyable than slogging up the very steep grass from the south. A good line but quite patchy rock.

Approach
This is above the col at the head of Gleann na Cloiche Sgoilte, which can be reached either by a long walk up Glen Scaddle, or a 7km walk up Gleann an Dubh Choirein from the head of Loch Doilet to the west (easiest), or (shortest but rough and steep) by working up Druim Garbh from the top of the Strontian to Polloch road and dropping northwards down a deer track from the notch at 869 682 before traversing east to the col. From the col go up northwards to a prominent steep buttress above a boulder field. There are a few enjoyable small outcrops below and left that make a good introduction.

The Route
From the right-hand edge of the steep cliff a grassy groove goes up left. Follow the left edge of this, then where it eases and starts to break up move right across the groove and onto the main buttress below two perched blocks. Pass these with care and go up the centre of the spur on shattered quartzy rock. Easy slabby scrambling continues for some distance before eventually fading out into the hillside. A few minor craglets can be found above on the way to the summit.

37 Right Spur   Grade 3 or Moderate
Alt 400m   Ht Gain + 150m   (NM 889 694)   Map p108   Diag p109

Longer and on better rock than the Left Spur but not as good a line.

Approach
As for the Left Spur, but start well below and right of the steep buttress at a long spur with a slabby left side.

The Route
Try to keep to the left flank of the spur, although the holds keep leading you up to the crest, which is easy. Reach a boulder field level with the one below the steep cliff to the left. Up right is another steep face, climbed right of centre by a rib just left of a grassy groove. Continue up the right side of the spur on steep stepped walls to reach a terrace.

Climbers will be tempted by the steep clean slab up left, V Diff centrally, Moderate up the airy left edge. Alternatively the right edge of the main buttress is easy and direct. More outcrops follow until the spur fades out. Up right is a steep wall below a large perched block, climbed by its easy left edge. A knobbly rib above is fun. This is started on the left, then slabs and minor outcrops continue most of the way to the ridge, which is reached just east of the summit.

SGÙRR DHOMHNUILL 888m

(NM 890 679)   Map p108

Although the highest hill in Ardgour, Sgùrr Dhomhnuill is a shy peak often hiding behind smaller closer neighbours. Both it and its subsidiary summits of Druim Garbh and Sgùrr na h-Ighinn are rocky and pointed but continuous lines are few, the best being on the north flank of Druim Garbh.

38 Druim Garbh, Left-hand Slabs   Grade 3   **
Alt 450m   Ht Gain +250m   (NM 884 689)   Map p108   Diag p111

Remote and north-facing they may be, but these fine clean slabs give 400m of entertainment and are well worth the effort of getting there.

Approach
Approach by any of the variants as for Route 36. The descent from the notch route fits well with a continuation over Sgùrr Dhomhnuill and Sgùrr na h-Ighinn, down Druim Leac a' Sgiathain to the lead mines and back over Druim Glas. This makes a great day out covering some marvellously rough and wild country.

The most sustained slabs are just left of the col, but these are quite steep and at least V Diff, so scrambling routes get forced off the rock onto grassy rakes. It is better to traverse left below these, cross a streamlet and pass below a large boulder to reach a wide clean slab, the start of the route. There is a much bigger easy angled slab below and left of this.

The Route
Climb the wide clean slab, which soon eases to almost walking, then either continue direct up easy slabs or go up left and across a small stream to climb a steeper slab with a vertical right-hand edge. This is quite smooth in places but a zigzagging scrambling route is feasible on superb rock. The two routes converge and become grassy, so go up left, aiming for another clean slab, which is quite tricky if tackled direct. Above this the rock steepens briefly and becomes knobbly before easing. Climb a rib just right of a small stream, which leads to more easy slabs. Head up left to a large hanging slab, easier than it looks, and continue to a large block below a wide grassy bowl. Move left to more slabs, then scrappier scrambling continues to the summit of Druim Garbh.

If continuing to Sgùrr Dhomhnuill, which is highly recommended as it's a splendid summit, then some good outcrops at about Grade 2 can be found a little left of the direct line, running up almost to the summit.

BEINN BHEAG 736m

(NM 915 635)   Map p108

The round of Coire an Iubhair is a classic day out, with Garbh Bheinn as the

GARBH BHEINN

scenic climax, Beinn Bheag is the highest summit on the northern arm, with an enjoyably lumpy ridge and great views of the north face of Garbh Bheinn.

39 East Face   Grade 2   *
Alt 400m   Ht Gain +200m   (NM 921 636)   Map p108

This is a wide expanse of gneiss slabs, easily accessible from the ridge, so easy to incorporate into the Coire an Iubhair circuit.

Approach
From the parking place at the foot of Coire an Iubhair head up open slopes northwards to follow the ridge of Druim an Iubhair to the summit of Sgòrr Mhic Eacharna. Descend westwards to Bealach nan Aingidh, then slant down rightwards, crossing two small streams, to arrive at clean slabs about 100m below the bealach.

The Route
Climb the first two slabs, then walking angle slabs lead to the right-hand end of a steep band. Go up the right edge of this, then head up right on minor outcrops to reach more sustained rock. A clean slab leads to a beautiful left-slanting groove with a steeper nose above. A little higher is a much bigger slab, with the best line starting just left of a slanting overlap and continuing up right to pass left of a perched block.

Above and left of this an airy rib is quite delicate (the scoop above the block is much easier). Small slabs now lead up to the left end of the vertical headwall. Start up a stepped rib just left of a small gully, then transfer to the right side of the gully as the angle eases. Easy ground arrives soon afterwards, with the summit 100m or so higher.

ARDGOUR & ARDNAMURCHAN

GARBH BHEINN 885m

(NM 904 622)   Map p108

One of the rockiest peaks on the Scottish mainland, with acres of gneiss slabs and a scatter of steeper cliffs. The rock climbs on the South Wall are justly famous, and the whole northern arc of the mountain offers great scope for exploratory scrambling. Four lines are described here but many more could be found.

40 Eagle's Nest Slabs   Grade 3   ***
Alt 150m   Ht Gain +450m   (NM 920 621)   Map p108   Diag p114

300m of superb gneiss slabs running up a blunt shoulder. A good general line with lots of possible variation in the details, up to about 4b in places if desired, although easier lines are always available. Makes an excellent warm up for either Great Ridge or Pinnacle Ridge.

Approach
From the parking place by the bridge at the foot of Coire an Iubhair take the

*Pleasant scrambling on Eagle's Nest Slabs (Route 40, Grade 3).
Scrambler: George Archibald. Photo: Noel Williams.*

path up the east bank of the stream for about 2km before crossing it below the route, usually easy. The route follows the left edge of the spur of Nead na h-Iolaire (Eagle's Nest, not named on the 1:50000 map). It is just right of a big open Y-gully (Coire Garbh Bheag). A steep band crosses the buttress low down and easy angled slabs lead up to its left end.

The Route
Amble up the easy angled slabs, with an optional steeper start. Traverse right onto the main slabs above the steep band and follow their left edge, quite sustained. The slabs broaden and get easier, usually easiest on the left, before eventually breaking up just right of a short overhanging buttress. Go right and climb a lovely clean staircase on the skyline to a grass terrace. A steep clean rib on the left, above a block, is Diff, while ahead is much easier, working up left to reach a big block above the rib. More super slabs follow, becoming a skyline rib and easing, with the best positions and most sustained rock on the left. Eventually the rib narrows and runs into the main hillside. Move right and climb another buttress to a step on the skyline where the slabs all converge to a more defined shoulder. There are outcrops above this which lead up to the summit of Sròn a' Gharbh Choire Bhig, or a long traverse leads to the foot of the Great Ridge, or a wide grassy rake leads down to the foot of Pinnacle Ridge, the latter option involving losing 100m of height.

41 Great Ridge   Difficult   ***
Alt 600m   Ht Gain +300m   (NM 908 624)   Map p108   Diag p114&117

An eye-grabbing line, airy positions, a wild setting and superb rock, what more could you want! Only the rather awkward and indirect approaches let it down. (The best option is the Direct Start, but that is quite a stiff Severe.)

Approach
Walk up Coire an Iubhair past the previous route then bear left up by the Allt a' Gharbh Choire Mhoir (not named on Landranger maps, but this is the stream descending directly from the summit of Garbh Bheinn). Go through the narrows at the foot of the corrie and the Great Ridge is unmissable ahead. Head up to the lowest rock.

The Route
a) Right-hand Start
From the lowest rock slant right up steep grass below a rock overlap. An awkward move round a prow leads to a grass ledge. Then go up to more grass below steep rock, with a thin grass ledge leading left. Go into the gully on the left and climb this, with either a thrutchy chimney to finish or airy moves on the spur out right. Arrive at the lower of two large grass terraces that slope up left below the Great Ridge proper. Follow this up left to the foot of a clean slabby rib. Climb this on good holds, with one energetic pull over a small overlap. At the top walk across right to the foot of the main ridge.

b) Left-hand Start
If approaching from the top of Eagle's Nest Slabs the left-hand start is more

*High up on Great Ridge, Garbh Bheinn (Route 41, Difficult).
Climber: Helen Watson. Photo: Scott Muir.*

convenient. Traverse horizontally right across a slabby rock face on ledges. Then enter and cross over a prominent gully before ascending grass and rock to the upper terrace. Descend a grass slope to the start of the ridge proper.

Climb a steep groove, almost blocked by a large flake, then up a sharp crest. Either a steep wide chimney with big flakes or an airier pad out left lead to easy ground below a steep wall. Walk left on a grass ledge then go back up right by one of two ramps, the first exposed and juggy, bordering on V Diff, the second easier. Another easy section leads to a steep tower, climbed by its left arête (avoidable further left). From a niche on the left move up right and follow a sharp crest to easier ground. The ridge now breaks up into outcrops, which can be clambered up or avoided as desired, leading enjoyably direct to the summit cairn.

42 Pinnacle Ridge   Moderate   **
Alt 350m   Ht Gain +500m   (NM 911 625)   Map p108   Diag p114

An excellent line with lots of variety and some good airy positions but a bit disjointed. The crux is quite hard and exposed, much harder than anything else on the route.

Approach
As for the previous route as far as the narrows, then cut sharply back right above the lowest steep cliff, following a well used path to the crest of the buttress.

The Route
Lots of outcrops lead up a minor top with a small pool beyond, then a slabby nose leads to easy ground. Walk up via a knobbly rib to a steeper cliff, the crux, arriving below an overhung niche. Go 10m left of this and climb a cleaned left-slanting groove. Work right up ledges, with a hard pull over a steep block. Directly above this climb a steep left-slanting groove on excellent holds, then traverse right airily below a perched block to arrive at easier ground on the skyline.

As the ridge narrows nice scrambling on the crest eases to walking, then becomes a sharp edge with two steeper prows (avoidable on the right, but fun direct). When the ridge runs into the hillside traverse hard left on a grass ledge to climb a lovely clean slab. Parts of this are ice-polished to a smooth sheen, other bits are rough and knobbly. At the top a sharp arête leads to an easier one and then open hillside. A few more outcrops can be found on the way up left to the summit.

43 Sròn Lag nan Gamhna   Grade 2   **
Alt 550m   Ht Gain +250m   (NM 902 630)   Map p108   Diag p114

An obvious inclusion if doing the classic round of Coire an Iubhair, a couple of rocky spurs providing plenty of entertainment on excellent rock.

Approach
If doing the anticlockwise round (the best way), then drop down from Beinn

ARDGOUR

Bheag (past a minor outcrop with a fun Grade 3 arête just left of the central groove) to the saddle bearing Lochan Coire an Iubhair. Sròn Lag nan Gamhna is directly ahead, the broad broken rib above the right end of the lochan.

The Route
Start on the left and follow vegetated ledges up right to the crest, then go up this. A clean slab on the left is good, then a tall rib right of an open groove is excellent. Smaller ribs then lead to the top of the spur. Cross a knoll and go down left to a small col. Climb a small buttress to a huge pile of blocks, then traverse left across a small gully to climb lovely striped slabs on knobbles to the top of the north face. The next section starts with easy slabs, then finishes up the left arête of a left-slanting groove on amazing contorted rock. The top of the north-east buttress arrives all too soon, then a short descent leads to more craglets and the top of Pinnacle Ridge, followed by yet more craglets and the summit.

The spur further right, at 898 626, is worth doing but not as good as it looks from the Strontian road. It is most easily approached from Coire an Iubhair and over the col at its head. Slant down once past the lochan to cross the foot of a deep gully, then separated outcrops leads up to more sustained rock. Where the buttress splits near the top the left half is better (Grade 2).

Eccentrics approaching Garbh Bheinn from Strontian can find some pleasant slabs on Sgùrr a' Bhuic, a spur of Sgùrr nan Cnamh, as well as some short harder slabs on the south flank of the latter.

CREACH BHEINN 853m

(NM 870 576)   Map p108

This Corbett is the highest of the Kingairloch hills. It has a classic southern horseshoe around Glen Galmadale, but the best scrambling round starts from Glen Tarbert to the north. This incorporates the slabs on the northern flanks of both Meall a' Bhràghaid and the eastern top of Maol Odhar.

44 Holly Tree Slabs   Grade 2, 3 or Difficult   **
Alt 100m   Ht Gain +300m   (NM 913 596)   Map p108   Diag p121
Superb gneiss slabs, giving over 300m of scrambling, albeit escapable, almost all the way to the summit ridge. The lower slab would be pretty serious in the wet.

Approach
There is a small parking spot – easy to miss – on the south side of the road about halfway between the mouth of Glen Tarbert and the bridge at the watershed. Otherwise walk down the glen from the parking place at the watershed. The slabs are obvious on the south side of the glen, slanting up right from about 100m above the road. The lowest slab on the left is the biggest and a couple of minor outcrops lead up to it.

122 ARDGOUR

*Holly Tree Slabs (Route 44, Grade 2, 3 or Difficult).
Scrambler: Iain Thow. Photo: Noel Williams.*

The Route
The Difficult variation starts at the foot of the cleaner left-hand slab and tackles it direct. It is easier to start up an easy rib on the right then either up the right-hand edge of the main slab (Grade 2) or traverse left onto the main slab above the steepest section. Go up the central crack for a few feet then slant left up a thin crack to climb a larger ragged one (Grade 3). Above the main slab all the routes rejoin and lots of smaller slabs lead up rightwards all the way to the summit ridge, with plenty of choice of route.

45 Coire Mheall Challuim Slabs   Grade 2
Alt 500m   Ht Gain +80m   (NM 892 586)   Map p108

A good follow on to Holly Tree Slabs, short but on excellent rock. It can be seen from the summit of Meall a' Bhraghaid (510m) by looking south-westwards across the corrie. It is much better than it looks from a distance.

Approach
From the top of the previous scramble head west to Meall a' Choirein Luachraich. Head down to the col below the north ridge of Meall Odhar's eastern top (715m). Then follow an easy traverse line leftwards for some distance to below the main crag. A few small craglets lead up to a grass terrace below the buttress proper, with blocky scree on the right and a prominent clean slab up left.

The Route
Start up the left-hand of two tongues which run into grooves leading up right. A broader spur leads up to a grass ledge below and right of the prominent slab. The slab itself is fairly easy V Diff. Climb a rib right of it, steep to start, to reach easy ground. There is another outcrop up right before the scrambling peters out to boulders.

It is worth continuing from the eastern top for 2.5km over the main summit of Maol Odhar (794m) to visit Creach Bheinn. Parts of a Voodoo aircraft, which crashed in 1964, can be seen on the summit of Maol Odhar. The remains of a very fine 'Colby Camp' are situated in a dip just before the summit of Creach Bheinn. This was built and manned by OS parties in the mid nineteenth century during the Principal Triangulation of Great Britain.

To get back to your starting point from here involves retracing your steps to the col west of Meall Odhar and slanting down north-eastwards to reach its north ridge. At about the 620m contour a steep grassy gully leads down into Coire nam Frithallt which can be followed down to the road.

BEINN RESIPOL 845m

(NM 767 655)   Map p108

A fine isolated rocky hill, Beinn Resipol dominates the landscape west of Strontian. The views down Loch Sunart towards Mull and out north-west to Rum and Eigg are tremendous.

46 South-West Flank   Grade 2
Alt 650m   Ht Gain +200m   (NM 763 654)   Map p108

Much of this is just walking up rock slabs but the scrambling sections are good and it makes an interesting way up the hill.

Approach
Follow the standard path up the Allt Mhic Chiarain from Resipole Campsite through lovely birch woods. As you approach the summit pyramid it appears to consist of three banks of slabs slanting up left to right. This route follows the lowest of these, starting at a group of sharp arêtes at the bottom left.

The Route
Start up the lowest left hand arête, which soon curves over into walking. More easy arêtes and walking slabs continue up right, with technical problems around if you want them, including several beautifully patterned schist slabs. Follow the slabs round onto the south flank and walk up to a steeper band, with several overhangs and a prominent quartz vein. Climb the vein and continue rightwards up knobbly slabs to easy ground. More slabby ribs lead up right (mostly walking) to reach another steep band on the skyline. Climb this by a rib on the left, then climb a clean slab on the right by a thin crack. Small outcrops carry on up to the summit.

Ardnamurchan

The ring of small gabbro peaks in the western part of the Ardnamurchan peninsula provide any amount of exploratory scrambling and many short rock climbs, the one often blurring into the other. Some examples follow to give the general idea.

CREAG AN AIRGID 257m

(NM 478 667) Map p125

This top on the south side of the Ardnamurchan Ring Dyke is easily reached.

47 Western Flank   Grade 3 or Moderate   **
Alt 50m   Ht Gain +100m   (NM 475 668)   Map p125

A roadside chain of outcrops leading to a fine viewpoint. There is a vast amount of route choice, so the following is merely one among many possibilities.

Approach
From Kilchoan take the lighthouse road for 1km, then turn right on the road to Sanna. Follow this for about 2km until it breaks through the rim of gabbro hills. Just around a right-hand bend is a parking place, with the crag clearly visible up on the right, about 50m above the road.

Cross the fence and slant up steeply between two minor outcrops to more sustained rock.

CREAG AN AIRGID

ARDNAMURCHAN

1. Creag an Airgid (Route 47) p124
2. Sgùrr nan Gabhar (Route 48) p127
3. Meall Sanna (Route 49) p127
4. Beinn na Seilg (Route 50) p131

The Route
Climb a crumbly wall in the centre, then a left to right scoop. A two-stepped wall follows with a steep finish (Moderate, or easier to the right), then go up right on a broad ramp of lovely knobbly rock. The right side of the crag ahead has a nice flake running from right to left, then easy slabs and grass lead to a knoll. On the other side of the dip beyond traverse left below vertical rock until you can pull up onto the top. Easy slabs now lead up to a steeper tier.

The Moderate option now climbs a steep nose 3m right of the obvious vertical arête (see photo overleaf, easier than it looks), then moves right along a small ledge to an airy move up onto slabs. An easy wide crack leads to the top. Alternatively you can work left up a ramp on the left hand side of the crag, not technically much easier but much less exposed.

The next craglet has a steep crack with a hard start (Moderate) or a slab on its right (Grade 3). The ground then eases to walking angle slabs and grass

Western Flank, Creag an Airgid (Route 47, Moderate).
Climber: Iain Thow. Photo: Jamie Hageman.

and another dip. Beyond this are broken outcrops, finishing up an easy left to right ramp, then more walking slabs leading to the summit cairn.

SGÙRR NAN GABHAR 132m

(NM 469 699)   Map p125

This is a small but prominent rock peak on the northern side of the Ardnamurchan Ring Dyke. It has a steep crag on its south-west flank, described in the climbing guide, but surprisingly it is unnamed on the OS Landranger map.

48 North-East Rib   Grade 1/2
Alt 50m   Ht Gain +60m   (NM 471 701)   Map p125

This route provides a good introduction to slab padding on rough gabbro. The built path from Glendrian follows the Allt Mhic Cailein through Bealach Mòr past the eastern side of Sgùrr nan Gabhar.

Approach
Follow the path to the ruined Glendrian village (478 689). Beyond the houses bear left through a gateway to the rather wet continuation. The path enters a narrow valley with Sgùrr nan Gabhar up on the left, then where it crosses the Allt Mhic Cailean stay on the west bank for 50m to the lowest outcrop.

The Route
Gain the first step from the left and go up to a groove. The left edge of this becomes a long clean slab, easing and widening before breaking up below a steeper face. Climb the left hand of two prows and the slab above, then swing up right onto another big easy slab which leads to the summit.

Also good are the south-facing slabs (NM 470 698) to the right of the climbing crag, starting either at a small grassy col at the same height as the climbs or by slabby outcrops below this. There is plenty of route choice, Grade 3 direct or Grade 2 by the easiest line. This is the 'easy slab descent' mentioned in the climbing guide.

Glendrian Caves
Well worth a visit when in the area are the Glendrian Caves (NM 462 705). The atmospheric fissure of the main cave lies about halfway along the west face of the leaning prow of Rubha Carrach. It goes in 100m or so, with interesting tufa formations at the end, so take a torch. The other cave is much smaller but was lived in in Mesolithic times. The top of Rubha Carrach is a dramatic spot too, a grassy platform undercut on three sides.

MEALL SANNA 184m

(NM 452 686)   Map p125

Although only 184m high, Meall Sanna has one of the best views in Scotland.

West Flank, Meall Sanna (Route 49, Grade 3).
Scrambler: Jamie Hageman. Photo: Iain Thow.

MEALL SANNA

It is poised above the gorgeous Sanna Beach, and looks out to Rum, Eigg and Ardnamurchan Point.

 49 West Flank   Grade 3   *
Alt 50m   Ht Gain +120m   (NM 448 688)   Map p125

The blunt spur running west-north-west from the highest point has lots of exposed gabbro to play on.

Approach
From Sanna car park follow the track southwards until just past the last cottage, then slant up south eastwards, skirting left of a pond to a painted corrugated iron shed. Carry on past a house ruin to the lowest outcrop on the left.

The Route
Climb either a thin black crack or easier rock to the right. Walk up slabs to a steeper nose, climbed direct on great friction. Only on gabbro could you pad up so easily at this angle! More walking slabs and boulder problem walls lead to a knoll and a slight descent. A smooth slab (quite technical) and a steep but knobblier wall above a small pool provide more fun. Above these move left via more small outcrops, aiming for a big clean slab on the left flank of the ridge. Climb this direct, keeping ahead up a rib when another parallel slab develops on the left. An even bigger exposed slab further left is good too, but harder to incorporate into this line. Above the rib go direct up the nose ahead, easier than it looks, with the summit only a few metres away at the top. Settle down to enjoy the magnificent view.

A satellite view of Ardnamurchan (Centre 3). Photo: Bing Maps.

Hebrides Rib (Route 50, Grade 3 or Moderate).
Climber: Iain Thow. Photo: Jamie Hageman.

The Ring Intrusion

It's impossible to describe scrambling in Ardnamurchan without mentioning the ultimate scrambling day out here – a complete round of the Ring Intrusion known as the Great Eucrite. All three of these scrambles can be incorporated into this, going anticlockwise, and many other outcrops can easily be added in too. Although only 18km, this has around 1200m of ascent, much of it on rock, so it makes quite a long day.

BEINN NA SEILG 344m

(NM 456 641) Map p125

This little summit is the highest top south of the road from Kilchoan to the lighthouse. Again the view from the summit is outstanding.

50 Hebrides Rib,   Grade 3 or Moderate   **
Alt 250m   Ht Gain +100m   (NM 456 645)   Map p125

A superb little route which would be worth another star if it was longer. Rough gabbro slabs, delicate in places and briefly exposed but not sustained.

Approach

From a small parking place at Lochan na Crannaig, 2km out of Kilchoan on the Lighthouse road, head south-west across pathless tussocks to pick up the north ridge of Beinn na Seilg. At about 250m on this is the stepped Eigg Buttress, and the left edge of this is worth including. Scramble to the big right-slanting shelf then climb the left-hand of two cracks (hardish Grade 2). From the top drop down right to pass below a line of steep buttresses, which give excellent short rock climbs. At the far edge of the last one it is possible to go round the corner to join the route at half height, but it is much better to go further down to the foot of the spur at a long overhang.

The Route

Climb a crack just left of the bottom overhang, moving right once above it to go up a slab to a shelf. Climb a stepped wall right of an open groove to a bigger shelf, then two more short walls lead to walking angle slabs. The access from the left comes in here.

A short step leads to a more substantial buttress. From the left edge of this move up right then delicately left to a comfortable ledge on the arête. Either step airily left (Moderate) to a small ledge then go up more easily or take an easier staircase on the right to reach the same place. The right edge of the main slab is also good (easier). Easy slabs follow to a final steepening, climbed by an orange rib on the left, finishing right at the cairn of the north top.

The main west summit is a superb viewpoint, and the slab below the east summit is worth including, although more or less walking after the first couple of moves.

MULL

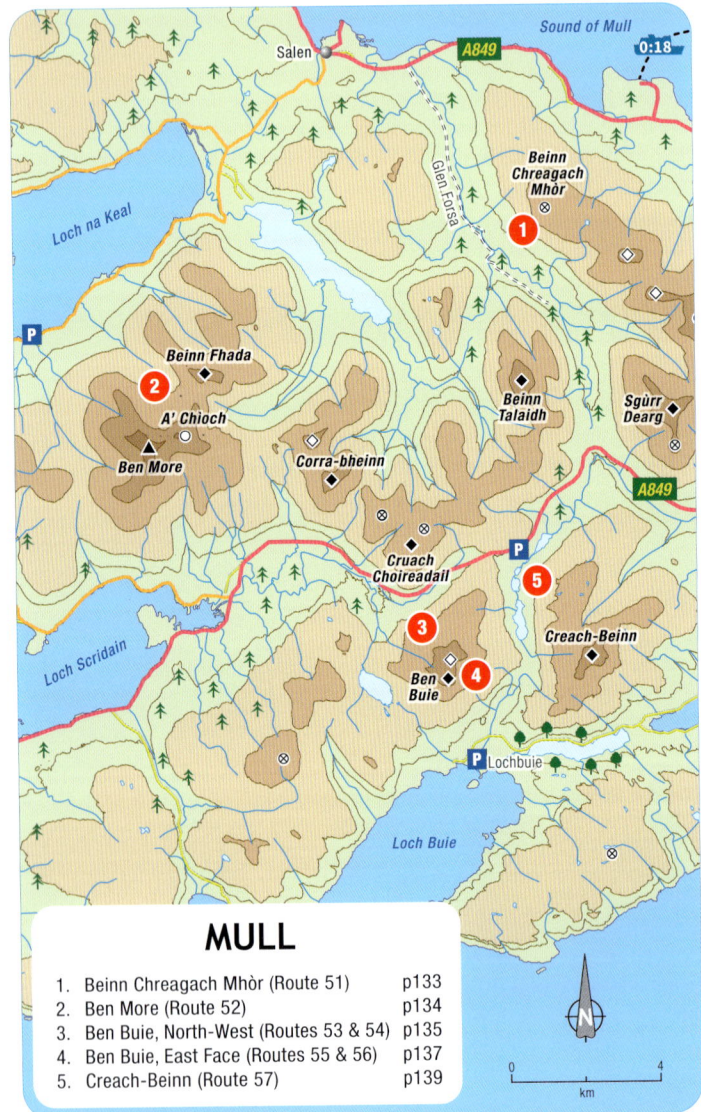

MULL

1. Beinn Chreagach Mhòr (Route 51) — p133
2. Ben More (Route 52) — p134
3. Ben Buie, North-West (Routes 53 & 54) — p135
4. Ben Buie, East Face (Routes 55 & 56) — p137
5. Creach-Beinn (Route 57) — p139

MULL

The Isle of Mull is carved from the remains of a Palaeogene volcanic complex, part of the vast sea of lavas poured out as the North Atlantic Ocean formed. Much of the island is basalt, which produces plenty of cliffs but not much scrambling, but luckily the south-central part of the island is built from the remains of the magma chamber from which the lavas issued, producing rough gabbro and other igneous rocks which are a delight to scramble up. Ben Buie in particular deserves to become a scramblers' mecca. By far the most popular route, however, is the narrow and shattered A' Chioch ridge of Ben More, although the fact that it finishes on the summit of the only island Munro outside Skye perhaps influences this! Mull is one of the best places in Britain for watching wildlife and this adds greatly to the pleasures of visiting the island, with Sea Eagles in particular being frequently seen.

There are plenty of hotels and B&Bs, an SYHA hostel in Tobermory, a bunkhouse at Craignure (<www.shielingholidays.co.uk>, tel:01680 812496) and a number of self catering cottages. Mull roads are nearly all still single track and getting around can take a while.

BEINN CHREAGACH MHÒR 579m

(NM 632 391)   OS Explorer 375   Map p132

On the north-east corner of the main group of hills is this steep-sided and flat-topped hill. The views out over the Sound of Mull are excellent.

51 South-West Face   Grade 2
Alt 450m   Ht Gain + 100m   (NM 631 389)   Map p132

Nothing special, but an opportunity to scramble on gabbro. Steep and serious low down, as well as rather heathery, but nice easy slabs higher up.

Approach
Follow the good track up Glen Forsa south-east of Salen (from NM 595 426) and cross the bridge at NM 613 386. The cliff is obvious, high up on the north side of the glen. Head up to the bottom left-hand corner, right of a boulder field, with a vertical wall running up leftwards and heathery crags to the right. There are some easy slabs on the way up.

The Route
Start just left of the bottom corner at a left-slanting slab with a vertical wall on its right. Climb the slab and step up onto a higher slab. At the top of this go up left on heather to a perch on the left arête (possible escape on left). Traverse right on steep heather then work up right to a large niche above the steepest part of the spur. Either make an exposed step up right or climb the back of the niche, which is less exposed but no easier. Rough slabs now lead to easy ground. Follow easy rock on the left edge of the spur past a brief

steepening until it runs out into the hillside. A short face just off left is fun, with the summit 100m further left.

There are some short but good slabs just left of the gully on the left flank of the spur. Start at the right edge and follow left-slanting cracks to the top.

BEN MORE 966m

(NM 525 331)   OS Explorer 375   Map p132

Mull's dominant peak is usually climbed by the good track from Dhiseig on the shores of Loch na Keal to the north-west but by far the best route is the classic northern circuit over A' Chioch, which includes two fine ridges. This is most easily started by walking up Gleann na Beinne Fada to the saddle north of A' Chioch. However, by including Beinn Fhada as described a little more scrambling can be included, as well as an enjoyable ridge and a fine rocky summit.

52 Northern Circuit   Grade 1   **
Alt 600m   Ht Gain +300m   (NM 537 340)   Map p132

Sharp ridges giving easy scrambling and airy positions. All the scrambling can be avoided, but this would miss the point (literally!). A good route on which to introduce people to the delights of scrambling, although a good head for heights is essential.

Approach
Start at the bridge over Abhainn na h-Uamha (NM 507 367) and follow a good path up the west bank past a gorge to the waterfall at 150m. If including Beinn Fhada then cross the river soon after this and go up steeply to the north-west top of Beinn Fhada. The slabs west of the summit are Grade 1 on quite shattered rock, with the grooves on the steeper short crag being Diff. Follow the ridge to the main summit (the slabs off right halfway along are very loose). Drop southwards to the col at the head of Gleann na Beinne Fada, where the direct route comes in.

The Route
The ridge to A' Chioch is easy at first, then steepens, narrows and gets rockier near the top. A good path zigzags up but the direct steps are easy enough. From A' Chioch a narrow ridge descends westwards before rising to Ben More. A good path avoids any problems on the left, but it is much more fun to tackle the arête direct. This is still easy but with a big drop on the right, and involves a couple of short descents. As you approach Ben More the ridge steepens, with the easiest line just left of the crest (further left is horribly scree-ridden).

The crest itself is still mostly easy, with an optional vertical wall on good spikes (Grade 2). The summit arrives all too soon, with views from Skye to Arran on a clear day. A good path runs north-westwards down to Dhiseig, meeting the road about 1.5km west of your start.

BEN BUIE 717m

(NM 605 271)   OS Explorer 375   Map p132

A wedge of rough gabbro sandwiched between Glen More and Lochbuie. The north and east sides are steep and rocky while the west flank descends gently (although still rockily) to the moorland around Loch Fuaron. Ramps of gabbro slabs run leftwards up the north face between Sròn Dubh and Creag na h-Iolaire, while the south end of the east face consists of three rocky buttresses, the northern one easy, the others both excellent scrambles.

53 Sròn Dubh Spur   Grade 2 or 3   *
Alt 250m   Ht Gain +200m   (NM 595 285)   Map p132   Diag p136

A long route with a good first half up slabs but a rather fragmented finish.

Approach

There is fairly limited parking at a pull off in Glen More opposite Sròn Dubh at NM 593 292. Cross the stream and head for the lowest rock on the face, about 100m left of where the face swings round to face west. There is a minor slab below the main spur.

The Route

After an avoidable steep start the spur becomes easy angled, with optional problems off to the right. It levels out at grass, with steeper rock above. Climb the nose direct, then another one above soon broadens out to easy slabs. A steeper slab above is Grade 3 direct, or easier coming in from either side a few feet up. Easy slabs run up for some way, finally breaking up below a long overhanging wall slanting up left. Directly above the highest slab of the lower spur a step off a boulder allows the wall to be climbed. Go up broken ground leftwards to another left-slanting vertical wall. The perched blocks on this are very loose, but just to the right an unlikely looking shallow groove is only Grade 3. Alternatively go round the wall to its left. Either way keep working up left, aiming for a prominent light coloured rib breaking through steeper cliffs. Climb this, followed by easier slabs to the top.

54 Sròn Dubh Central Slabs   Grade 3   **
Alt 250m   Ht Gain +200m   (NM 601 289)   Map p132   Diag p136

Rough gabbro slabs leading up to a superb exposed finish. Technically quite hard in places but escapable fairly frequently.

Approach

As for the Spur but head about 400m further left to where a band of easy angled slabs slants up left. The next stream to the left is the most prominent on the face and the route stays well right of this.

The Route

Start at a short steepish nose just left of a small stream and go leftwards up the easy angled slabs until they run out at a dip with big boulders. Go up

right past a small steep slab to a much bigger one. Start diagonally down and left from a small rowan, at a thin crack with grass tufts. Go up left of the crack and continue up left on superb rock. As this steepens it gets rougher and more holds appear. Break through an overlap just left of its lowest point and go up to heather. Move right and go up easier but more shattered slabs to a big perched block. Work left and up a steep slab on very rough rock, then an easier slab leads to an extensive boulder field, with intimidatingly steep rock ahead. On the top right-hand edge of the boulders climb a delicate slab to a perched block below the steep cliff. Start at the lowest point and go up right to a grass ledge. Traverse scarily left past loose blocks to better rock right on the nose, a spectacular perch. Go up and right on excellent rock to arrive suddenly at the top. Above are scattered outcrops and a long low wall with lots of problems, then easy rock leads up to the top of Cnap nan Gobhar

55 Summit Buttress   Grade 2/3
Alt 450m   Ht Gain +200m   (NM 607 272)   Map p132   Diag p138

Nicely positioned and a good line from a distance, but quite broken on closer acquaintance, becoming quite loose after a nice start.

Approach
From Lochbuie head up the slopes past Cnoc Reamhar. The route is the prominent buttress directly below the main summit on the east, with an obvious scree gully just to its right. Start at a rib just left of the scree gully.

The Route
Climb the crest of the rib, with good holds at the only steep bit. Eventually it becomes a slab slanting up left to more broken ground. Keep ahead to reach more steep rock as the spur becomes more defined again. Carefully surmount a rather shattered overlap, move up right and go through another small overhang to easier ground. The prow ahead is very loose so finish up its right edge, with an avoidable hard start if desired. The summit is only just above, with a superb view.

56 Juniper Buttress   Grade 3   **
Alt 450m   Ht Gain +250m   (NM 607 273)   Map p132   Diag p138

A succession of fairly steep walls of rough solid gabbro with lots of route choice and nice positions.

Approach
As for the previous route but go further right to the buttress on the right side of the scree gully. Start at the lowest rock, well right of the gully.

The Route
Climb a short groove, harder than it looks, then a left-slanting ramp leads through a steep tier to heather. On the next tier step off a block to surmount a short wall, step left and then work up right on easier rock to stones and heather. Above this climb the buttress centrally on good rock to another steep

*Summit Buttress (Route 55, Grade 2/3).
Scrambler: Pete McLeod. Photo: Gordon Rothero.*

wall. This goes direct at Difficult, or is avoidable on the right. Cross a large boulder field to a larger tier. Start right of centre on big steps then move left above the first prow. Zigzag up fairly steep rock just right of the crest to reach a large area of juniper and scree. An easy buttress leads to more juniper and scree, then easy rock runs up to a vertical wall crossing the buttress. Surmount this by a weakness left of centre, then go up more broken rock, aiming for the left-hand of two small towers. Either go up the easy groove between them or (better) start up the left tower direct, step left onto a slab, then work up right to the crest on good holds. Easy ground now leads to the central summit of Ben Buie.

The long spur running east from just north of Cnap nan Gobhar is mostly walking but has some Grade 1 scrambling (and steep short problems on the left), starting as low as the 350m contour.

CREACH-BEINN 698m

(NM 643 276)   OS Explorer 375   Map p132

An isolated mountain scattered with numerous small gabbro outcrops, Creach-Beinn is the southernmost big hill on the island, with a super view across to the Argyll hills.

140 MULL

CREACH-BEINN
North-West

57. Loch an Eilein Shoulder   Grade 2 *

CREACH-BEINN

Lochan an Eilein Shoulder (Route 57, Grade 2). Scrambler: Colin Moody.

 57 Loch an Eilein Shoulder   Grade 2   *
Alt 200m   Ht Gain +120m   (NM 626 295)   Map p132   Diag p140

An easily accessible scramble on rough gabbro. Nice moves and positions but a rather wandering line

Approach
From the parking at NM 623 303 descend to either of the narrows on Loch an Eilein (both crossable in most conditions, despite what the map implies). Go up to the lowest rock on the end of the broken spur where the face curves round from north-facing to west-facing, with steeper cliffs off to the left.

The Route
Start up a crack just left of a long vertical wall. This soon leads to easy slabs. Where these open out traverse left to a projecting rib, then climb a steeper band right to left past white intrusions. More easy slabs follow, then traverse left across grass to much more sustained slabs. Climb these on superb rough rock to a steeper finish on good holds right at the top of the crag.

An alternative finish carries straight on up from the first buttress instead of traversing left to the projecting rib. It climbs a succession of steeper faces, still Grade 2. This is not as good as the main route but has the possibility of including harder problems.

If going on to the summit of Creach-Beinn, then working round left over Beinn Fhada gives lots of small gabbro outcrops to play on. The crags shown on the OS Landranger map west of Creach-Beinn are mostly scree.

CAIRNGORMS

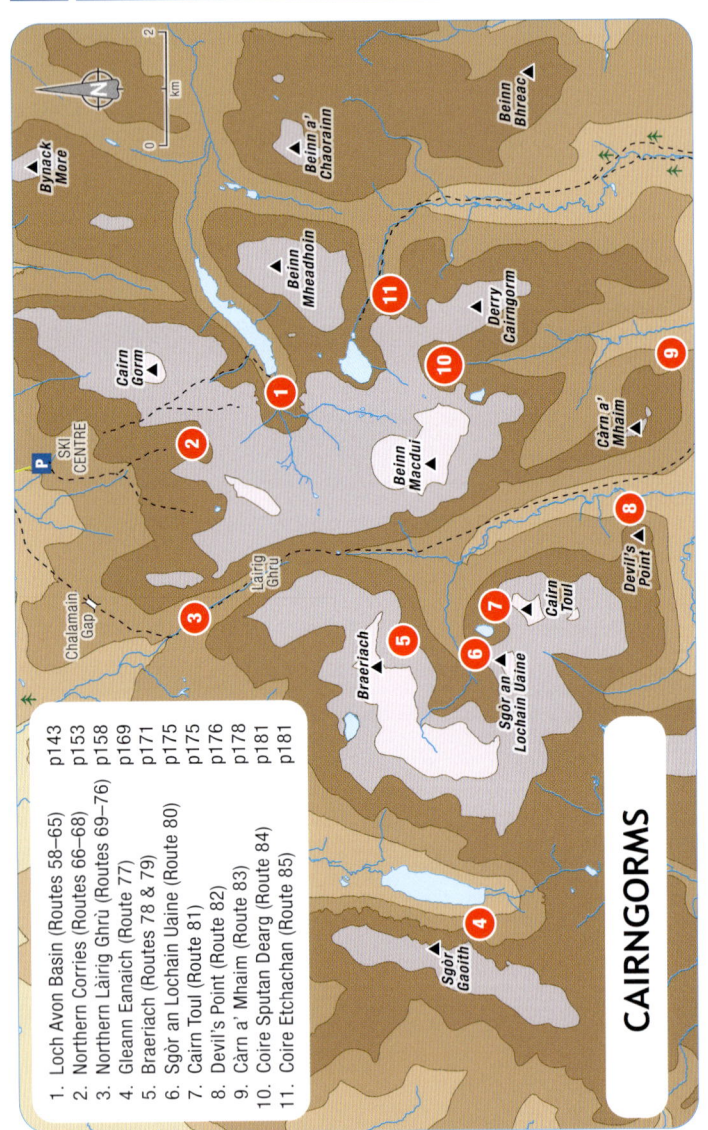

1. Loch Avon Basin (Routes 58–65) p143
2. Northern Corries (Routes 66–68) p153
3. Northern Làirig Ghrù (Routes 69–76) p158
4. Gleann Eanaich (Route 77) p169
5. Braeriach (Routes 78 & 79) p171
6. Sgòr an Lochain Uaine (Route 80) p175
7. Cairn Toul (Route 81) p175
8. Devil's Point (Route 82) p176
9. Càrn a' Mhaim (Route 83) p178
10. Coire Sputan Dearg (Route 84) p181
11. Coire Etchachan (Route 85) p181

CAIRNGORMS

'Nevis is bulk, the Cairngorms are space', as Jim Crumley puts it. Lots of space in fact, the biggest expanse of high mountain country in Britain, and an arctic environment where snowfields last long into the summer. Nowhere else can you walk for miles in a straight line without dropping below 3000 feet. Navigation in poor weather is notoriously tricky and a mistake can leave you a long way from home. Even cliffs of the size of those that ring Loch Avon are dwarfed by the openness of the scenery.

The granite of which virtually all of this massif is composed has been carved by the ice into a variety of towers and slabs. Where the rock is monolithic this has produced clean slabby cliffs such as Hell's Lum or Stac an Fharaidh and steep buttresses such as Mitre Ridge or Shelter Stone Crag which are home to tremendous rock climbs. Where the rock contains more weaknesses these have been exploited to leave rows of more broken buttresses, and many of these make excellent scrambles, albeit with some loose rock – Lurcher's Crag, Stag Rocks and Coire Bhrocain each provide several examples. At its extreme the rock has become so deeply weathered that doing anything on it in summer conditions is not to be recommended – the Eanaich cliffs spring immediately to mind.

Although there are few of the very best scrambles in the Cairngorms there are many that are hugely enjoyable, especially at the upper end of the grades, and the wildness and scale of the setting is second to none.

The various sections are described starting with the Loch Avon basin and then moving anticlockwise around the massif.

Loch Avon Basin

The deep basin of Loch Avon is the heart of the Cairngorms. It is surrounded by massive cliffs, ranging from the awe-inspiring Shelter Stone Crag to the clean slabs of Hell's Lum Crag and Stac an Fharaidh and the jagged ridges of Stag Rocks.

The basin is most easily approached from the north via the Fiacaill a' Choire Chais, which is the right-bounding ridge of the Coire Cas ski complex. Loch Avon itself can then be reached by descending Coire Raibeirt. There is a popular howf called the Shelter Stone (*Clach Dhion*) situated some 400m beyond the western end of Loch Avon. The routes are described in a clockwise direction starting below and north-west of Càrn Etchachan (1120m) on the south side of the basin.

GARBH UISGE CRAG

OS Landranger 36   (NH 998 014)   Map p144

This is the small cliff just right of the mighty Shelter Stone Crag and separated from it by Pinnacle Gully, in which lies the distinctive Forefinger Pinnacle – a very loose Moderate.

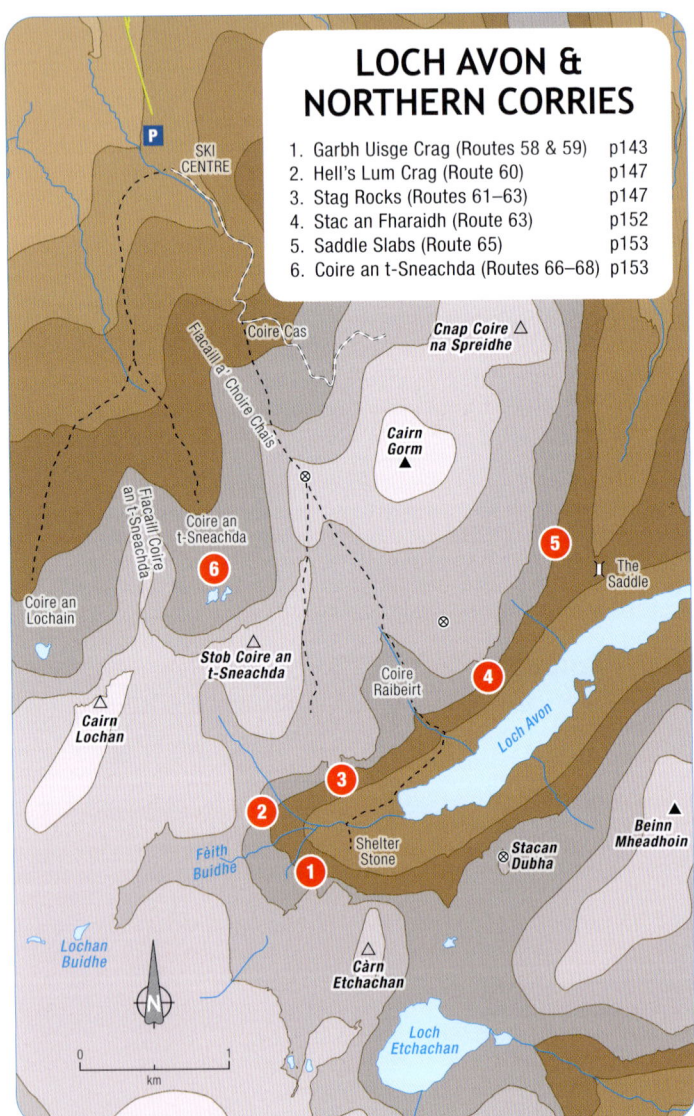

LOCH AVON BASIN   145

 58 Feld Spur   Grade 3
Alt 900m   Ht Gain +100m   (NH 999 014)   Map p144   Diag p146

This spur is the slightly separate buttress on the right edge of the crag. It is right of the distinctive Quartz Gully (Grade 3, steep to start). Quite intimidating but not hard, worth doing if passing and would be worth a star if cleaner. Unusually it is slightly easier in descent, as Patey originally did it.

Approach
Either descend from the plateau on the eastern side of the Garbh Uisge or slant up from the Shelter Stone to the foot of the spur.

The Route
Start up the cracked slab on the right-hand side and go up to the crest. Continue past blocks and up left to the edge. The spur then steepens, forcing a move right and up into a mossy niche. Climb the back right corner of this steeply on good holds to an easing. Continue up the left edge of the spur to easy ground where the gully on the left opens out, then go up right of a prominent block on the skyline to boulders. Avoid an overhang by steps on the left and do the same at the vertical wall above. The rest is easy but very loose, finishing on steep rubble.

 59 Feith Buidhe Slabs   Grade 1   *
Alt 850m   Ht Gain +250m   (NH 998 016)   Map p144   Diag p146

It is unlikely that anyone would walk in just to do this route, but these easy open granite slabs are in a magnificent situation and are a lovely way of gaining height. They are usually covered in snow until at least July.

Approach
Whatever way you get to the head of Loch Avon head up to the lowest point of the triangle of slabs between the two streams of Feith Buidhe and Garbh Uisge.

The Route
Follow the Feith Buidhe (the right-hand of the two sets of waterfalls), with odd slabs in the stream bed if the water is low. Where it steepens and enters a small gorge go up left and slant left up walking angle slabs. Where these meet a small stream on the left go right up more slabs and short steps. Where a small waterfall comes over a steep wall on the left cross below it and climb a juggy flake.

Above is a huge expanse of easy slabs, feeling more like Norway than Scotland. Walk up these to a steeper tier, banked out by snow for most of the year but when clear it provides lots of possible finishes. Perhaps the most in keeping is to start at the right edge of the large central recess and traverse up and right to go up slabs and steps just left of Feith Buidhe.

146 LOCH AVON BASIN

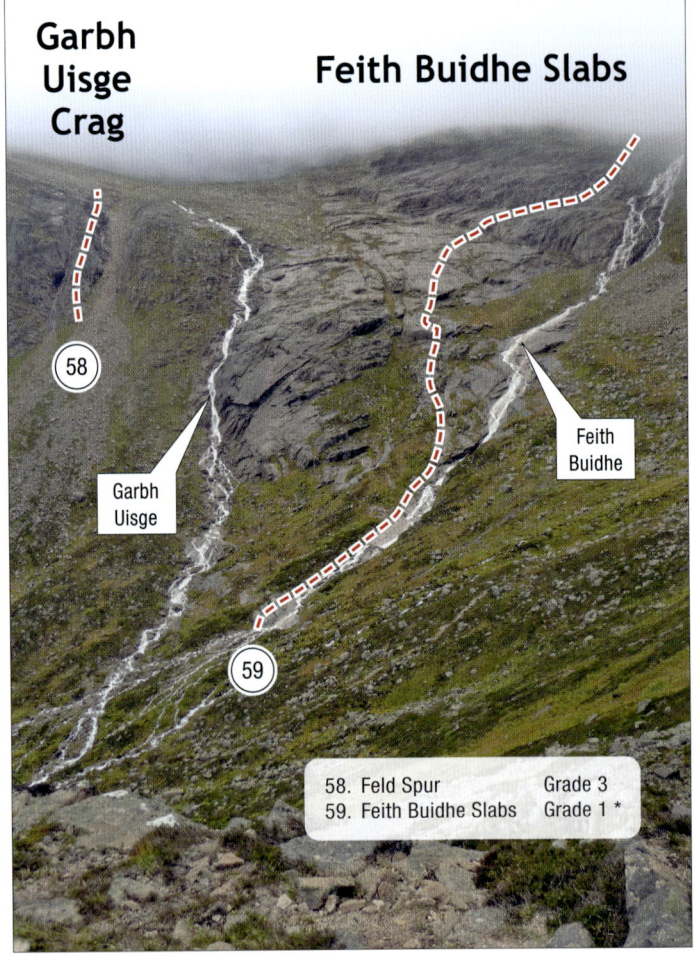

HEAD OF LOCH AVON

Garbh Uisge Crag

Feith Buidhe Slabs

58

Garbh Uisge

Feith Buidhe

59

58. Feld Spur   Grade 3
59. Feith Buidhe Slabs   Grade 1 *

STAG ROCKS

HELL'S LUM CRAG
OS Landranger 36 (NH 996 018) Map p144
This is the steep slabby east-facing crag high up above the head of Loch Avon, home to some classic rock climbs and one poor but well known scramble.

60 The Escalator Right-hand   Moderate
Alt 950m   Ht Gain +150m   (NN 996 018)   Map p144

The route lies on the right-hand part of the crag. It is full of snow for much of the year and almost always wet when not. The top half is damp and lichenous even in a drought so a cleaner right-hand finish is described.

Approach
Most easily reached from the Cairngorm car park by following the path into Coire an t-Sneachda as far as the lochans then slanting right up the obvious Goat Track to reach the plateau (rough near the top). Follow the path down the east side of Coire Domhain and down the first part of the steep descent, then cross the stream and traverse across to the crag. The route follows the obvious large straight wet fault near the right-hand edge of the cliff.

The Route
Climb slabs just left of the fault until it steepens to a crack with a corner on the right. Climb a slight arête just right of the crack and step up to reach a small sharp jug (crux). Just above this an obvious escape line appears on the right. The fault continues straight up, always slimy and rather loose. Better is to go easily rightwards up a ramp as far as the crag edge (where it splits the upper branch is harder but better). A clean rib goes direct up the right edge, perhaps Moderate at the top.

STAG ROCKS
OS Landranger 36 (NJ 001 020) Map p144
The westernmost of the crags above the north side of Loch Avon, split into two main sections by Diagonal Gully. The left half consists of stepped ridges, of which Afterthought Arête is a classic. It is normally approached by descending a broken gully at the western end of the crag.

61 Afterthought Arête   Moderate   ***
Alt 900m   Ht Gain +150m   (NJ 001 020)   Map p144   Diag p148

One of the best easy routes in the Cairngorms, airy and spectacular on excellent rock. After an avoidable hard start there are numerous variations, but it is best to stick to the crest as far as possible.

Approach
The quickest route is to go up Fiacaill a' Choire Chais from the Cairngorm car park. From the 1141m summit head right along the cliff edge to the first saddle, then traverse southwards along the slope to reach the summit of Stag

148 LOCH AVON BASIN

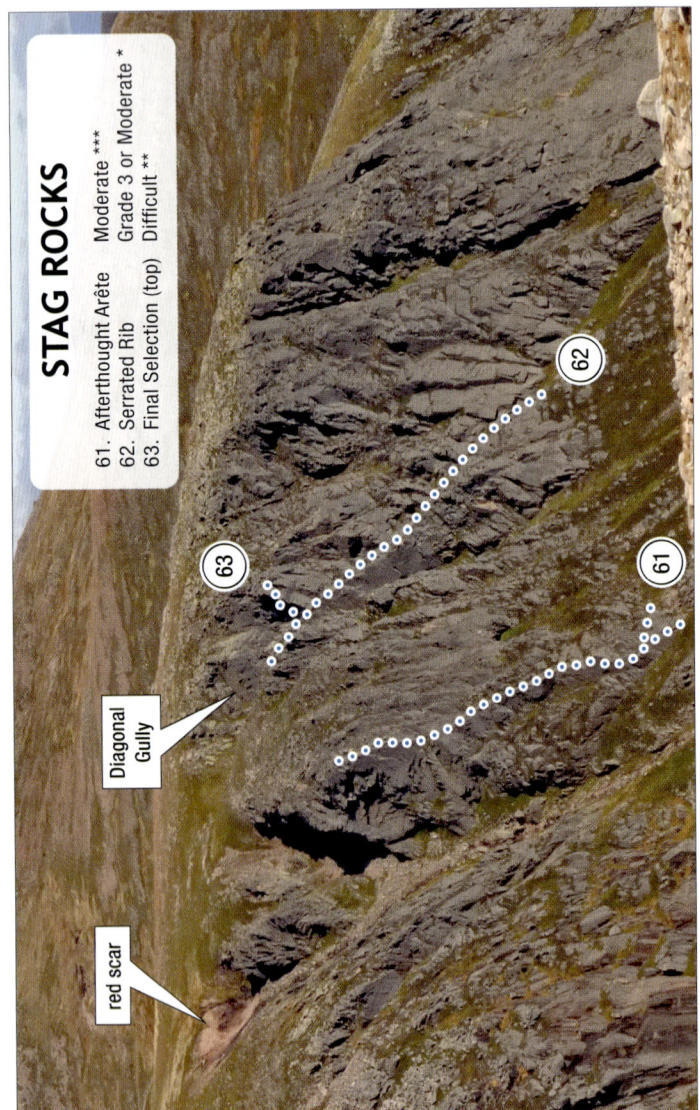

STAG ROCKS

61. Afterthought Arête — Moderate ***
62. Serrated Rib — Grade 3 or Moderate *
63. Final Selection (top) — Difficult **

Afterthought Arête (Route 61, Moderate).
Scrambler: Richard Merryfield. Photo: Noel Williams.

Rocks. West of this is Diagonal Gully, then a flattish grassy area, then the main descent gully, with prominent red patch on its far side. Descend this until below the lowest rocks. Traverse back left (looking out) for 100m or so to a well trodden spot at the foot of the ridge.

The Route
At the bottom of the arête is a steeper buttress, with direct routes up it that are much harder than Moderate. The easiest way is to avoid this on the right and come in higher up, joining the described route just above the first big platform. Alternatively, start on the right and work up left, crossing a delicate slab, to reach a big flake below a vertical wall. Go left along the top of the flake, then weave a way up leftwards to a big platform left of the main ridge. Pull up right and continue up right to climb either an easy groove or the arête to its left, arriving at another big platform above.

Step left off the platform to climb the surprisingly easy arête, sharp and juggy. At the next big ledge make an awkward step right and go up the right-hand side of the now steeper crest. The last move is quite awkward and exposed, but is avoidable on the right. Easier ground now leads to a groove on the right, from the top of which you swing left on a conveniently jammed block to regain the crest. An easy slab leads to a harder one, then the crest breaks up into minor ridges. Probably the best line is the groove on the left-hand arête, finishing up a steep wall of blocks.

62 Serrated Rib   Grade 3 or Moderate   *
Alt 900m   Ht Gain +120m   (NJ 002 021)   Map p144   Diag p148
The broken rib that bounds the right-hand side of the western half of Stag Rocks. Not sustained but with some airy positions. The rock climb version finishes up a jagged rib further left, but this is harder and more sustained.

Approach
As for the previous route to the summit of Stag Rocks, then descend the western gully and traverse across below the whole of the western section to the foot of Diagonal Gully. Alternatively descend Diagonal Gully (loose, steep and not very pleasant). Serrated Rib starts at the lowest rocks on the western side of the gully (left-hand side looking up).

The Route
From a niche at the base of the arête head up right, then cracks lead back up left to easier ground. Wind up blocks and heather close to the crest until it opens out into a large heather field. On the top right-hand edge of this is a prominent sharp arête. Either traverse out onto this using the lowest two breaks (Moderate), or come in higher up just below the overhang (much easier). Tackle the arête direct in a great position, with the top overhang proving to be easy. Move left and climb the next blunter arête direct too, with a delicate step onto a slab halfway up (avoidable on the left). Pleasant easy rock leads to the top.

STAG ROCKS

63. Final Selection — Difficult **

LOCH AVON BASIN

63 Final Selection   Difficult   **
Alt 950m   Ht Gain +60m   (NJ002 021)   Map p144   Diag p151

This route is situated on the eastern section. Another great easy climb, steep, sustained and exposed, but on excellent holds. Well protected for those using a rope and rock gear.

Approach
Since the start lies towards the top of Diagonal Gully the route is best accessed from above. Descend Diagonal Gully for about 100m. The route is the well-defined second rib down the left-hand side of the gully (looking out), after a rather amorphous higher one.

The Route
Start up the groove just left of the arête, then go right up cracks to the crest. Climb this, then cracks on the left, past one ledge to reach a larger ledge backed by an overhang. Go right and up a chimney to reach the top.

STAC AN FHARAIDH 1082m

OS Landranger 36   (NJ 008 030)   Map p144
This minor summit is on the eastern side of Coire Raibeirt. The cliffs lie south-east of the summit directly above Loch Avon.

64 Broad Buttress   Grade 3
Alt 900m   Ht Gain +120m   (NJ011 027)   Map p144

A broken buttress left of the main cliff has a fun top half after a vegetated and rather scary start.

Approach
Although the crag can be approached directly from Loch Avon, the loch is a long way from anywhere, and most will come in from the Coire Cas car park. Go up Fiacaill a'Choire Chais and follow the path down into Coire Raibeirt. At the 1000m level bear left to reach the top of the cliff. Descend steep broken ground well south-west of the main cliff. Just left of the main slabs is the well-defined Narrow Gully and Broad Buttress is just left of this.

The Route
Climb the left arête of the lowest steep tier by heather ledges, then an easy slab leads to another steep buttress. Get onto this from the left then go up steep flake holds left of centre to reach a prominent vertical red rockfall scar. Avoid this on the right and go up a steep corner to heather. An insecure step up right onto slabs leads to another steep corner, then traverse left to the edge of the buttress. Another short steep corner leads to easier ground, where things get much more pleasant.

Go up bouldery steps right of a central groove, using it at one point, with one steeper but still easy wall. Eventually the buttress steepens again and is split by a square gully. The arête right of the gully is good (but Moderate), or climb the easier chimney just right. Juggy right to left steps up the final tier make a fine finish.

THE SADDLE 807m

OS Landranger 36   (NJ 018 033)   Map p144

The Saddle is the high col linking Cairn Gorm (1244m) with A' Chòinneach (1016m), the south-western top of Bynack More (1090m). Saddle Slabs can easily be incorporated if travelling between the two.

65 Saddle Slabs   Grade 2 or 3
Alt 900m   Ht Gain +80m   (NJ 015 036)   Map p144

Short and not worth a special trip, but a worthwhile diversion if climbing Cairngorm from The Saddle. Excellent rock but the glacial polish makes it slippery in the wet.

Approach
The Saddle can be reached up Strath Nethy, over Bynack More or from Loch Avon. The slabs are obvious 100m up and right from the Saddle. The centre of the largest slab has parallel faults slanting up right. Start just left of the left-hand one.

The Route
Follow pink slabs up left, passing left of a steep wall to reach ledges. Traversing right here onto the easier angled main slab is feasible but leads to smooth slabs in a serious position (Difficult). Scramblers should carry on up left via slabs and faults, aiming for two large downward pointing overlaps. Go left of these to the edge of the slab and cross a wide stepped groove to a steeper tower. Either climb this direct (Grade 3) or go up the stepped groove (Grade 2, often wet). Either way soon reaches easy ground.

Northern Corries of Cairn Gorm

Their easy accessibility from the Coire Cas ski road has made the twin corries of Coire an t-Sneachda and Coire an Lochain popular honeypots. Despite this they still retain an air of the high mountains and the described scrambles are all excellent.

STOB COIRE AN T-SNEACHDA 1176m

OS Landranger 36   (NH 996 029)   Map p144

This top of Cairn Gorm overlooks the left-hand of the twin corries. The two routes described are both steep but easier than they look. Both routes have substantial areas of loose rock.

COIRE AN T-SNEACHDA

66 Pygmy Ridge   Moderate   **
Alt 900m   Ht Gain +80m   (NH 995 029)   Map p144   Diag p154

Small but perfectly formed, this steep tower provides a choice of line in a fine position. Both approaches are fairly loose as is the upper half of the route.

Approach
From Cairngorm car park take the path south-west, forking left into Coire an t-Sneachda. Pass the lochans and a rougher path slants up rightwards below the cliffs. This is the Goat Track, which exits up steep ground onto the col east of Cairn Lochan. Pygmy Ridge is on the skyline up right from the large central Aladdin's Buttress, with broken slabby rocks below it. Go up just left of the first scree shoot that crosses the Goat Track. Where this becomes a steeper gully work leftwards up the slabby broken ground to reach a platform at the foot of the ridge. The same point can be reached by descending from the plateau, enabling it to be combined with Fingers Ridge. The upper tower is a prominent landmark just west of the summit of Stob Coire an t-Sneachda and the gully west again can be descended with care.

The Route
Start steeply direct on good holds, then climb a steep flake chimney on the right. Continue up a shallow central groove to a large niche. Climb the left arête to another niche, then go steeply up to the crest. Direct from the first niche is also good (Difficult). Follow the crest on good holds to a level arête. The avoidable tower above has big holds but is not as solid as the lower rocks.

67 Fingers Ridge   Difficult   *
Alt 1000m   Ht Gain +150m   (NH 993 029)   Map p144   Diag p154

A fine line, but with intricate route finding and some very loose sections.

Approach
From Cairngorm car park take the path south-west, forking left into Coire an t-Sneachda. The route is near the right end of the headwall, easily identified by the two fingers high on the skyline with a tall clean narrow slab below them and well defined gullies either side. From the pools below the headwall the Goat Track goes up right and about halfway up it crosses a scree shoot coming out of Red Gully. Just before this go up left to the foot of the slab.

The Route
Climb easy angled slabs and a left slanting groove. A steeper move up a cracked wall leads to a boulder covered ledge, then go left to the edge of the gully (Broken Gully) and climb more steeply up a crampon scratched rib. Make an awkward move up a leaning flake and continue up the long groove left of the main slab. This eventually joins the arête, which is followed airily to the pinnacles. Pass between them and move up left to climb a delicate final slab by a thin crack.

*Pygmy Ridge (Route 66, Moderate).
Scrambler: Ben Lowe. Photo: Iain Thow.*

COIRE AN T-SNEACHDA

Coire an t-Sneachda, Fiacaill Ridge on the skyline (Route 68, Grade 1 or 2). Photo: Iain Thow.

CAIRN LOCHAN 1215m

OS Landranger 36 (NH 985 025) Map p144

This top of Cairn Gorm overlooks the right-hand of the twin corries. It is conveniently reached from the ridge dividing the corries.

68 Fiacaill Ridge   Grade 1 or 2   **
Alt 950m   Ht Gain + 100m   (NH992 034)   Map p144

A popular and fun way up onto the plateau, nicely positioned, on excellent rock and with lots of choice of route. A good introduction to scrambling. The Twin Ribs start is slightly harder but still good.

Approach
From Cairngorm car park take the path south-west, forking left into Coire an t-Sneachda. Most of the west side of the corrie is bouldery but halfway along is a buttress of clean steeper rock, the Twin Ribs. This start can be avoided by walking up the ridge crest from further down to reach the minor summit of Fiacaill Coire an t-Sneachda (c.1120m), making the route Grade 1.

The Route
At the Twin Ribs climb either of two grooves to the top of the first step (the right one is easier). Climb another steep step, then cracked slabs. Boulders lead to the ridge near the top of Fiacaill Coire an t-Sneachda, where the easier route comes in.

Beyond the summit follow the narrow but easy rocky arête over minor tops to reach the main scrambling section. At the first steepening go right and then either step awkwardly left to the crest or go straight up an open groove to meet the crest higher up. Carry on up well scratched slabs and ledges to a levelling. Go left above a leaning wall then up shelves and over a minor bump. Finish up the crest on blocks. All difficulties are avoidable on the right. Continuing up the ridge soon leads to the summit of Cairn Lochan.

Northern Làirig Ghrù

Arguably the most famous pass in the country, the Làirig Ghrù debouches into Speyside between the imposing but broken cliffs of Lurcher's Crag and Sròn na Làirig. Both consist of several pinnacled ridges which make interesting climbs and scrambles. The rock needs treating with care in places, and although Lurcher's has cleaned up in the last few years, it is a crag for experienced climbers with sound judgement of rock quality.

LURCHER'S CRAG   1063m

OS Landranger 36   (NH 968 033)   Map p142

Guarding the northern portal of the Làirig Ghrù, Lurcher's Crag throws down a line of ragged ridges into the mouth of the pass. Seven of these make

scrambles/easy climbs of varying degrees of looseness. The most straightforward approach, allowing for familiarisation on first visit, is via steep scree from the Làirig Ghrù path. For those familiar with the crag, it is possible to take the path from the Cairngorm car park below Coire an t-Sneachda, up the spur between Coire an Lochain and Lurcher's Gully, then cut across to the flat area above the south end of the crag. For the first two routes descend rough steep ground south of the cliffs for 100m or so until possible to cross the southernmost ridge (Deerhound Ridge) at a notch, or pass below it.

69 Collie's Ridge   Moderate   *
Alt 900m   Ht Gain + 120m   (NH 969 029)   Map p142   Diag p159

A blunt buttress, mostly only Grade 2, but with a dramatic crux in an airy position, only avoidable by leaving the ridge altogether.

Approach

Approaching from the Làirig Ghrù path, the broad ridge on the right-hand end of the crag is Deerhound Ridge, which descends lower on the slope than the other ridges. The next buttress left is much too steep for scrambling, then Collie's is the one left again, with the Amphitheatre on its left. It has broken rocks directly below it. If arriving by crossing the notch in Deerhound Ridge as described above then a descending traverse below the steep rock leads easily to Collie's Ridge, the first buttress to look at all feasible for scramblers (although still quite steep and intimidating).

The Route

Start up the left arête of the buttress, avoiding two steeper steps on the left to reach a vegetated easing. Go up blocks on the right arête to another easing, then clamber rightwards up piles of boulders to the crest, where easy ground comes in on the right. Go up the steepening crest to a tower. Climb this on its exposed right arête by an exciting pull up on jugs. Above this an easy blocky arête leads to the top.

70 Drystane Ridge   Moderate   **
Alt 900m   Ht Gain + 100m   (NH 969 029)   Map p142   Diag p159

A good direct line, more sustained than Collie's Ridge, with clean solid holds in a good position.

Approach

This is the gradually steepening narrow ridge bounding the left-hand side of the Amphitheatre left of Collie's Ridge. Either approach up the scree from the Làirig Ghrù path below, or cross the notch in Deerhound Ridge as described above then traverse downwards below Collie's Ridge to reach the Amphitheatre.

The Route

Start on the left edge of the Amphitheatre up easy-angled shattered rocks, then when the ridge steepens move onto the crest to better rock. The line is obvious, with the first steep step being the hardest. There are two more steep

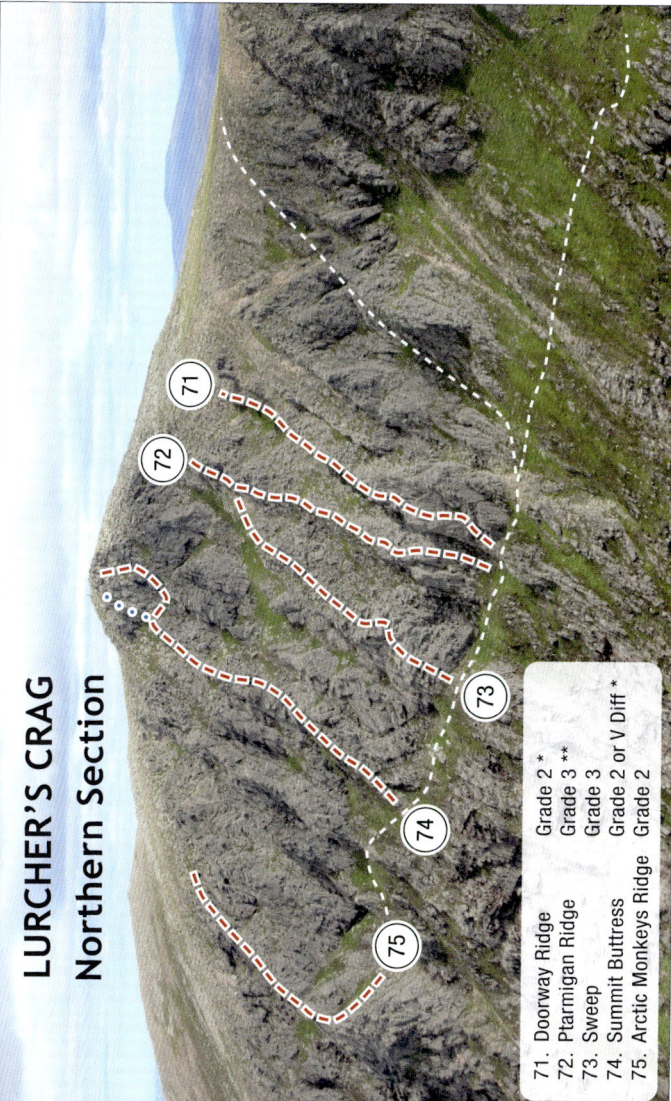

steps above, climbed on good flakes, the second on the right arête. Higher up, bypass an overhanging tower on the right, after which the ridge opens out to easy blocks.

71 Doorway Ridge   Grade 2   *
Alt 900m   Ht Gain +150m   (NH 967 032)   Map p142   Diag p161

A broad buttress with quite sustained scrambling, finishing with a narrower but easier ridge. Like the following routes it starts from the terrace at half height on the crag.

Approach
This can be approached from below by traversing in from the right above the lowest rocks. However, it is much quicker to start from the Coire Cas car park and follow the path across below the Northern Corries and up the spur east of Lurcher's Gully to about 1000m. Traverse right to the slight col (997m) south of the summit of Lurcher's Crag. Where the ground starts to rise up to the summit, before it gets rocky, is the wide top of South Gully, with red scree at the top and a tall sharp pinnacle 50m down on the left. Descend this with care, awkward at the bottom, then traverse north below the main cliff on deer paths. Round the first steep buttress then from its left edge a grassy runnel slants up right to the skyline. The route starts up this.

The Route
Go halfway up the runnel then take the first weakness in the left wall up onto open slabs with lots of large square holds. Go up these to a broad square tower and dodge this on the right (Moderate direct). Regain the crest via a steep niche on sharp jugs. Beyond a minor col a step off a pointed block leads to easy clambering up a blocky crest and over the top of the doorway to easy ground. Climb a loose outcrop on its right, then a steeper more solid buttress by the groove just right of a jutting prow.

72 Ptarmigan Ridge   Grade 3   **
Alt 900m   Ht Gain +150m   (NH 967 032)   Map p142   Diag p161

Quite lichenous, so not a good choice in the wet, but with a tremendous finish.

Approach
As for the previous route, then round the first steep buttress is a usually wet gully, the rather unprepossessing start of the route.

The Route
Climb the gully on good holds, moving left at a steeper section to enter the easier angled upper gully. Go up left on blocks and steps to reach the arête just behind a square pinnacle. Follow a groove just right of the arête, then the excellent crest direct. This soon eases to broken ground, rather loose, before steepening again. Tackle the first steep step on the left, then work up right to left to arrive at another sharp arête. Across a small col is an intimidating vertical tower. Climb this left of centre on big holds, (stepping

LURCHER'S CRAG

Typical Lurcher's ground on Doorway Ridge (Route 71, Grade 2).
Scrambler: Iain Thow. Photo: Paul Buchanan.

*Ptarmigan Ridge (Route 72, Grade 3).
Scrambler: Iain Thow. Photo: Paul Buchanan.*

right onto the detached pinnacle at the top helps). When you've finished whooping an easy crest leads to the plateau.

73 Sweep   Grade 3
Alt 900m   Ht Gain +150m   (NH 967 032)   Map p142   Diag p161

An intimidating and serious start leads to easier scrambling up the crest and an optional steep finish.

Approach
As for Route 72, then round the first steep buttress and along below a diagonal overhanging wall. Above the spur beyond this are intimidating looking slabs, broken but quite steep.

The Route
Gain the slabs (easiest on the left) and go up right to climb a heathery groove just left of the crest. A little below where this is blocked by overlaps move up right to the crest just as it conveniently eases in angle and go up past the overlaps. Climb a blocky rib to an easing, then climb a steep groove just right of a prow on big spikes, easier than it looks. Carry on up the crest to easy ground, then move up right to the tower finish of Ptarmigan Ridge and either climb its left side easily or move right and finish direct up the steep juggy groove left of the pinnacle. Easy rocks remain.

74 Summit Buttress   Grade 2 or Very Difficult   *
Alt 900m   Ht Gain +200m   (NH 966 033)   Map p142   Diag p161

Good sustained scrambling interrupted by one much harder step which will force most scramblers into an indirect finish.

Approach
As for Doorway Ridge (Route 71) but carry on traversing below the main cliff past a long low overhanging wall. Round the next spur and pass below an occasional waterfall, then at the far edge of the next spur the ground opens out and grass reaches higher up. Start here.

The Route
Follow open grooves up the left edge of the buttress with the odd bit of greenery. There are easy escapes on the left at regular intervals. Where the ridge breaks down into boulders go up right to the crest, with easy ground now off right. The ridge continues up left, over a steep blocky tower, then more blocks lead up left to a straight slabby section. Climb this, with a steep section at twin cracks, then cross a minor summit to a grass col.

Ahead is an overhanging prow, and it is possible (V Diff) to swing right below this into a large niche, then go back left to the crest, where cracks and big holds lead directly to the summit. The grassy groove left of the prow avoids the steep part but has an insecure grovel at the top which is no easier than the right-hand line. It is much easier to traverse well to the right (slightly down) on grass and climb the top section of the next ridge on huge blocks, which keeps the standard at Grade 2.

NORTHERN LÀIRIG GHRÙ

75 Arctic Monkeys Ridge   Grade 2
Alt 900m   Ht Gain + 150m   (NH 966 033)   Map p142   Diag p161

Nicely positioned bouldery scrambling on reasonably solid rock.

Approach
As for Doorway Ridge (Route 71) but continue the traverse below a long low overhanging wall and a couple of other buttresses to reach an amphitheatre backed by steep slabs. The ridge ahead has a prominent pyramid on the skyline, the line of the route.

The Route
The lowest part of the ridge, where the amphitheatre narrows, is steep and broad. Go up grass right of this and move left as soon as possible to gain the ridge above the steep part. This is easy clambering at first, then becomes more of an arête. Pass right of the pyramid to a grass notch. Climb the bouldery crest above to an easing below an overhanging prow. Go up the groove right of this, with the steep left fork being Difficult. The groove can be followed to easy ground, but more exciting is to swing (or crawl!) left below a small overhang to rejoin the main crest. Choose between the big slab on the left and either of the grooves on the right for a good finish.

76 Lairig Ridge   Difficult   **
Alt 850m   Ht Gain + 150m   (NH 964 024)   Map p142

This fine route is situated on the west side of the Làirig Ghrù opposite Lurcher's Crag. A steep start and easy slabs lead to an excellent pinnacled arête with spectacular positions.

Approach
The route can be approached using the Làirig Ghrù track from Whitewell (916 085) but it is quicker to start at the Sugar Bowl car park (985 074), take the path on the outside of the hairpin down to the river, then up the far side and along the crest to go through the Chalamain Gap. Descend to the Làirig Ghrù and go up it for 1km, then slog up the steep scree to the most obvious ridge on the west side, with a steep slabby wall at its foot.

The Route
Climb steeply up the right edge of the wall, soon easing, then at its top move left along a ledge below an overhang. Make awkward moves up past a loose flake to easy ground. Scramble up easy slabby rock to the foot of the ridge proper. Climb this direct, with the steepest bit avoidable by using a groove just left, to a lovely perch as the angle eases. Follow the sharp arête over pinnacles, with superb positions but no real difficulty.

Other possibilities nearby
There are some fun outcrops on the north side of the Chalamain Gap at 965 052, notably a clean buttress near the east end. Start up the corner on its left side and move out onto the front above the steepest section (Moderate). The westernmost buttress has quite sustained slabs at Diff (or harder).

LAIRIG RIDGE 167

Lairig Ridge (Route 76, Difficult).
Climber: Noel Williams. Photo: Iain Thow.

SGÒR GAOITH

Gleann Eanaich

A lovely quiet glen leading to a wild loch dominated by the huge cliffs buttressing Sgòr Gaoith and Sgoran Dubh. Usually approached from Whitewell, starting as for the Làirig Ghrù, but the scramble described is more easily reached from Glen Feshie.

SGÒR GAOITH 1118m

OS Landranger 36   (NH 903 989)   Map p142

At the north west corner of the Cairngorms the broad ridge of Sgòr Gaoith runs northwards from the Moine Mhòr plateau, its east flank dropping to Loch Eanaich (Einich) in 600m of shaggy cliff and steep heather. Much of the rock is horrendously loose, especially on Buttresses 3 and 4, making the crag much better suited to winter than summer.

77 Corner Ridge   Grade 2
Alt 900m   Ht Gain +200m   (NH 906 982)   Map p142   Diag p168

The best known route is Pinnacle Ridge on Number 5 Buttress above the head of Loch Eanaich, which is Moderate by the easiest route, with impressive situations, especially around the pinnacle, but much of the rock is abominably loose. 100 metres or so to its left is the following route, which follows the blunt spur bounding the northern edge of the high level corrie of A' Phocaid. The rock is still far from perfect, but much better than on Pinnacle Ridge. It follows a good line but is escapable in many places.

Approach
A good track leads to the foot of Loch Eanaich (mountain bike useful), where the outlet can usually be forded to gain a stalker's path along the loch shore and up into A' Phocaid. This can be reached more quickly (but with more ascent) from the foot of Glen Feshie. From a parking place at 852 013 take a good path eastwards up the Allt Ruadh. This carries on further than the map shows to reach the broad saddle between Sgòr Gaoith and Càrn Bàn Mòr. From the spring and hut ruin at Fuaran Diotach (900 977) head a short distance south-east and descend a steep spur with care to the south edge of A' Phocaid. There appear to be good scrambling possibilities on the corrie headwall but be warned, they're steeper than they look! From the north edge of A' Phocaid go up between two steep screes to the foot of the ridge. A few unimpressive lower craglets can be included by starting further right.

The Route
Start by climbing broken outcrops to reach steeper cleaner rock. Climb this by right to left flakes, then go up a narrow ridge leading up to a knife edged flake. This can be avoided on the right or tackled awkwardly à cheval. From the col behind the flake step right into a niche, then go up right then left to regain the ridge. Go up this to heather. Corner Ridge itself now goes up easily

170 GLEANN EANAICH

The blunt rock spur below the summit of Sgòr Gaoith (Grade 3).
Scrambler: Iain Thow. Photo: Paul Buchanan.

to join the next ridge to its right, but more fun can be had by traversing right to join this ridge lower down. Go up this on big spikes, avoiding the top block on the left. An easy slabby ridge carries on up to the plateau.

Other possibilities nearby
Directly below the summit of Sgòr Gaoith is a blunt rock spur, which gives a good short Grade 3. Slant down from south of the summit to the foot of the spur. After an easy start avoid a steeper section on the right by a ridge between two chimneys (direct is V Diff). The rest of the ridge is excellent fun, taken direct on good holds, emerging suddenly at the summit, usually to the shock of anyone sitting on it!

Braeriach & Cairn Toul Massif

The block of high ground west of the Làirig Ghrù contains two of Scotland's highest peaks, reachable from either Deeside or the Spey.

BRAERIACH 1296m

OS Landranger 36   (NH 954 999)   Map p142

A vast, sprawling, fairly remote hill with a plateau summit and numerous steep corries. Several of the latter have superb climbing, both winter and summer, but the long walk in deters many. There is scope for far more exploratory scrambling here, but the unfrequented nature of the corries mean that a great deal of the rock is looser than you would like.

78 Near East Buttress   Grade 3
Alt 1150m   Ht Gain +100m   (NN 957 999)   Map p142   Diag p172

Quite broken scrambling but with some good sections and a fine finish. Possibly worth a star for the situation rather than the scrambling.

Approach
As for Route 76 from the Sugar Bowl car park to the Làirig Ghrù path, but then soon after joining it take a recently rebuilt path up south-westwards and up onto Sròn na Lairige. Continue across the col linking this to Braeriach and up to a minor saddle, where the path turns right. Leave it and descend scree ahead into Coire Bhrocain, traversing right once below the cliffs. The prominent gully in the upper right corner of the corrie is East Gully (often a stream), and Near East Buttress is just to its right, starting broad and fairly easy angled, then with much steeper rock up right.

The Route
Start just right of East Gully and work up right on rather mossy rock and grass ledges. After about 50m a cleaner rib develops on the left, close to the gully, while the right side becomes a grassy field. Climb the rib, with the steep section having good holds, to reach broken ground with rock towers up right. Climb an exposed rib on the gully edge to easy ground and an obvious easy

172 BRAERIACH & CAIRN TOUL MASSIF

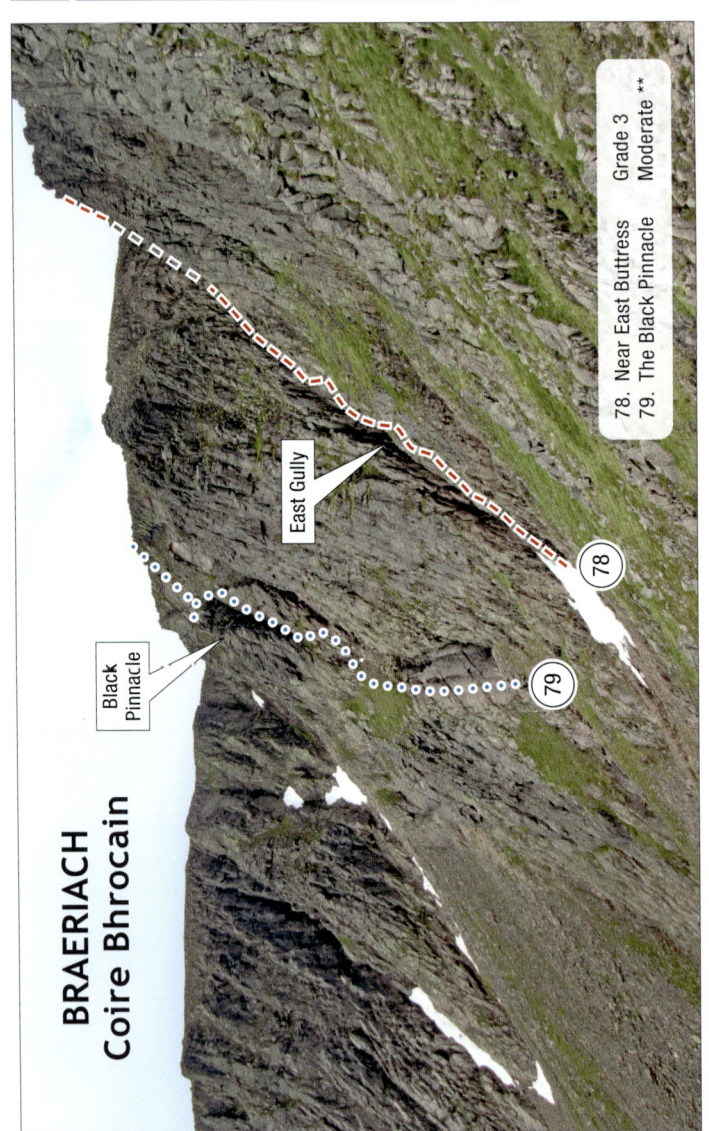

escape up left (very loose). Directly above steep steps and ramps lead up to the top of the buttress and you can either climb these, avoiding the top one on the right, or slant right lower down to climb just left of the arête of the buttress.

The exposed rib can be avoided on the right and the easy escape used to make an easier but much looser scramble (Grade 2), and with care this line can be descended to reach the grassy field, which is escapable at its bottom left corner (looking out). This enables you to use Near East Buttress as a warm up for the Black Pinnacle, which is only slightly harder technically, albeit much more exposed, serious and intimidating.

79 The Black Pinnacle   Moderate **
Alt 1150m   Ht Gain +150m   (NN 955 999)   Map p142   Diag p172

An intricate and intimidating expedition around the most impressive buttress on the cliff, with superb situations but low in the grade technically. Although meandering, the line falls into place logically when you are on it and despite the odd bit of vegetation the route deserves the classic reputation it used to have. Snow can linger a long time in the corner behind the Pinnacle which can force you to use the Slab Variation (Difficult) well into the summer.

Approach
As for the previous route into Coire Bhrocain, then continue traversing to reach the main buttress in the centre of the cliff. This has a slabby ramp running up leftwards from its right flank, and above the upper end of this the Black Pinnacle itself projects outwards, a wing of slabs separating it from the Y-shaped Central Gully to its right. Start at the foot of the slabby ramp.

The Route
Climb the slabs or the easier broken ground just left, then continue in the same line on grass until below and right of the Pinnacle and left of Central Gully (easily identified by a huge jammed boulder near its foot). Go up just left of the gully and take a small shelf left to grass below the wall of the Pinnacle, which is followed up to the rather grassy corner between the Pinnacle and the slabs. Climb the corner, using the slabs in places. Taking the slabs direct on sharp quartz edges is Difficult, nicer climbing but exposed and serious.

Either version takes you to an easy angled but airy arête overlooking the left branch of Central Gully. At the top of this move right to reach a ledge on the inside edge of the Pinnacle. An easy but exposed detour takes you to the pinnacle top. It's quite a place – you can see down a hole right through it!

Return to the ledge and make an awkward step down to the neck between the pinnacle and the main headwall, then cross an easy arête to grass. The rock above feels steep and quite rounded at first but is well supplied with jugs (easiest going left to start). At the top are two small pinnacles and stepping across the gap makes a spectacular finish (or squirm up thankfully between them).

The top of Angel's Ridge (Route 80, Grade 1).
Scrambler: Gareth Lynn. Photo: Andrew Gifford.

SGÒR AN LOCHAIN UAINE 1258m

OS Landranger 36 (NN 953 976) Map p142

Christened Angel's Peak by the Victorian mountaineers to match the Devil's Point on Cairn Toul's other shoulder, this is one of the few pointed summits in the Cairngorms. Its finest feature is the graceful North-East ('Angel's') Ridge, a classic line in both summer and winter.

80 Angel's Ridge   Grade 1   **
Alt 950m   Ht Gain +300m   (NN 957 981)   Map p142

Beautifully positioned easy scrambling up the crest of the ridge in a wild and remote setting. One of those routes that shouts 'come and climb me'.

Approach
One of the most obvious lines in the Cairngorms, if you can't find this then there's no hope for you! It is reachable in a long day from Linn of Dee or the Sugar Bowl Car Park below Cairngorm (mountain bike useful from the former) but most will either camp or use Corrour Bothy. Whichever way you come in reach Lochan Uaine either by steep broken ground above Garbh Coire Bothy, right of the waterfall, or by slanting up scree and steep grass from the stream junction at 972 985. Both routes are hard work.

The Route
The ridge is walking at first, then gradually steepens to easy scrambling, with minor problems available (including a lovely à cheval crest at about two-thirds height). The final tower is steeper and looks intimidating from below, but turns out to be a zigzag up huge boulders, arriving exactly at the summit, always a satisfying moment.

CAIRN TOUL 1291m

OS Landranger 36 (NN 964 973) Map p142

The most shapely of the Cairngorms major peaks, with a definite summit giving splendid views out over the Làirig Ghrù. As well as the scramble described the South-East Ridge finishes with a sharp rocky arête that affords brief airy fun (Grade 1).

81 Solitude Rib   Grade 2
Alt 1100m   Ht Gain +200m   (NN 963 974)   Map p142

Pleasant clambering up a broken spur in a lovely setting high above the wild Lochan Uaine. Low in the grade. The approach holds snow until well into the summer, although it is easy angled and can add an Alpine ambience to the route rather than being a problem.

Approach
The route follows the central rib in the North-West Face of Cairn Toul,

overlooking Lochan Uaine and dropping directly from the summit. The lochan is usually reached up steep broken ground above Garbh Choire Bothy (right of the waterfall). An alternative option is to slant up scree and steep grass from the junction of the stream draining Garbh Choire with that coming down from the Pools of Dee (971 984). Both ways are steep and distinctly hard work.

The Route
From Lochan Uaine walk up to a shelf at the foot of the face. Go up scree then work rightwards through a band of broken slabs to reach the foot of the rib. Go up the rib, which is easy at first, then gradually becomes steeper and better defined. At half height a steeper rib just right gives a Grade 3 variation, or just keep on up. Soon after the two ribs rejoin the ground eases to boulders with a few minor outcrops and these continue almost right to the summit cairn.

THE DEVIL'S POINT 1004m

OS Landranger 36   (NN 976 951)   Map p142

The huge broken face that dominates the lower part of the Làirig Ghrù unfortunately consists largely of broken and occasionally rotten rock. Guesachan Gully round on the left-hand side is a vegetated Moderate, and another grassy line can be found right of centre. Luckily the slabs on the northern end of the crag, above Corrour Bothy are considerably more solid. A meandering Diff picks out the more sustained rock, but a direct line up the central weakness of the slabs makes a good scramble, worthy of far more attention than it gets.

82 Corrour Slabs   Grade 3   **
Alt 650m   Ht Gain + 350m   (NN 979 954)   Map p142   Diag p177
An excellent start up clean sound slabs, then more broken but still enjoyable slabs and craglets.

Approach
Corrour Bothy is easily reached in 11km from Linn of Dee (063 897) by following the main Làirig Ghrù path past Derry Lodge and crossing the bridge just before the bothy. The Devil's Point is obvious above, with the lower right-hand side of the face having clean slabs facing the bothy. Near their right edge is a pale coloured right-facing blind flake/shallow groove.

The Route
Climb the flake/groove and continue up the slabs in the same line, quite sustained, to reach grass ledges below the right end of the long overlap. Climb the weakness right of the overlap to reach a grass strip with small juniper scrub, then go up the edge of the slab on the left to a left-slanting weakness. Ignore this as it leads to a hard corner and instead go up right to climb an easier slab to grass at the top of the main slabs.

Go up escapable slabs, then slightly steeper steps. At a much bigger and steeper buttress walk left across a gully above its obviously hard section. Gain the left skyline and go up past a big boulder, then walk left up stony ground to the next skyline. Climb an avoidable rib to grass, then pass right of a vertical tower to reach the neck behind it. Boulders lead to a nice rough slab, then more boulders and minor outcrops continue almost all the way to the summit.

Other possibilities nearby
On the other side of Glen Geusachan the slabby stream of Caochan Robidh provides some entertainment on the way up Beinn Bhrotain, starting conveniently close to the end of the track up the west bank of the Dee. The left edge of the prominent slabs higher up (972 911) also provides brief fun.

Ben Macdui Massif

The highest of the Cairngorms is surrounded by several smaller peaks and is much more complex than it seems on first acquaintance, with numerous corries at several levels and some wonderful 'lost world' corners.

CÀRN A' MHAIM 1037m

OS Landranger 36   (NN 994 952)   Map p142

A twin summit on the southern edge of the Macdui massif, with an enjoyable north ridge and a fine view. Scattered around its slopes are several plates of slab, one of which gives the following scramble, which is only a minor diversion from the main path up the hill.

83 Creag Coire na Poite   Grade 2
Alt 650m   Ht Gain +100m   (NO 006 945)   Map p142

A pleasant slab, if a bit gritty in places.

Approach
From Linn of Dee (NO 063 897) take the path through the woods to reach the Glen Lui track and follow this to Derry Lodge. Continue up Gleann Laoigh Bheag then fork left and cross the Luibeg Burn. After a few hundred metres the path up Càrn a' Mhaim forks right. Use this to gain 100m or so of height then traverse right across heather to the foot of the east facing slabs.

The Route
From the bottom left edge of the left-hand slab work rightwards to reach a crest overlooking the central gully, avoiding the lichenous areas as far as possible. Carry on up the crest until a short distance below the large overlap, where slightly steeper slabs force you into the gully. Finish up this.

Crystal Ridge (Route 84, Difficult).
Climber: Helen Watson. Photo: Scott Muir.

BEINN MACDUIBH (BEN MACDUI) 1309m

OS Landranger 36 (NN 989 989) Map p142

Scotland's second highest summit is a vast sprawling plateau with corries bitten into it at several levels and rather random angles, a tricky place to navigate in mist, as many have found out the hard way. The huge face above the Làirig Ghrù is steep, but bouldery rather than craggy, so scrambling interest is concentrated on the north-east, in Coire Sputan Dearg and Coire Etchachan.

84 Crystal Ridge   Difficult   ***
Alt 1000m   Ht Gain + 100m   (NO 003 989)   Map p142   Diag p179

This ridge is situated in Coire Sputan Dearg on the east flank of Beinn Macduibh. It is arguably the best route of its grade in the Cairngorms, a keen edge, sustained and exposed but in balance and on good positive holds.

Approach
From Linn of Dee (063 897) follow Route 83 to Derry Lodge and continue up Gleann Laoigh Bheag. Then fork right up the Luibeg Burn to where the track veers left up towards Beinn Macduibh. Carry on up the stream into Coire Sputan Dearg. The biggest buttress on the left side of the corrie is the Grey Man's Crag, with Crystal Ridge being the slabby spur running up its left flank, with a sharp left-hand edge.

The Route
Start on the bottom right of the spur (delicate) or on the left arête (easier). Either way leads to ledges below more sustained rock. Climb the arête on good holds, mostly on the right but with a detour onto the left side at about 15m. As the angle eases move left again to a good ledge, then step up to regain the crest almost immediately. Soon after this the ridge breaks down to rubble. The top of Pinnacle Buttress up left makes a good finish, reached by traversing left above the rubble. Cross the gully and work left up blocks to the crest, following it to the top.

The bottom of Pinnacle Buttress on the left is graded Moderate but the start of the main long groove is quite hard. Left again is an easy angled slab high up. The left edge of this is good, gained by linking easy slabs and grass up left from the foot of Pinnacle Buttress and climbing a steep corner onto the slab (Grade 3).

85 Quartzvein Edge   Moderate   **
Alt 850m   Ht Gain + 120m   (NO 015 997)   Map p142   Diag p182

Creagan a' Choire Etchachan dominates the head of the corrie above the Hutchison Hut, and this follows the left edge of the main cliff, just right of the prominent Forked Gully. Steep walls with good holds are separated by (mostly) easier slabs, making a popular route, quite exposed in places.

BEN MACDUI MASSIF

CREAGAN A' CHOIRE ETCHACHAN

Far Left-hand End

Bastion

Forked Gully

85

85. Quartzvein Edge — Moderate **

Approach
From Linn of Dee (NO 063 897) take the path through the woods to join the main path up Glen Lui. Beyond Derry Lodge cross the stream and turn right up Glen Derry. The path recrosses the stream as it comes out of the woods and about 3.5km later fork left to go up to the Hutchison Hut. Start up the main track from the hut, but soon after crossing the first stream bear up leftwards, aiming for the left-hand edge of the cliff. Walk up Forked Gully for 50m or so to a detached boulder just next to the cliff. The route starts just above this.

The Route
Pull up steeply past a quartz knob to ledges, then climb a V-groove and the crest to reach grass ledges. Continue steeply up the crest to a quartz vein, from where there are two usual options. Those who prefer balance to thuggery can traverse right along the vein and climb slabs, quite delicate for a move or two, to reach a scree shoot. Alternatively, carry on up the crest until it curves over into a slabby ramp overlooking the gully. This is steeper and much more exposed, but on positive holds. Where it becomes horizontal and grassy clamber onto a block on the right and make a long exposed step up right on sharp but rather dubious holds to arrive suddenly at the scree shoot mentioned above. The left edge of the scree shoot makes a nicer finish than the shoot itself.

Other possibilities nearby
The rib left of Forked Gully is better than it looks (Grade 3). A steep start is followed by an easy juggy crest, followed direct. The steeper finish is Moderate if tackled direct, but is easily avoidable. The East Face of Càrn Etchachan has a pleasant rib just right of the grassy runnel about 100m right of the loch (Grade 3, a chain of non-serious but sometimes quite tricky problems). High up left of the runnel are some nice easy slabs with a scrappy start. The South Face of Stob Coire Etchachan has lots of rock, but most of it is atrocious and the cleaner sections are too hard for scrambling. The two ribs on the right-hand side start reasonably but soon lose themselves in amorphous scraggy ground.

Eastern Cairngorms

Two major hills and many smaller ones hide some remote corries, of which those on Beinn a' Bhuird provide by far the best scrambling.

BEINN A' BHÙIRD 1197m

(NJ 093 006) Map p184

A vast sprawling high plateau, deeply bitten into by four remote eastern corries. The crags in these are rather dwarfed by the scale of their

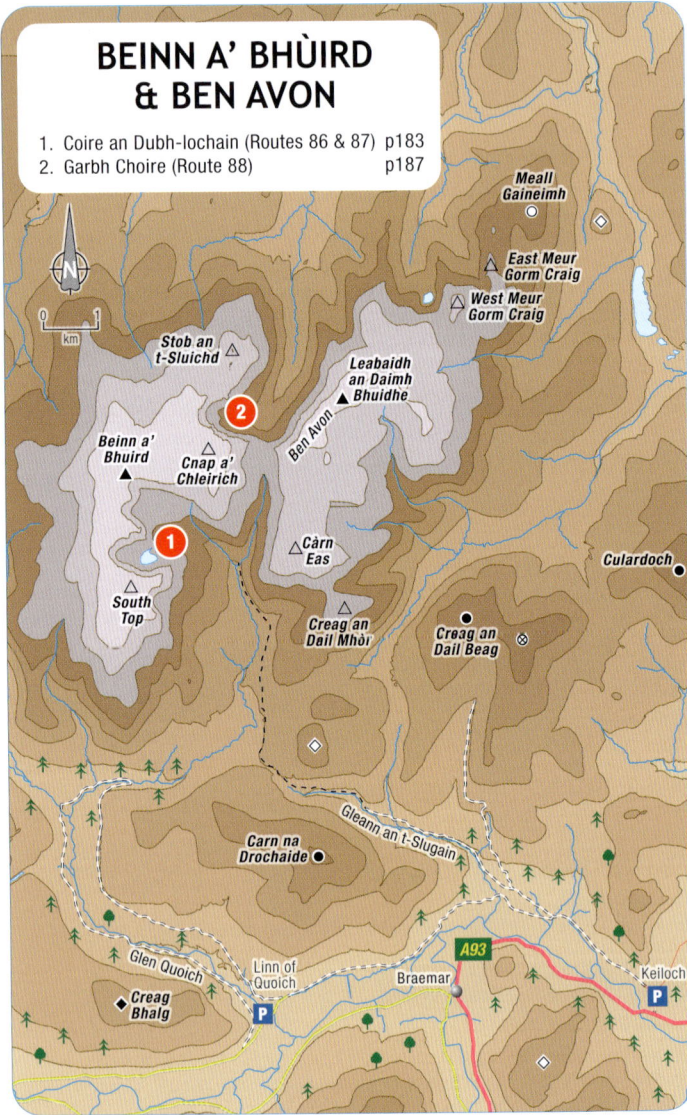

surroundings, despite being up to 200m high. *Mitre Ridge* and *Squareface* in Garbh Choire are the classic rock climbs but there are many other fine routes and a few good scrambles.

The first two routes are situated south of the summit, on the north side of Coire an Dubh-lochain.

86 Dividing Buttress   Difficult or Grade 3   **
Alt 950m   Ht Gain +200m   (NO 097 994)   Map p184   Diag p186

Excellent slabby granite in airy positions, quite serious, although it can be escaped from in several places.

Approach
The easiest route in is from Invercauld in Deeside (pay and display car park at Keiloch NO 188 911). Take the path up Gleann an t-Slugain and over into the upper reaches of Glen Quoich. Just before the prominent boulder of Clach a' Chlèirich, at NO 113 990, fork left up Allt Dearg and bear left to follow the stream up into Coire an Dubh-lochain. Dividing Buttress is the right bounding edge of the corrie.

The Route
There is an optional start up awkward mossy slabs from the lowest rocks on the left side of the buttress (lower than the lip of the corrie). These soon lead to a big ledge below a superb rippled slab, where an easier access comes in from the left.

Climb the slab (sustained Grade 3) past a huge perched block to easy ground. Surmount a small tower on jugs to reach a much bigger tower behind. The Difficult variation slants leftward up a slab and round the corner on the left to climb the tower by steep twin cracks. Scramble airily up the crest to a narrow col. A Grade 3 alternative starts up a chimney groove on the right of the slab then skirts rightwards below the tower, climbs a short arête and zigzags up left to the narrow col.

Continue along a sharp arête, then up easy rocks to much less serious ground. The scrambling can be prolonged by transferring to the arête on the right above its sharp nose, then climbing a final mossy tower, descended awkwardly on the left. The left slanting crack facing the plateau is a fun problem at Difficult.

An easier option (Grade 2 *) is the slabby rib starting well inside the corrie (not the smooth lower slab, which is much harder). This starts level with the tower of the main route and is easily reached from the ledge below it. There is a wide choice of route, but keeping to the left arête is both better and easier than the slabby right flank.

87 Addition Buttress   Grade 2
Alt 1000m   Ht Gain +150m   (NO 094 994)   Map p184   Diag p186

Not as good as it looks from a distance but enjoyable all the same. A broken slabby rib with the odd tricky bit.

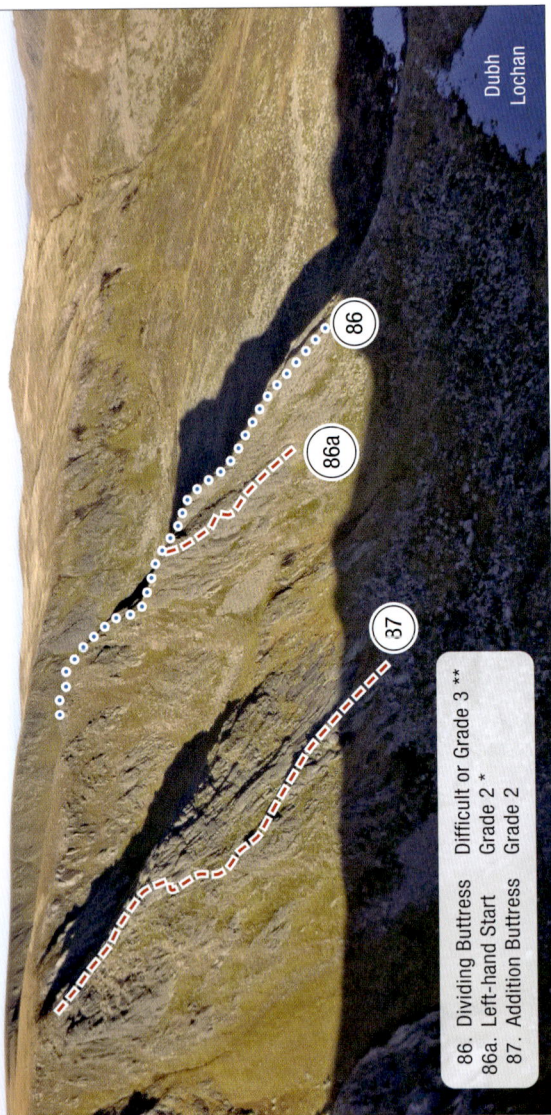

Approach
As for the previous route but continue further into Coire an Dubh Lochain. Alternatively come in by the track up Glen Quoich to the plateau edge then descend steep grass just right of the final tor of Dividing Buttress (looking out). This of course allows the route to be included as an add on to the latter, although it would be a bit of an anticlimax. Addition Buttress follows the parallel spur about 100m left of the left-hand start to Dividing Buttress. The clean slabs at the foot are sadly just too steep for scrambling and the route starts up the broken spur just left, above piles of boulders.

The Route
Climb the right-hand of two mossy lines of slab, the lowest continuous rock on the face. Pass right of a huge flake which forms an overlap, then continue up the rib to a perched block. Carry on up in the same line, mainly grass and crowberry, to reach a steeper slabby prow. Climb this by a weakness on its left and go up to easy ground. Here it is possible to traverse rightwards onto the broad crest of the main spur and zigzag up this. More entertainment can be found, however, by going straight up an easy broken rib until it runs into the steep sidewall of the main spur and using a good flake crack to swing right to a niche. Descend a little and move right around the rib to grass, then climb a crack just left of a huge block (the slim might fit through the hole underneath it but the present writer doesn't). All ways now carry on up the broad crest, finishing with a couple of short stepped towers to reach grass slopes just below the plateau edge.

88 M & B Buttress   Grade 3   *
Alt 950m   Ht Gain +120m   (NJ 112 019)   Map p184   Diag p188

This broad buttress is situated in Garbh Choire north-east of the summit. It has a definite crux, starts with slabs and finishes with a well defined arête.

Approach
It's a long way to the Garbh Choire whichever way you come in. The quickest method is by mountain bike up Glen Avon from Tomintoul as far as the footbridge at 126 059 then head south up Slochd Mòr to the foot of the route. From the south-east a good track leads up Gleann an t-Slugain from Deeside and on to the Sneck between Beinn a' Bhuird and Ben Avon. From there descend into the Garbh Choire and cross rough ground on the floor of the corrie north-westwards. On the northern side are a series of broken buttresses, M&B Buttress being the right-hand and longest one, with a broad apron of slabs at its foot. It is also feasible to come in from Glen Quoich over the summit of Beinn a' Bhuird and descend eastwards from Stob an t-Sluichd once beyond the cliffs, then cut back underneath to reach the buttress.

The Route
Start at the lowest rock and climb rough slabs direct to a perched block. Climb a central groove past two steeper sections (or easier steps to the right). Either way leads to a steep prow as the ridge narrows. Either go left up a slanting

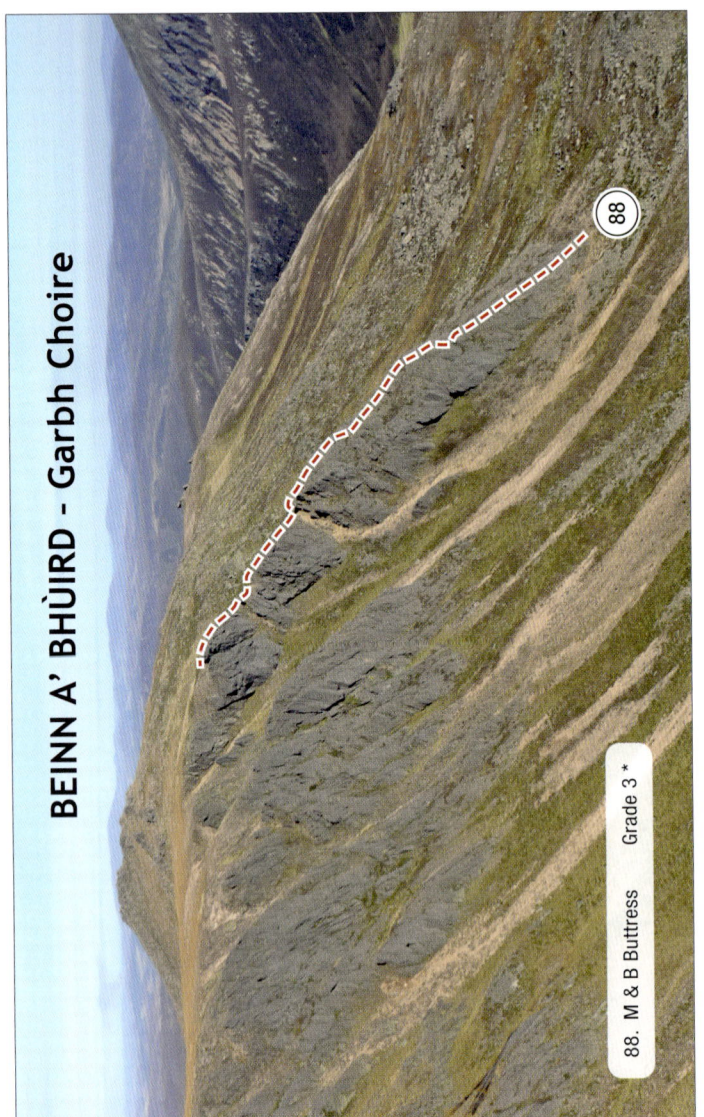

M & B Buttress (Route 88, Grade 3). Scrambler: Peter Pollard. Photo: Scott Muir.

groove to make an exposed step round left into a broken slabby gully before going up right to the crest, or go right below the prow and rejoin the ridge as soon as possible. Above a short arête the ground eases, with a few optional boulder problems (the steep corner off right is excellent at Moderate). As the ridge narrows again go up steps right of an easy central groove, with a steep pull up on juggy flakes. Cross a minor top and an easy ridge to another col, then clamber over two small pinnacles to a third col. Climb the steep pinnacle beyond to step rightwards off the top, the last bit being easily avoided on the right. Bouldery steps lead easily to the top.

BEN AVON 1171m

(NJ 133 019) Map p184

Another sprawling high plateau, one of the biggest in Scotland, and a long walk from anywhere. Ben Avon lacks the steep cliffs of its neighbour but has over a dozen minor summits, many of which take the form of isolated rock tors reminiscent of Dartmoor or the Peak District but with a much greater degree of isolation. Defined routes have been named and described on these tors, but they seem more suited to a free and easy approach. Plan your day to take in a few of them and climb any line that takes your fancy.

LOCHNAGAR

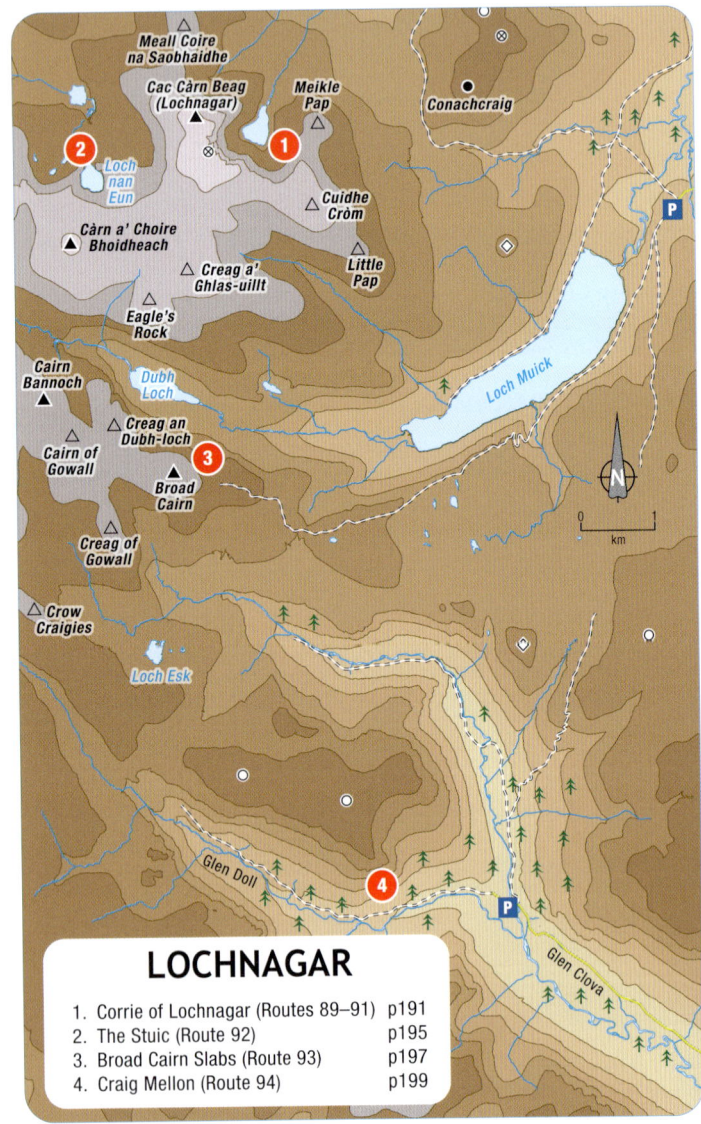

1. Corrie of Lochnagar (Routes 89–91)   p191
2. The Stuic (Route 92)   p195
3. Broad Cairn Slabs (Route 93)   p197
4. Craig Mellon (Route 94)   p199

LOCHNAGAR & GLEN CLOVA

From Deeside the main Cairngorm massif hides away behind lower hills, but on the south side Lochnagar flaunts its wares for all to see. The magnificent North-east corrie is a prominent feature in many well-loved views and is the spiritual heart of the area's climbing, particularly in winter. Eagle Ridge is the gem, but a couple of the easier buttress climbs make good targets for experienced scramblers. Tucked away behind Lochnagar is the mighty Creag an Dubh Loch, a contender for the best rock climbing venue in Britain. Sadly the few easy lines here are very vegetated and not worthwhile in summer, so scramblers have to be content with the nearby slabs on Broad Cairn. Further south and east, Glen Clova too has a few scrambling possibilities, although tolerance for a little vegetation is a must here.

Lochnagar Massif

The presiding hill of Deeside, and the heartland of Aberdonian mountaineering, has a couple of hundred climbs in its superb north-east corrie.

LOCHNAGAR 1155m

(NO 243 861) Map p190

Two of the easier rock climbs on the magnificent north-east face make good objectives for ambitious scramblers. Other atmospheric lines are scattered around.

89 Central Buttress   Moderate or Grade 3   *

Alt 850m   Ht Gain +250m   (NO 250 855)   Map p190   Diag p192

The left edge of the main cliff, sometimes a sharp ridge, sometimes more of a blunt buttress. Quite exposed in places, especially near the start.

Approach

Follow the main Lochnagar path as far as the saddle below Meikle Pap. A much smaller path continues ahead, descending slightly, then splits to traverse around the corrie. The higher path loses less height but is rougher. Central Buttress is the first big mass of rock reached, splitting the corrie into two and rising directly above the stretcher box.

The Route

From the lowest rocks a grassy gully goes up left in two sections. In the higher section both arêtes provide better and only slightly harder alternatives. Reach open ground on the left, with very steep rock ahead and another gully coming up from the right.

The next section is the crux, and can be avoided by grass on the left,

LOCHNAGAR

89. Central Buttress — Moderate or Grade 3 *
90. Black Spout Left-hand — Grade 1
91. Black Spout Buttress — Difficult **

reducing the difficulty to Grade 3. It is better, but distinctly harder, to follow an exposed ledge rightwards above the steepest section. Where it ends climb steps back up left to grass ledges (possible escape left). Climb a steep blocky groove from the right-hand corner of the ledges, with a steep exposed finish.

The easier option comes in here. Go out right on a small ledge above the void to an airy perch on the arête as the angle eases. Now romp up the crest on well-scratched jugs, with occasional minor detours on either side, to a levelling at a notch with jammed blocks. Pass right of a small tower, then avoid a larger one by a groove on the left. The ridge now merges into the general hillside, although some minor clambering may be found on the way to the plateau.

90 Black Spout Left-hand Branch   Grade 1
Alt 950m   Ht Gain + 120m   (NO 245 858)   Map p190   Diag p192

A traditional scramble that may appeal to historically-minded masochists and frustrated cavers. Bizarrely, it was once popular.

Approach
As for the previous route, but continue the traverse past the stretcher box and below the left-hand half of the main cliff to enter the obvious large open cleft of the Black Spout, the largest gully on the face. About halfway up this a branch goes off left.

The Route
Crawl through the unpleasant hole to reach scree. This leads without incident to the cliff top, but further masochism can be found by climbing the well named Crumbling Cranny. This is the first opening in the cliff on the right above the hole. It is mostly steep loose rubble, but the steeper top 10m or so is proper rock and almost pleasant.

91 Black Spout Buttress   Difficult   **
Alt 950m   Ht Gain + 250m   (NO 246 859)   Map p190   Diag p192

A varied route that starts quite grassy but improves as it rises, finishing with a couple of steep exposed steps on superb juggy rock.

Approach
As for the previous route to the mouth of the Black Spout then move right to gain steeply sloping grass just right.

The Route
From the top right-hand corner of the grass move up right and climb a grassy chimney (not the steeper chimney just left). Where the ground opens out keep ahead up another chimney. Continue up boulders on the left edge and cross a horizontal arête to a saddle. The better upper part of the route can be started here by coming in up the Black Spout and slanting up right to the saddle.

Go up piled blocks and a short crack to climb an awkward steep chimney

Black Spout Buttress, Lochnagar (Route 91, Difficult).
Climber: Nate Webb. Photo: Iain Thow.

(avoidable by steep grass on the right or an airy step on the left). Zigzag up to a steep wall, climbed delicately left to right. Take the final wall direct on good holds. Both the last two steps can be avoided in the gully on the right, no easier but much less exposed, although this misses out the best part of the route.

Other possibilities nearby
The adventurous may enjoy the trip out to Lochnagar Pinnacle (Moderate). Walk down the crest just east of the Left-Hand Branch of the Black Spout until it steepens, then descend an insecure groove just right of the arête (looking out). Grassy steps lead down right to the col. Five metres down the right-hand gully climb a steep right-slanting crack, then a wider ramp goes more easily up left to the Pinnacle summit. Remember that all this has to be reversed as it is by far the easiest way off. The descent from the Pinnacle itself is often abseiled.

CÀRN A' CHOIRE BHOIDHEACH 1110m

(NO 226 845) Map p190

This plateau summit is Lochnagar's western extension, but counts as a separate Munro. The cliffs on the northern flank are divided by a prominent spur, which finishes on a minor top called The Stuic (1093m).

92 Stuic Buttress   Grade 1   *
Alt 950m   Ht Gain +80m   (NO 227 854)   Map p190

An easy spur with minor rock steps, not exposed. A good introduction to scrambling and an enjoyable way onto the plateau.

Approach
The spur rises from the west side of Loch nan Eun, a walk in of at least 8km from any direction. The shortest route follows good paths through the pines of Ballochbuie Forest from Invercauld Bridge (186 909). Follow the track on the south side of the Dee and take the first fork right, leading up to the falls of Garbh Allt (198 895). Swing right below these and turn left up the track following the Feindallacher Burn. At around the 600m contour cross the stream and plod up pathless heather to Sandy Loch and then Loch nan Eun, with the Stuic prominent above.

An equally scenic but longer route follows the north side of Loch Muick to Glas-allt Shiel, then up a good path past Glas-allt Falls to 1000m. Traverse west to the col at 240 852 where an easy descent leads to Loch nan Eun. The summit of Lochnagar is a fairly minor diversion from this route and many treat The Stuic as an add-on after the more substantial routes on the reigning peak. The round from Spittal of Glen Muick of Lochnagar via Central Buttress and Càrn a' Choire Bhoidheach via The Stuic, descending past Creag an Dubh Loch, is a classic day out.

Stuic Buttress (Route 92, Grade 1). Photo: Nick Bramhall.

The Route
The spur is easy to start, then narrows and steepens. The first steep step can be tackled direct but is much easier on the left, traversing back right just above. An easy crest leads to a squeeze between two flakes, then a well trodden route follows the arête up short steps to the Stuic's pointed summit. Halfway round the corrie rim rightwards the well-named Stegosaurus Rib is a nice short Grade 2, best reached from above by the gully to its right.

Loch Muick Hills

South and west of Loch Muick is a range of plateau summits running across to Glens Clova and Callater. Broad Cairn, the most accessible of these, has a good scramble on its north side, Further up the glen is the huge crag of Creag an Dubh Loch, home to some of Britain's best rock climbs. Sadly the few easier lines here are mostly grass and it offers little or nothing to scramblers.

BROAD CAIRN 998m

(NO 240 815) Map p190

A rounded stony hill usually climbed as part of a group of Munros at the head of Glen Muick. On a dry day the described route makes an enjoyable detour from the usual way up the hill.

93 Broad Cairn Slabs   Moderate   *
Alt 850m   Ht Gain +80m   (NO 244 817)   Map p190

A sweep of clean ice-scraped slabs, not steep but quite smooth. Lots of route options but all converge at a short sharp crux where many will want a rope. Thoroughly nasty if wet.

Approach
From the Glen Muick car park (pay and display) take the track along the south side of Loch Muick and up to the stable at 256 808. A well used track leads up Broad Cairn from here, followed to reach a flattening at 850m. Slant right from here, slightly down, to reach the foot of the slabs in about 400m.

The Route
Start centrally and pad up the easy lower slabs, moving left into slightly steeper but still slabby grooves. Go up these to a left slanting grassy weakness that divides the gentler lower slabs from the more tiered ones above. Go up the weakness towards an inverted V of steeper rock. Either do two awkward mantelshelves left of the apex to reach easier slabs and the continuation of the weakness, or work up and right from 5m below the apex then go back left once the angle eases (easier but more serious). There are many possible lines above (and an easy escape left), but probably the best is to slant rightwards up easy slabs to climb a thin crack just left of a bigger weakness about halfway across the slabs. Continue in the same line to the top.

198 BROAD CAIRN

Broad Cairn Slabs (Route 93, Grade 3).
Scrambler: Nate Webb. Photo: Iain Thow.

CRAIG MELLON

Glen Clova

The most dramatic of the Angus Glens, Glen Clova is best known in the outdoor world for the Munros of Driesh and Mayar and the roadside rock climbing on the Red Craigs, but the following scramble is well worthwhile.

CRAIG MELLON 866m

(NO 263 774) Map p190

This plateau hill separates Glen Doll from Upper Glen Clova and has very steep flanks on both north and south. Mostly they are very vegetated, but the fine finish on the route below makes it worthwhile.

94 Craig Mellon   Grade 2/3
Alt 400m   Ht Gain +400m   (NO 267 763)   Map p190   Diag p200

Although containing a fair amount of steep walking, the described route includes over 200m of rock too, mostly Grade 2 but with a couple of short sections bordering on Grade 3. Being unfrequented it has its fair share of loose rock, but the underlying rock is sound. It is quite lichenous so a poor choice if wet.

Approach
From the Braedownie car park at the Glen Clova road end (pay and display) follow the main forest road to the junction at 268 759. Go steeply up rightwards towards the left-hand of the two lowest buttresses (currently up unpleasant recent tree felling and bog).

The Route
The bottom of the first buttress is steep, so gain it from the left and slant right up a heathery groove (or rock just to its right) to the crest. Work back left up heathery slabs to finish up a steep groove on good holds. The top groove can be avoided on the left.

Walk up to the left edge of the next crag and either clamber up an easy broken spur or (much better) climb the clean rib right of this, with a steep start on positive holds. Carry on up the rib until it eases to walking. It is possible to continue straight up from here, linking minor outcrops, but better is to slant up left towards a prominent steep crag high on the left skyline. Pass below a short steep craglet, then 100m left of this scramble up a more broken blunt buttress to reach the left edge of the main steep crag.

Climb an introductory outcrop, then the left flank of the main crag. The easiest line starts just right of the left-hand rib, slants up left then goes back right, but this is rather heathery. It is better to gain the next rib to the right from the left about 10m up, above its steep start, then zigzag up it to the top of the buttress.

Scramble up a short rock step, then progress is apparently barred by an intimidating leaning wall. This succumbs surprisingly easily on the left, using

big holds just right of a perched block. Above is a short thuggy wall, then easy minor craglets and walking lead up to the plateau.

Other possibilities nearby

On the other side of Glen Doll from Craig Mellon and further up is Craig Maud. The Pinnacle Ridge up its front provides a very vegetated scramble, much better in winter. Further round on Driesh the left-hand edge of the Winter Corrie has a few minor outcrops, while lower down on the Red Craigs, on the two crags closest to the road, are the short Moderate rock climbs of *Ant Slab* and *Twenty Minute Route* (see the North-East Outcrops guide).

The south-west corner of Clachnaben summit tor. Photo: Eric Taylor.

Further east, Glen Esk has a few cliffs but all are very vegetated. Much more promising is the stubby granite wart of Clachnaben which dominates Glen Dye. From the car park on the Cairn o' Mount road at NO 649 869 a well used path goes south-west to the stream at 642 861 then up past a high wood to the summit. Even the easiest route to the tor's top requires using hands, and lots of fun can be had clambering about. The best line starts steeply at the south-west corner then follows the skyline, with a hard move above a big ledge at two-thirds height (avoidable on the left).

MEAGAIDH & ALDER

Although separated by the broad valley containing Loch Laggan, these two ranges have much in common. Creag Meagaidh and Ben Alder themselves are high plateaux bitten into by numerous deep corries while their satellite peaks are shapelier with the odd rocky spur. Both areas have excellent winter climbing on the corrie headwalls but the rock is rather too shattered for good summer rock climbing. However both ranges have spurs between the corries which make fine scrambles. All the routes can be done in a day, especially if a mountain bike is used, but for Ben Alder many will prefer to wild camp or to overnight at Culra Bothy (currently closed but the intention is to reopen).

Monadhliaths

These plateau summits sprawl between Speyside and Loch Ness, with scenic deep valleys and a remote feel. In general they are not a happy hunting ground for scramblers but a few possibilities exist, mainly amongst the rockier hills on the north-west flank.

BEINN SGÙRRACH   470m

OS Landranger 35   (NH 503 147)

About 15km north-east of Fort Augustus the B862 road along the east side of Loch Ness passes through the small clachan of Whitebridge. Prominent to the south-east from here is the rock spike of Beinn Sgùrrach, which provides an easily accessible scramble good for an evening.

95 North-West Ridge   Grade 3
Alt 350m   Ht Gain + 140m   (NH 500 147)   Map inside front cover

Mossy slabs but with plenty of good holds. Very slippery in the wet.

Approach
A track leaves the minor road to Loch Killin at NH 504 124 and descends to the power station. Follow the east bank of the River Fechlin for 1km before traversing up to the west nose of the hill. Just above the highest point of the deer fence is a small col backed by mossy slabs.

The Route
Climb the slabs then go left up heather and broken rock, aiming for the prominent slabby rib on the skyline. Climb this direct, sustained but always on good holds (easier slightly right). More broken rocks lead to the summit. The next hill, Leac nan Cisteachan, has a line of slabs running up its west end, mostly walking angle but very pleasant all the same. Left of the lower scramble are more slabs, but these are much more broken and vegetated, far less fun.

BEINN SGÙRRACH 203

*North-West Ridge, Beinn Sgùrrach (Route 95, Grade 3).
Scrambler: Marco de Man. Photo: Iain Thow.*

MEAGAIDH & ALDER

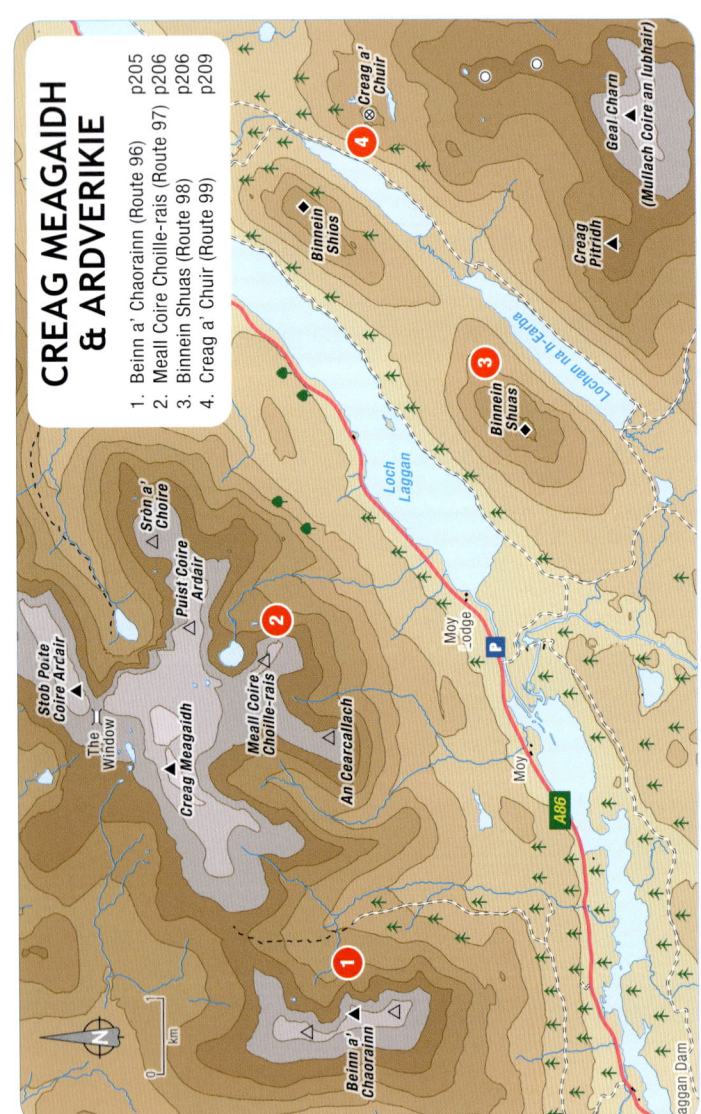

CREAG MEAGAIDH & ARDVERIKIE

1. Beinn a' Chaorainn (Route 96) p205
2. Meall Coire Choille-rais (Route 97) p206
3. Binnein Shuas (Route 98) p206
4. Creag a' Chuir (Route 99) p209

Other possibilities

A little further north, the Beinn Dubhcharaidh flank of Cona Gleann has a lot of slabby rock, unfortunately linked by man-eating steep heather (583 203). In upper Strathspey the Allt Chnaimeanaich (895 985) can be worthwhile (Grade 3), but only in very low water as the narrow stream bed quickly becomes full. Stac Ghorm in Strathnairn (631 273) has lots of rock but most of it very mossy and lacking in lines.

The Creag Meagaidh Massif

A huge sprawling plateau mountain with half a dozen deep corries. Coire Ardair on the east is the most spectacular and the best known, particularly for its fine winter climbing. However, much of the schist in this dramatic corrie is vegetated and fragile so best left alone in summer. Beautiful Coire Choille-rais on the south-west side of Puist Coire Ardair (1071m) is smaller but has a more attractive offering.

BEINN A' CHAORAINN 1052m

OS Landranger 41   (NN 385 851)   Map p204

The mountain to the west of Creag Meagaidh has a broad whaleback with three summits above a craggy East Face. The ridge descending from the central and highest summit is a fairly popular easy scramble.

96 East Ridge   Grade 1   **
Alt 750m   Ht Gain + 250m   (NN 392 851)   Map p204

A succession of outcrops running up a well-defined spur, not difficult but in a superb position.

Approach
Park at Roughburn (377 813) and take the forest road north-westwards and then back round east. After 5km or so this leads out of the mature forest and from here there are two possibilities. Either slant up to around 650m and then traverse north to the foot of the ridge (shorter but rougher), or follow the track into newer forestry until a small path runs up the Allt Ban to reach the ridge directly.

The Route
A short steep ascent leads to a level ridge, then the spur gets steeper and rocky, although never difficult. Climb it direct up little outcrops and arêtes or avoid them easily to arrive at the central and highest summit. To descend, the south-west shoulder takes you down to a stile on the forest edge above Roughburn.

MEALL COIRE CHOILLE-RAIS 1028m

OS Landranger 42   (NN 432 862)   Map p204

This south-eastern top of Creag Meagaidh overlooks a large lochan which nestles in the floor of the delightful Coire Choille-rais. The left bounding rim of the corrie gives the following route.

97 East Ridge   Grade 2
Alt 850m   Ht Gain +120m   (NN 435 862)   Map p204

Quite vegetated scrambling but a good line, with the inward dipping strata making it easier than it looks.

Approach
Park at either end of a blocked off loop in the old road (445 842) about 1km east of Moy Lodge. A path runs up through the woods just east of the stream to open country. A sketchier path then continues up the east bank past a fine waterfall, switching to the west bank at around the 500m contour. At around 650m bear up left towards the East Face, which is split by a straight central gully with a prominent rock spur left of it. Go up grass and avoidable minor craglets to the foot of the spur.

The Route
Climb a broken rock rib about 10m left of the gully, avoiding the bulging prow at its top by grass on the left. Continue up grass to another broken rib. This is quite steep in places but good positive holds make it much easier than it looks, and all difficulties are avoidable by winding about a bit. It rises to a fine climax at two jutting boulders right at the top. Climb a short groove just left of the first boulder, then pull up leftwards to surmount the second. The top arrives suddenly, with the summit of Meall Coire Choille-rais 100m or so further on, giving superb views down to the lochan below. A loop round the top of the corrie is the obvious continuation, perhaps with a detour to the summit of Creag Meagaidh itself. If doing the latter in mist, note that the very substantial *Maclaren's Cairn* (commonly called Mad Meg's Cairn) at 424 876 is not the summit!

Ardverikie

Several rocky peaklets flank the main Ben Alder Forest hills on the north, providing a scenic backdrop to Loch laggan and a couple of good scrambles.

BINNEIN SHUAS 746m

OS Landranger 42   (NN 464 826)   Map p204

The prominent knobbly hill on the south side of Loch Laggan, well known to climbers because of the classic severe Ardverikie Wall. The described scramble

Ardverikie Rib, Binnein Shuas (Route 98, Grade 3).
Scrambler: Jamie Hageman. Photo: Iain Thow.

is further right at the far end of the cliffs, well beyond the main climbing area. Sadly it is not as good as it looks from a distance as the lower section is steep and vegetated, but the main slabby ramp is excellent, on superb knobbly pegmatite.

98 Ardverikie Rib   Grade 3
Alt 550m   Ht Gain +200m   (NN 469 831)   Map p204   Diag p207

Rough pegmatite slabs in a serious position, not hard but quite intimidating in the middle. Not a good choice in the wet.

Approach
From Moy Bridge (NN 433 830) follow the estate roads to the west end of Lochan na h-Earba, then just before the bridge turn left on a rough path slanting up towards the classic rock climb Ardverikie Wall. Leave this as it starts to gain height and keep traversing round until past the obvious cliffs. Go up past two small outcrops to reach more cliffs set further back, the last ones on the East Face. The left-hand buttress is roughly diamond shaped, with a clean slabby top and a steeper more vegetated lower half. Go up the gully on the left until it is feasible to get onto the lower buttress above the steep part.

The Route
Go out right to the skyline and climb an airy rib to a big heather shelf below the upper buttress. Climb the slabs on lovely knobbly pegmatite, probably dodging the steep top wall on its right, to reach another heather shelf. The buttress up right is much steeper, but more knobbly slabs slant up left from its foot. Follow these up and left, until it is possible to move up right above the overhangs (or carry on up left, more serious but no harder). The slabs gradually ease over into walking, then another rib develops over to the right, leading to the north-eastern top of Binnein Shuas. More outcrops can be found on the way to the main summit, including an excellent long slab.

If descending the south-west flank there are lots more outcrops of excellent pegmatite to play on, Of course this is also true if coming up this way, but sadly they don't form much of a line, involving lots of zigzagging about to include the best bits.

CREAG A' CHUIR 643m

OS Landranger 42   (NN 505 847)   Map p204

A minor peak on the fringes of Ardverikie Forest with a nice pointy summit and a rocky north-west face above Lochan na h-Earba.

99 Central Buttress   Moderate or Grade 3   *
Alt 450m   Ht Gain +100m   (NN 500 848)   Map p204   Diag p210

Slabs of excellent pegmatite, a bit vegetated low down but improving higher up. Very slippery in the wet.

Approach
The shortest route is from Kinloch Laggan, crossing the bridge by the gatehouse and following the private road to Ardverikie. Once the castle comes into view fork left and left again to go up to Lochan na h-Earba on a forest road. It is longer but more scenic to come from Moy Bridge (433 830) along estate roads (bike option) past the western lochan. The latter fits in well with a continuation over the Munros of Geal Charn and Creag Pitridh.

By either route, from halfway along the eastern lochan go steeply up through trees towards the biggest and cleanest face on the central buttress.

The Route
Go up broken outcrops covered in pine needles, then pad up a cleaner slab slanting up left to the main face. At the foot of this go right to easier rock close to the right-bounding gully. Take a slabby rake up left, getting harder with height (keep left) and culminating in an awkward and exposed move left to a heather alcove. This is worth Moderate, harder than anything else on the route, but the whole section can be avoided on the right if required.

Above this section go up right and climb much easier ribbed slabs to a blaeberry field. Climb the first part of a steep groove, traversing right below a pointed overhang when it gets harder. Go back up left and up nicely positioned easy slabs running up leftwards. A couple more outcrops can be found on the way to the summit, with a good finale up a clean rib.

Geal Chàrn & Ben Alder

These huge rounded hills feature prominently in views from many directions. Although not particularly rocky they have a sub-arctic feel and hold snow well into the summer. Three of the subsidiary ridges are well known scrambles and the two other routes mentioned here are excellent too.

Ben Alder (l) and the Lancet Edge (r) from the east. Photo: Peter D Smith.

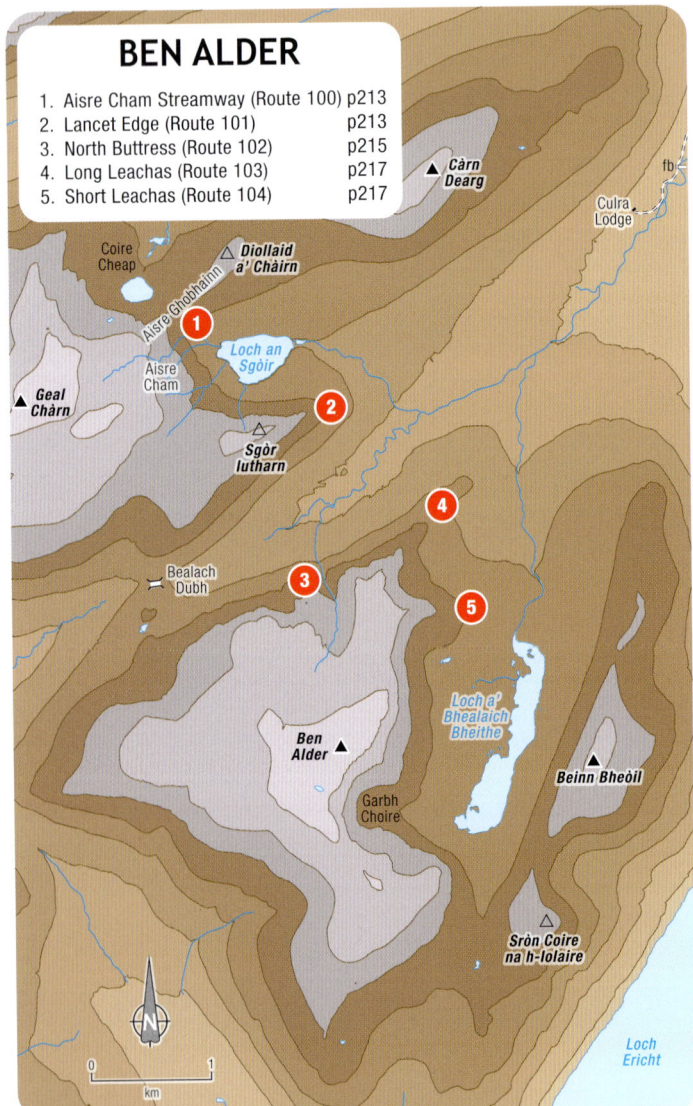

BEN ALDER

1. Aisre Cham Streamway (Route 100) p213
2. Lancet Edge (Route 101) p213
3. North Buttress (Route 102) p215
4. Long Leachas (Route 103) p217
5. Short Leachas (Route 104) p217

GEAL CHÀRN

All five routes are usually approached from a camp/bothy at Culra / *Caol Rèidh* (NN 523 762). (Culra Bothy is currently closed but the intention is to reopen it.) To reach Culra either cycle along Loch Ericht from Dalwhinnie or up by the River Pattack from Inverpattack 554 897. On the latter option a short detour to the Falls of Pattack is recommended.

Culra can also be reached over the Bealach Leamhain from Moy (432 829) or even from Corrour Station by going along Loch Ossian, up the Uisge Labhair and crossing the Bealach Dubh. This latter route lends itself to a return over the three Munros Geal Chàrn, Aonach Beag and Beinn Eibhinn.

GEAL CHÀRN 1132m

OS Landranger 42 (NN 470 745) Map p212

The highest of the ridge of Munros north of Ben Alder has a broad summit plateau and narrow but easy connecting ridges. The unnamed corrie on its south-east flank boasts two excellent scrambles, one following the stream gully closest to the north-east ridge (Aisre Ghobhainn), the other being the sharp spur that forms the southern rim of the corrie, running up to Sgòr Iutharn.

100 Aisre Cham Streamway   Moderate or Grade 3   *
Alt 800m   Ht Gain +150m   (NN 484 751)   Map p212

An often wet gully scramble, tricky in places and occasionally exposed. The top section holds snow well into late spring, in which case a right-hand finish may be necessary.

Approach
From Culra follow the path towards Bealach Dubh for 2km, then turn right and head up by the stream to Loch an Sgòir. Go round the north side of the loch and follow the stream from its far north-west corner up to where it issues from a narrow gully in the backing cliffs. If climbing Càrn Dearg first this point can easily be reached by an 80m descent from the narrow saddle below the steep rise of the north-east ridge (Aisre Ghobhainn) of Geal Chàrn.

The Route
Enter the gully and climb the left side, gradually steepening to an airy step on good holds. Escape right here is possible and if the upper slot is full of snow or has too much water the rib right of it is an enjoyable Grade 3 on good rock. The slot itself is Moderate, climbed mostly on the left until a steepening forces you to cross the stream on a slanting slab. Above this the angle eases and the slot soon opens out to boulders.

101 Lancet Edge   Grade 1 or 2   *
Alt 650m   Ht Gain +350m   (NN 497 744)   Map p212

The ridge itself is sharp with some easy well-positioned scrambling, while there are some optional outcrops lower down.

*Aisre Cham Streamway, Geal Chàrn (Route 100, Moderate).
Photo: Robin Wallace.*

BEN ALDER

Approach
The very fit may consider incorporating the ridge into a traverse between the trains at Dalwhinnie and Corrour. Whichever way you come in the first rocks are found just up westwards from where the Allt Loch an Sgòir crosses the path from Culra to the Bealach Dubh.

The Route
Climb a delicate slabby rib below and left of a leaning wall, then break through steeper rock by a pink staircase. Walk right to more slabby ribs, then go up heather to the ridge proper. The middle of three outcrops is fun, then climb another rib on the left, hard to start. Go up a broken crag on the crest, the only unavoidable scrambling on the entire route. Now follow the lovely narrow arête to the top, a bit shattered in places but beautifully airy.

BEN ALDER 1148m

OS Landranger 42   (NN 496 719)   Map p212

The dominant hill of the area, whose huge plateau is easily identified from many hills in the southern half of the Highlands. The 300m cliffs on the north and east are mostly quite vegetated and broken but provide excellent winter climbing. The pair of ridges on the angle of these two faces are well known easy scrambles, while the central buttress on the north face is excellent too, and deserves to be better known.

102 North Buttress   Grade 3   **
Alt 750m   Ht Gain +200m   (NN 493 733)   Map p212   Diag p216

An intimidating route up a wild and unfrequented part of the mountain. A scary crux but the rest is much easier.

Approach
Reach Culra bothy either by the path along the shore of Loch Ericht from Dalwhinnie or up Glen Pattack from 554 897 (detour to the Falls of Pattack recommended). Carry on up the north bank of the stream for 3.5km, then cross it and go up to the blunt buttress that projects out just west of the impressive waterfalls dropping from the plateau.

The Route
The bottom of the spur is too steep for scrambling so go round right and up past a reddish wall slanting up right. Take the first prominent grassy ledge up left to an easing on the crest of the buttress. Ahead is steep again but an awkward move left gains a slab with small sharp holds. Cross this leftwards then make an exposed traverse further leftwards to reach more broken rock. Go up this, working back up right to regain the crest above the steep section.

Slabs with sharp rippled holds lead to another grass terrace. Keep on up the crest on more excellent slabby ribs with plenty of route choice until it curves over into walking and merges with the plateau in the base of a shallow

216 MEAGAIDH & ALDER

BEN ALDER
North Buttress

102. North Buttress   Grade 3 **

corrie. Crossing the stream and heading up south-east takes you to the ridge above the eastern cliffs, which (hopefully!) provides spectacular wild views on the way to the summit.

103 Long Leachas   Grade 1   **
Alt 800m   Ht Gain +200m   (NN 503 735)   Map p212

This is the north-east spur of the mountain, the right-hand of the pair facing Culra. It gives easy scrambling up a narrow ridge. The stars are more for atmosphere than the scrambling itself, which is fairly minor.

Approach
There is a footbridge 500m north-east of Culra Lodge. Cross this and follow the path on the south bank of the Allt a' Chaoil-rèidhe. Just over a kilometre from Culra the path climbs southwards and eventually follows the stream which flows from Loch a' Bhealaich Bheithe. At about 700m cross the stream and go west to reach the easy angled spur at the foot of the ridge.

The Route
A good path zigzags up the first steepening, then at the next tower the path goes up right of centre, with more direct routes possible at higher grades. Now just follow the crest, narrow and easy angled at first, then rising into a series of broken towers with huge holds, usually avoidable on the left using well-travelled paths. If using the ridge for descent in bad weather, a very useful cairn marks its top.

104 Short Leachas   Grade 1 or 2   *
Alt 750m   Ht Gain +300m   (NN 506 729)   Map p212

This is the left-hand of the pair of spurs facing Culra, slightly harder than its twin.

Approach
As for Route 103 but continue along the path as far as Loch a' Bhealaich Bheithe. The ridge lies a few hundred metres off to the west. Cross the stream and start at the lowest rock, just up and left of a small lochan.

The Route
Move up right then left to large boulders on a ledge, then tiptoe up a left slanting crack to easy ground (Grade 2 but the buttress is easily avoided on the left). At the next steepening go up a grassy groove left of centre, then the ridge eases to walking. The tremendous East Face makes a superb backdrop. The upper ridge is sharper, with easy but shattered scrambling. Near the top a steep tower gives pause for thought, Grade 2 direct or easier by a groove on the right.

The three Ben Alder routes can be combined by going up left from the top of North Buttress, descending Long Leachas, then climbing Short Leachas.

NEVIS RANGE & MAMORES

Clustered around Ben Nevis is the biggest concentration of high summits in Scotland, linked into two chains of sweeping ridges either side of the deep trench of Glen Nevis. Occasionally these ridges run to scrambling, as in the Ring of Steall, but most of the routes described here are on the faces below them. Supreme amongst these is the North Face of Ben Nevis itself, a honeypot for winter climbers from all over the world and with superb (if comparatively neglected) rock climbing. The most prominent lines up the face, however, straddle the boundary between climbs and scrambles. Of the five main ridges only Ledge Route is a pure scramble, the others, although they contain scrambling, all have sections where the vast majority will want a rope. Whatever you define them as though, these are iconic routes deserving all the superlatives that have been heaped upon them.

The Grey Corries

This ridge of quartzite peaks east of Nevis Range proper makes a classic hill day, but the best scrambling is on nearby subsidiary summits, the Munro of Stob Bàn off to the south, and the jagged spike of Sgùrr Innse across the Lairig Leacach to the east.

SGÙRR INNSE 808M

OS Landranger 41   (NN 290 748)   Map p219

Small it may be relative to its neighbours, but this thrusting peaklet will grab the attention of any keen scrambler. The actual scrambling isn't as good as you initially expect, being fairly broken and lacking in well defined lines, but it's well worth doing all the same.

105 South-East Slabs   Grade 3   *

Alt 550m   Ht Gain +200m   (NN 293 746)   Map p219   Diag p220

Steepish slabs separated by heather leading to a definite crescendo and a splendid summit.

Approach
It is usually possible to drive up the gravel track from Corriechoille and park at NN 255 789. Walk up the track from here into the Lairig Leacach until just before the bothy. Sgùrr Innse is obvious up on the left. Slant up to the col south of it, then traverse eastwards on deer tracks below the lowest tier of cliffs for about 0.5km.

The Route
The face is in three tiers, the lowest fairly heathery, with the more-or-less lowest outcrop having a large pink boulder sitting on its top. Climb to the

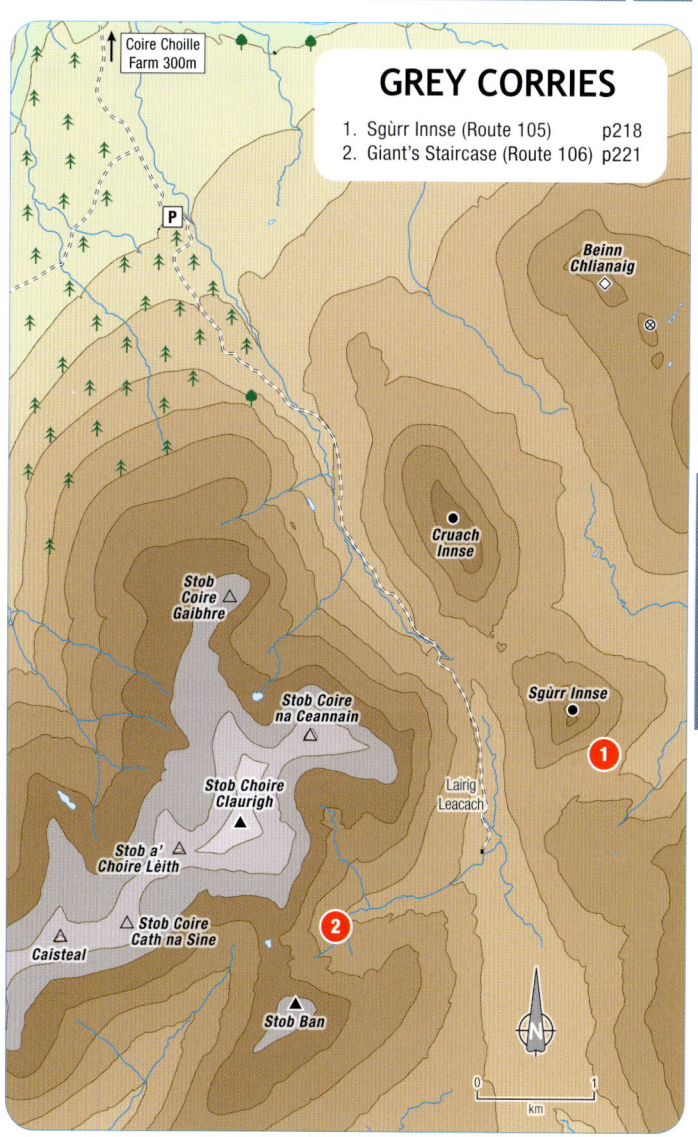

220 GREY CORRIES

SGÙRR INNSE
South-East Face

105. South-East Slabs — Grade 3 *

boulder then walk up to a steeper crag, which is climbed by a right-slanting weakness on its left. The next step has a nice pillar, climbed steeply on good holds. Walk right below steep rock to a clean slab with good sharp holds, quite hard if tackled direct. Above this is a shorter slab then walking leads to a wide bouldery terrace.

Above the boulders is a steep face with flaky right-facing cracks, harder than scrambling but definitely attention grabbing for climbers. The outcrop is easily avoided on the right, then follow a line of clean craglets which give fun scrambling with good holds appearing just where you need them. Easy slabs lead to another bouldery terrace.

On the top tier there is an easy finish up right, but a more fitting climax follows the clean left edge of a heathery ramp up leftwards to an overhanging prow. A precarious move takes you up left again into a vegetated niche, where after a few steps up left good flakes give you confidence to swing airily rightwards to a sudden arrival at the top.

STOB BÀN 977m

OS Landranger 41   (NN 267 724)   Map p219

A distinctive pointed peak set apart from the main Grey Corries ridge. The ribs just below the summit are fairly broken, although some scrambling can be contrived. Far better are the slabs below the saddle linking Stob Bàn to the main Grey Corries ridge, which make a splendid scramble.

106 Giant's Staircase   Grade 2/3   **
Alt 650m   Ht Gain + 100m   (NN 269 729)   Map p219   Diag p222

A succession of clean quartzite slabs separated by grassy ledges. A climbers' scramble which can be made quite technical if desired but is also easily escapable. Very slippery in the wet.

Approach

As for Sgùrr Innse to Lairig Leacach bothy, then follow either bank of the Allt a' Chuil Choirein up into Coire Claurigh. The slabs are obvious ahead, on the corrie headwall.

The Route

The slabs are in three tiers, with loads of possibilities on each one. The following is just a suggestion, many will prefer to simply follow their nose. Climb the lowest slab by cracks on the right, delicate at the top, to a sloping shelf. Go up a thin crack, then easier slabs to the top of the first tier. Climb either a delicate slab on the left or an easier one further right, right of a wet corner. More easy slabs take you to the top of the second tier and a small lochan. Climb the ledgy right-hand side of the slab above this, then traverse left and bear left up slabby ribs. Either a delicate slab off left or a rounded nose directly above make a fine finale.

106. Giant's Staircase Grade 2/3 **

GIANT'S STAIRCASE 223

*On the second tier of the Giant's Staircase (Route 106, Grade 2/3).
Scrambler: Tim Taylor. Photo: Noel Williams.*

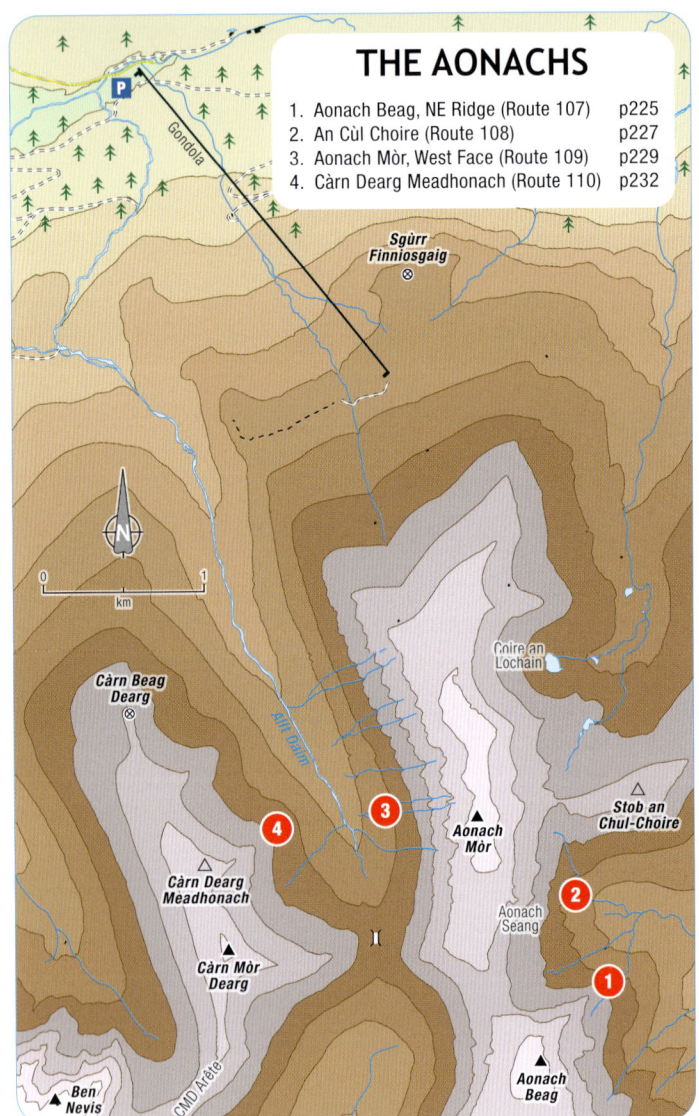

AONACH BEAG

The Aonachs

The two broad steep sided summits just east of Nevis itself are easily accessed using the ski development and have become very popular. Both have scrambling on them with an Alpine feel about it, especially in Spring.

AONACH BEAG 1234m

OS Landranger 41   (NN 197 715)   Map p224

A rounded topped hill with steep craggy sides except on the south. The West face is largely too steep for scrambling and the East face very broken, but the North-East Ridge is a winter classic and a worthwhile trip in summer too.

107 North-East Ridge   Very Difficult   *
Alt 700m   Ht Gain +450m   (NN 203 720)   Map p224   Diag p226

A very long route in a wild and remote corrie and probably the most serious route in this guide. Although much of it is walking, the complicated crux section is quite hard. The airy arête after it comes as enjoyable light relief.

Approach
The traditional approach is from Glen Nevis through Nevis Gorge and over the saddle between Aonach Mòr and Sgùrr Choinnich Beag, then traversing north-west across very rough ground (in mist beware the false ridge halfway across). It is much easier to take advantage of the Nevis Range gondola and either a) go over the summit of Aonach Mòr to the saddle beyond it, then descend eastwards below steep cliffs to reach the foot of the ridge or
b) approach as for An Cul Choire Headwall (Route 108) but carry on across the lower corrie and up to the foot of the ridge.

The Route
From the foot of the ridge go up a left slanting grass weakness, then back up right to easy ground. Go up right towards a minor gully and climb easy slabs on its left. If coming over from Glen Nevis the ground logically leads you in here. Zigzag up rightwards to the crest and follow it easily. After a while it narrows and steepens to an enjoyable clamber over blocks and spikes. Arrive at some huge pinnacles which signal the start of much more serious terrain. The direct route, which ascends a greasy chimney below and left of a conspicuous mass of white quartz, is much harder than scrambling.

Instead follow vegetated steps up right, rising slightly until a grassy break (awkward to start) cuts back up leftwards towards a short quartzy wall. Climb this (crux) to a larger grass ledge about 10m below the crest of the ridge. The same point can be reached by continuing slightly further right after the vegetated steps and ascending to a comfortable grassy nook with a good flake belay at its left-hand end. Traverse horizontally left past a bulging wall (crux) to reach the same grass ledge.

Whichever version you use, continue by slanting up rightwards on a good

AONACH MÒR

ledge until a short juggy wall leads up to a bouldery niche and the crest. The short exposed arête beyond is the best bit of the route, then a broader ridge runs up to the top, with occasional outcrops to add interest. The summit is a short distance up to the left.

AONACH MÒR 1221m

OS Landranger 41   (NN 194 729)   Map p224

A long thin plateau with steep craggy flanks, the easy accessibility provided by the gondola on the northern slopes has made Aonach Mòr a popular winter climbing ground. The longer west face has one excellent scramble, while An Cùl Choire on the south east has acres of rock with a remote feel.

108 An Cùl Choire Headwall   Grade 3   **

Alt 750m   Ht Gain +400m   (NN 199 725)   Map p224   Diag p228

A winding but logical line up a big face in a wild situation with some excellent positions and good rock. It is quite committing and often holds snow until June, which makes it feel very Alpine.

Approach

Purists will walk in up the glen from Leanachan Forest, but most will take advantage of the Gondola to gain 600m. From the top station traverse round into Coire Choille-rais north-east of Aonach Mòr and go up this to the col at its head, just west of Stob an Cùl Choire. The stream at NN 204 738 provides en route fun at Grade 1, starting up the slabs on the left, and just before reaching the col at the head of the corrie there is a very pleasant slabby buttress of the same grade up on the right.

The descent from the col into An Cùl Choire needs care. Either keep well right of the stream with an awkward slab at the bottom or start down the true left side of the stream then at half height take a well used deer track leftwards down slabby ramps and cut back right below the cliffs. The latter option takes you past lots of superb short slabs – exploring too many of them might leave you without enough time for the main route! Either way takes you to the lowest rock on the main face at the head of the corrie. The route starts at the top of an earthy runnel about 100m left of the waterfall coming down from the col. The general line zigzags around a prominent straight black stream slot coming down from the right-hand side of the obvious tower of the Aonach Seang on the skyline.

The Route

Go up slabby steps just left of the stream then cross it and go up to a large clean slab. Go up the grass ramp right of this (or climb it direct at Diff) and follow its crest up left to reach a large walking angle slab. At the top of this go up a groove for 10m to a sharp wedged flake. Step left here to go round onto the front face and keep going left to reach an open groove which leads up leftwards to the crest. Go directly up just right of the stream, with the first

108. An Cùl Choire Headwall   Grade 3 **

awkward step helped by a square hold in the groove just left. Rough easy angled rock now leads to a slab, then another awkward rounded step leads to a big grass terrace.

Cross left over the stream and follow an easy rib. Climb the right edge where it steepens then traverse left below another steepening (possible escape left here). Work back up right to the crest and go up to a ledge. Climb a broken groove to a triangular grass patch below a wet slot, step right and climb just right of the slot on big jugs. Continue to a steep wall then move right into the stream bed. On the other bank climb steeply on good holds to easy ground.

Up left is the tower of the Aonach Seang (Diff by the groove in the front) but a good continuation at the grade strings together outcrops just right of the stream. All are possible direct on excellent rock, with occasional thought-provoking moves. After the first two it is also possible to go left across the now usually dry stream and clamber up onto the Aonach Seang at a notch above the main climbing. The top section is easy fun, with any difficulties avoidable if required. All variations finish up steep grass to reach the plateau a few hundred metres south of the summit.

109 Golden Oldy   Grade 2   **
Alt 800m   Ht Gain +350m   (NN 188 730)   Map p224   Diag p230

A rather scrappy lower half leads to a hugely enjoyable sharp arête.

Approach
Although walking up the lower glen is still perfectly feasible almost everyone approaches this from the top of the Nevis Range gondola. Take the path westwards to the minor col south of Meall Breac, slant down into the glen of Allt Daimh on a sketchy path to pass below slabby outcrops and traverse along to join the stream. Follow this up until opposite the East Ridge of Càrn Dearg Mheadhonach. Up left is a complex of ridges, with six main ones. Golden Oldy is the second from left, the first thin one, and the only one whose boundary streams join before reaching the main river. The join is just above a prominent slabby waterslide and opposite the stream that drains the corrie between Càrn Dearg Mòr and Càrn Dearg Mheadhonach. Slog up steep grass to the foot of the buttress.

The Route
At first there are a few minor outcrops scattered over the slope, then more consistent rock materialises on the right edge. Climb this to a bouldery arête then zigzag up easy ground left of the crest. Climb a steeper bluff left then right to an easy angled ridge, where the fun begins. Follow the superb airy arête to the top, although many avoid the later pinnacles on the right. The ridge finishes a little below the plateau and hard snow can linger here well into the summer. If in doubt take an axe. The summit cairn is 100m off right.

230 THE AONACHS

AONACH MÒR
West Face

109. Golden Oldy   Grade 2 **

AONACH MÒR 231

*High on Golden Oldy (Route 109, Grade 2), with Route 110 in the background.
Scrambler: Nate Webb. Photo: Iain Thow.*

The Ben Nevis Massif

Although most people know it either for its hugely popular tourist track or for the climbing on the vast North Face, 'The Ben' is really a range in itself, with several subsidiary summits with routes hidden away on them and an outdoor playground down on its lower flanks in Glen Nevis.

CÀRN MÒR DEARG 1223m

OS Landranger 41 (NN 177 722) Map p224

Ben Nevis's little sister, often used as an approach to it from the north, a classic expedition. The arête linking it to Nevis is sharp and rocky, but with only very minor scrambling. The ridge dropping east from the northern top offers more sustained rock, especially if the slabs below are included.

110 Càrn Dearg Mheadhonach, East Ridge   Grade 1 or 2
Alt 620m   Ht Gain +550m   (NN 182 735)   Map p224

A pleasantly sharp arête (Grade 1), which can be started up slightly harder slabs.

Approach
The ridge itself can be approached from Glen Nevis via Nevis Gorge, up Coire Giubhsachan and over the saddle at its head, which lends itself well to a circuit over the Ben. It is easier (and a much longer scramble) to take the path westwards from the top of the Aonach Mòr Gondola to the minor col south of Meall Breac and slant down into the glen of Allt Daimh on a sketchy path. Follow the stream to where a tributary stream comes down from the corrie between Càrn Dearg Mheadhonach and Càrn Beag Dearg.

The Route
Follow the right-hand streamlet, then when it gets mossy transfer to the left one. Go up the right edge of the slab left again to gain the first level of the corrie. Walk left across scree to steeper rocks and climb the first clean rib, mostly on its right side. Work left up easier slabs until they peter out into boulders, then move up left to steeper padding slabs which lead up to the foot of the ridge proper. Clamber up boulders on the crest, which narrows to a fine arête over a minor top. More ridge leads to a second pinnacle with an airy descent. Easy broken rock leads to the summit of Càrn Dearg Mheadhonach where a pleasant stroll leads to the Munro summit.

BEN NEVIS 1344m

OS Landranger 41   (NN 167 713)   Map p233

Scotland's highest mountain may be a huge whaleback from the south but its North Face is an altogether different proposition. Five major ridges and innumerable lesser spurs tumble intricately into the huge trench of the Allt

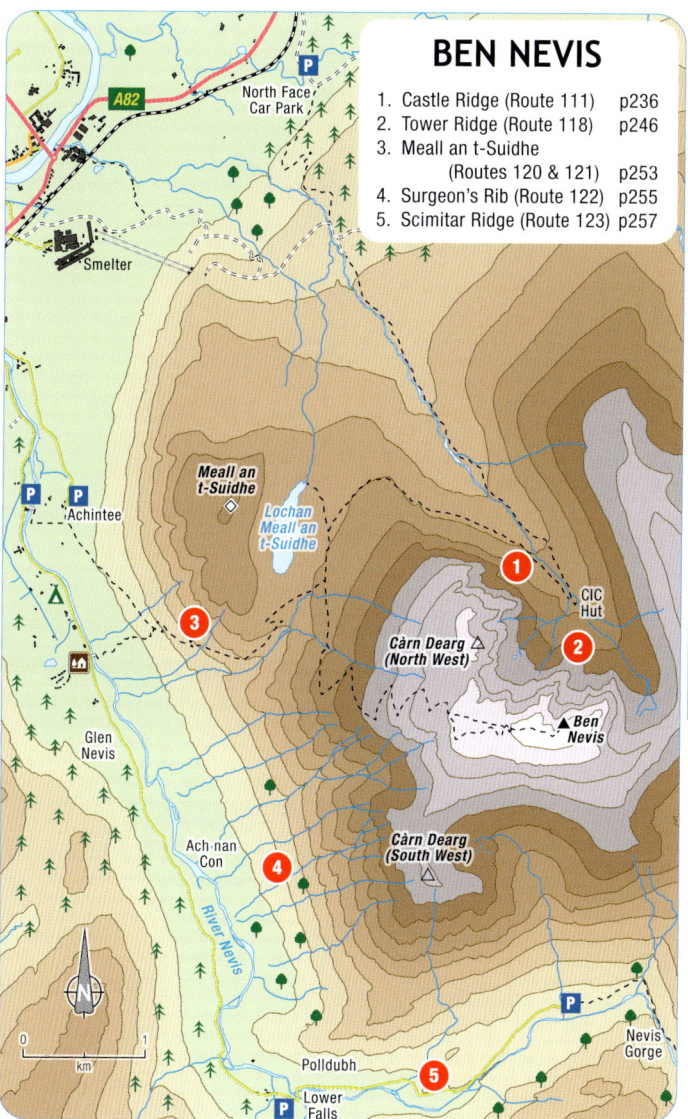

NEVIS MASSIF

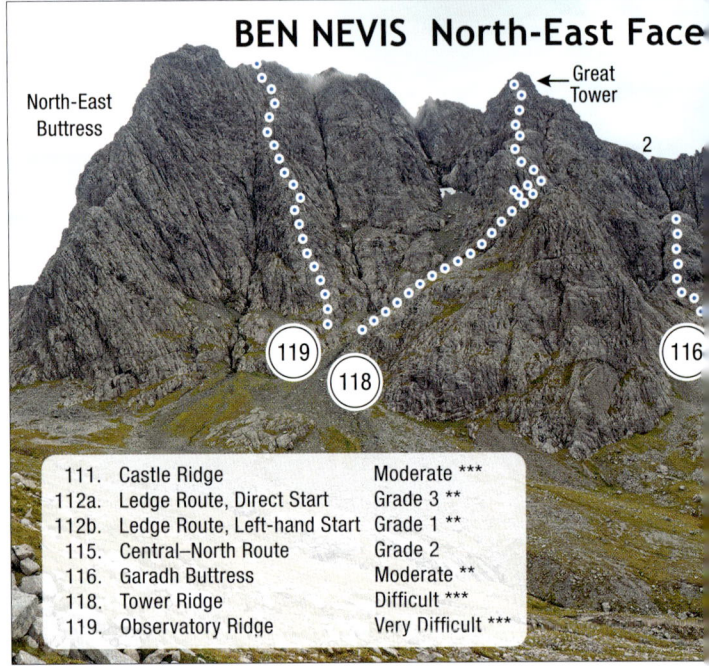

The North-East Face of Ben Nevis. Photo: Noel Williams.

a' Mhuilinn. Two kilometres long and over 600m high, this is the grandest rock face in these islands, home to routes of an Alpine scale. With the exception of Ledge Route none of the routes here are easy and all are intimidating and serious, but the rewards are correspondingly great. Ascents of the major routes here will live with you for the rest of your life.

Descents

In poor weather the descent from the summit is notoriously tricky, especially with snow on the ground (i.e. most of the year!). A dogleg is necessary, first to avoid the top of Gardyloo Gully which cuts in from the right (often with a large cornice), then to stay clear of Five Finger Gully, which drops away left a little further on. From the summit trig point walk 150m on 231° (grid), then follow a bearing of 282°(grid) to pick up the zigzags at the top of the Mountain Track. These two bearings are marked by large cairns at 50 metre intervals, which can be helpful when the path is covered in snow.

BEN NEVIS

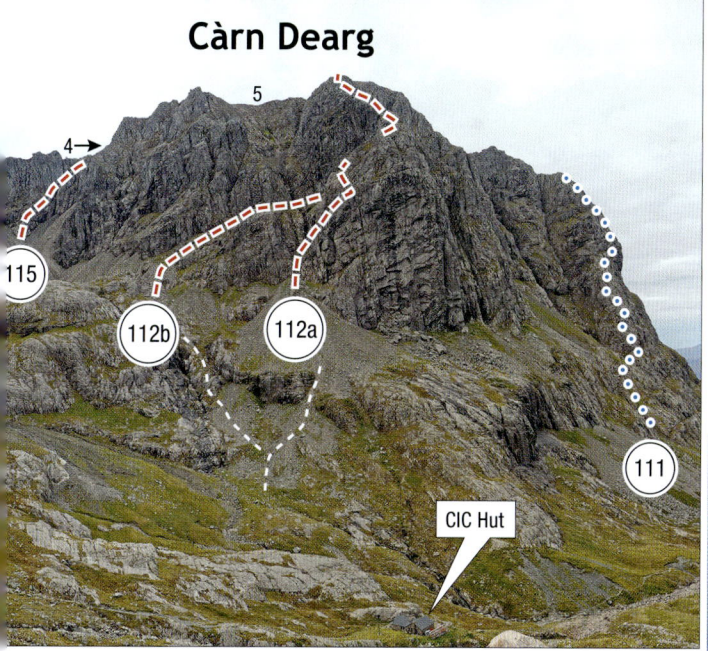

Càrn Dearg

This photograph was taken in October.
Please be aware that much snow may still be present in the spring and summer.

Route to the CIC Hut

All the Ben Nevis routes except Castle Ridge are best approached via the CIC Hut, stunningly set in the Allt a' Mhuilinn. There are two main approaches. If staying in Glen Nevis the simplest option is to follow the hordes up the Mountain Track from Achintee in Glen Nevis (parking at NN 123 728) until it cuts sharp right above Lochan Meall an t-Suidhe (3.5km). At this point turn left and follow a different path in a northerly direction which slants down to the outflow of the loch. After almost 400m fork right and take an older and boggier path round into the Allt a' Mhuilinn and the CIC Hut (6.5km).

The normal approach for climbers starts from the North Face car park near Torlundy (NN 145 764). Follow a path which zigzags up through the forest to the dam on the Allt a' Mhuilinn (2km). Continue on a short section of forest track and turn right at a junction. Cross a stile and follow a path (much improved) up the east bank of the Allt a' Mhuilinn as far as the hut (5.7km).

NEVIS MASSIF

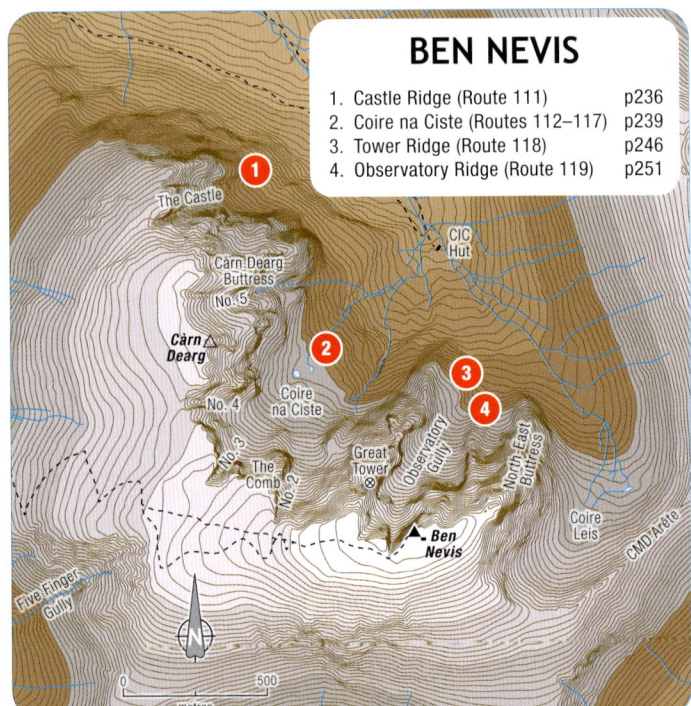

BEN NEVIS

1. Castle Ridge (Route 111)   p236
2. Coire na Ciste (Routes 112–117)   p239
3. Tower Ridge (Route 118)   p246
4. Observatory Ridge (Route 119)   p251

111 Castle Ridge   Moderate   ***
Alt 650m   Ht Gain +400m   (NN 163 725)   Map p236   Diag p235

This is the rightmost ridge on the North Face, slanting up rightwards about 600m north-west of the CIC Hut. One of the best routes in this guide, long, varied and on superb rock. The hard bits are well separated but the crux is quite tough.

Approach
Use either of the approaches described for the CIC Hut. The route from Achintee in Glen Nevis passes directly beneath the ridge. Leave the Ben path by turning left above Lochan Meall an t-Suidhe and after some 400m fork right. From a point overlooking the Allt a' Mhuilinn descend gradually some 30m and continue as far as the Lunching Stone (1615 7278), an enormous split boulder situated beside the path.

To reach the same place from the North Face car park follow the path up

*Castle Ridge (Route 111, Moderate) with the Castle to its left.
Photo: Noel Williams.*

On the crux of Castle Ridge (Route 111, Moderate).
Climber: Mike Bauermeister. Photo: Noel Williams.

the east side of the Allt a' Mhuilinn until opposite the ridge. Cross the stream (at a height of about 530m) and ascent a grassy slope direct to the Lunching Stone.

Up and left from the Lunching Stone, and about 50m left of a waterfall, a shallow grassy gully slants up to the ridge proper.

The Route

Start just right of the gully and climb a tongue of slabs, then move left to a larger area of easy slabs. Go up grass and more slabs just right of a scree shoot with a vertical left wall. These lead to an open grassy shelf with the tower of the Castle prominent high up ahead and Castle Ridge up right. This point is also easily reached by traversing up rightwards from the CIC Hut.

Cross the stream and go right up a grassy groove to the ridge crest. Carry on up this on lovely rough rock, well marked with crampon scratches. Turn a steeper wall by going right along a ledge then taking a steepening groove back up left. The steepest part of this can be bypassed by moving left and up slabby steps, exposed but much easier. Dodge another steep wall on the right to reach ledges below a much bigger prow, which provides the crux.

Climb a short steep corner then cross rightwards to a nest of boulders on the edge of all things. If you are going to rope up do it here, as the crack above is steep, exposed and quite sustained. The hardest part is reaching the foot of the crack proper, using awkwardly placed holds that aren't as good as you would like. The crack is steep but is well supplied with big friendly jugs. Pull out to easy ground with relief. Above is a short steep chimney then lots of excellent easy scrambling on a sharp arête and optional juggy steps. Eventually the ridge runs out into the main bulk of the hill at about 1060m.

It is possible to descend rightwards from here but it is unpleasantly bouldery. It is better to head up left, cross the summit of the Castle and continue up the north-west flank of Càrn Dearg. Then from the first top (1214m) either descend Ledge Route (the next outing described), or continue in a southerly direction to a low point on the plateau rim (top of Number 4 Gully). Then head south-west to pick up the Mountain Track. Descend this or pop up the the summit of Ben Nevis first.

 112 Ledge Route   Grade 1 or 3   **
Alt 650m   Ht Gain +400m   (NN 164 723)   Map p236   Diag p240
Much of this is walking, but in impressive situations. By the left-hand start it is the best easy scramble on the mountain.

Approach
From the CIC Hut head up easy slabs to a flatter area behind. After crossing a stream, the two starts separate (see Diagram p235). The right-hand start climbs a scree slope slightly rightwards at first then aims for the mouth of Number 5 Gully, the large cleft left of the obvious huge steep face of Càrn Dearg Buttress. The left-hand start finds a way up beside a stream issuing from the right-hand side of a rock band guarding Coire na Ciste.

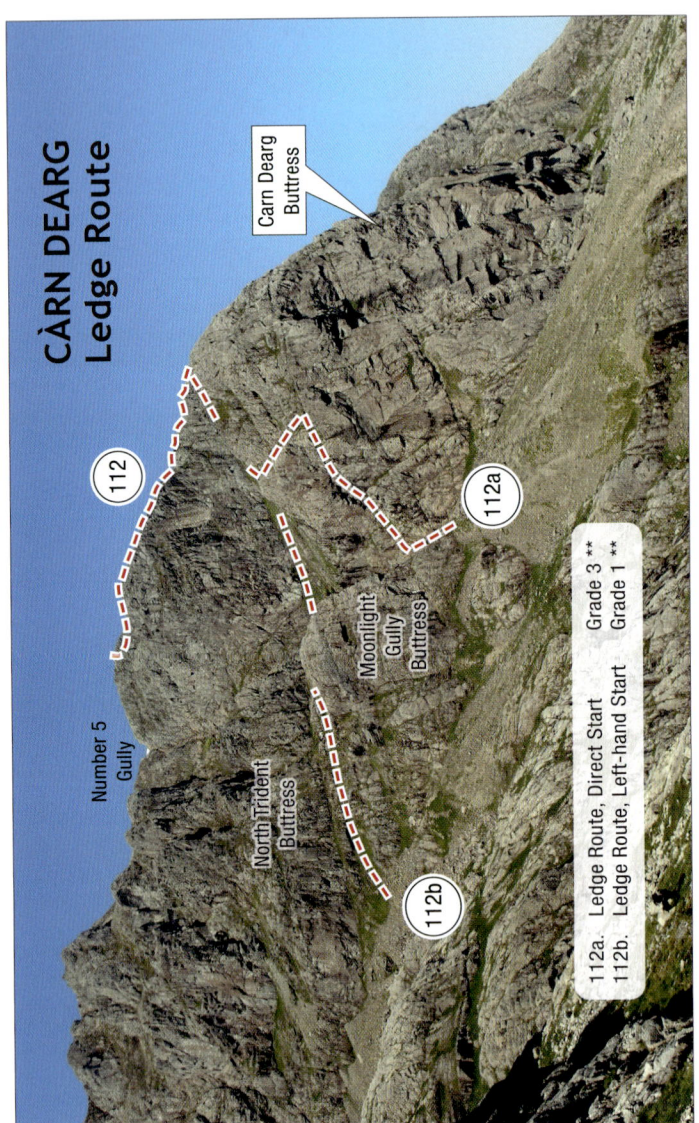

BEN NEVIS 241

On the optional exposed fin of Ledge Route (Route 112, Grade 1).
Scrambler: Iain Thow. Photo: Noel Williams.

The Route
a) Direct Start   Grade 3
Start up Number 5 Gully. If this is full of snow, as it often is until late Spring, then climb the slabs immediately right (Grade 3, quite loose). Leave the gully rightwards on the first large shelf by a scree path. Then cross easy-angled slabs (exposed and often wet) to an airy perch on the lip of big cliffs. Take a shallow chimney back up left, moving to the more pleasant rib just left of it as soon as possible. Reach a large shelf, turn right and soon join a faint path used by the alternative approach which leads to the crest of the buttress.

b) Left-hand Start   Grade 1
Leave the stream (which drains from a lochan in Coire na Ciste) and head up rightwards to a prominent rockband forming the base of North Trident Buttress. Head hard right for about 100m to reach a large shelf above the first tier of Moonlight Gully Buttress. Then turn left and head uphill, until it is possible to cross over the stream in Number 5 Gully. Follow a faint path in the scree which curves up rightwards across a huge hidden recess. Go past a prominent tower to reach the buttress skyline at a perched boulder.

Turn left and go up the bouldery crest to a sharp fin. Clamber along its narrow crest (or avoid it on the right), then more easy crest follows to an easing of angle. A final rise can be tackled direct at Grade 2 or walked round on the left to arrive on the plateau at the northern top of Càrn Dearg.

 113 Number 4 Gully Buttress   Grade 3
Alt 1000m   Ht Gain +100m   (NN 161 717)   Map p236   Diag p243
A route in two sections, an awkward groove and a more broken upper section.

Approach
From the CIC Hut take the path right up slabs and across a stream to go up into the right-hand side of Coire na Ciste. Go up past the lochans to the scree coming out of Number 4 Gully in the top right-hand corner. Below and right of this a wide sloping shelf goes out right. A little above this is a left-slanting groove with a vertical right wall and slabs to its left. This looks feasible but becomes quite hard and is definitely not the route. The proper start is reached by going rightwards below a steep rib to arrive at a slightly wider chimney/groove hidden round the corner.

The Route
Bridge up the hard start to the chimney (crux) and follow it steeply to easy ground (big holds on the right help). Move left and climb a rib on more big holds. This ends at a grass ledge below a steep wall. Follow this left (a field of wild flowers in early summer) to climb a rib left of a damp gully on mixed rock and grass, then either slant easily up left to the plateau or go up direct on juggy rock past a small pinnacle to finish just right of a vertical wall.

An alternative finish follows the grass ledge rightwards below the steep wall and up to a notch on the crest above South Trident Buttress, where the following route starts.

114 South Trident, Upper Arête   Grade 2
Alt 1100m   Ht Gain +60m   (NN 160 717)   Map p236   Diag p243

An enjoyable clamber up a blocky ridge, the towers being much easier than they look.

Approach
Although this can be approached by a long traverse leftwards from the easing of angle near the top of Ledge Route it follows more naturally on from Number 4 Gully Buttress, as mentioned above.

The Route
From the notch go up a broad rocky crest to a steep prow. Climb this right to left on big holds. Easier rock leads to another steepening which succumbs surprisingly easily, with the plateau not far above. The top of Number 4 Gully is about 200m off south-west.

 115 Central-North Route, Creag Coire na Ciste   Grade 2
Alt 1000m   Ht Gain +150m   (NN 162 716)   Map p236   Diag p243

Rather a wandering line but winds through some impressive scenery. Delicate in places but not sustained.

Approach
As for Number 4 Gully Buttress (Route 113) to the lochans in Coire na Ciste, then go up scree to the lowest point of the spur between Number 3 and Number 4 Gullies.

The Route
Climb the spur on good holds to easier ground. Head for a prominent corner with a smooth right wall and climb the easier corner 10m left of this. Work up right to another steepening and go out right to climb a nose on big sloping holds. Carry on up and right to reach vertical rock, then go right onto a large right-slanting shelf via the higher of two traverse lines. Walk right across the top of North Gully to scree, then tiptoe up mossy slabs on the right. The slightly steeper top succumbs on either arête to arrive on the plateau just left of Number 4 Gully.

 116 Garadh Buttress   Moderate   **
Alt 850m   Ht Gain +100m   (NN 165 716)   Map p236   Diag p245

A blunt spur of excellent rock which is often sheltered from the wind when other parts of the Ben are not. The lower and hardest section is poorly protected and surprisingly exposed but soon eases.

Approach
From the CIC Hut go up the slabs to the grassy area where the path into Coire na Ciste crosses the stream, then go up left to the mouth of a small gorge. (See the diagram on p235.) Right of this is a smaller chimney. Climb a wall just right again and continue up slabs to grass. Carry on up left and climb a steeper face starting at a sharp arête above boulders to reach scree in the left

side of the corrie. Garadh Buttress is situated up left, tucked into the side of Tower Ridge, with a small waterfall issuing from the gully between them. Start at the left edge of the slabby apron that foots the buttress, about 10m right of the waterfall.

The Route
Climb steeply up left on good holds to a good ledge leading left towards the top of the waterfall (reasonable nut crack if a belay is required – not much afterwards). From the left end of the ledge make an exposed traverse left on small sharp holds, then a delicate step up reaches juggier rock (crux). Carry on up direct to much easier rock, then either climb a steep prow on big holds or an easier angled more delicate ramp to its right. Now follow the more broken crest on delightfully rough rock, passing another steepening by positive holds on either side. All too soon you reach the rocky summit of the buttress which is called Garadh na Ciste – a great viewpoint.

Descending right beyond here, down a rather shattered band of rock into Coire na Ciste is one option, as is following a broken grassy groove up left over two minor cols to reach Tower Ridge just below the Little Tower. In late summer in dry weather, however, the next route makes an enjoyable finish.

117 Raeburn's Easy Route   Grade 2/3
Alt 1100m   Ht Gain +250m   (NN 163 715)   Map p236   Diag p245

A surprisingly easy line winding its way through some impressive ground. It holds snow until August and weeps heavily after rain, so is very mossy in places, but in good autumn conditions is well worthwhile.

Approach
Could be reached directly up Coire na Ciste from the CIC Hut, but more likely to be used as a finish to the previous route.

The Route
From the screes at the top left corner of Coire na Ciste (just down and right from the top of Garadh na Ciste) two gullies sprout upwards, with the huge tower of the Comb just to their right. Go into the mouth of the left-hand gully (Number 2 Gully), then move up left to a long mossy pink wall. Go left then right to bypass this and reach a scree patch above it. From the top left corner of this work left up mossy ramps to cross a slimy streamlet, then climb a nice rib on big square holds. Move further left to reach the lower left end of a big scree ramp (another juggy rib makes a nice shortcut). Follow the ramp up right to its end, where it becomes a mossy groove. Climb this, with one slightly precarious move, then move out right onto a rib, which leads more easily to the plateau.

118 Tower Ridge   Difficult   ***
Alt 650m   Ht Gain +500m   (NN 167 718)   Map p236   Diag p247

The most famous rock route on the mountain, long, varied and with a thrilling climax at the wildly exposed crossing of Tower Gap.

*Halfway on Tower Ridge (Route 118, Difficult).
Climber: Nate Webb. Photo: Iain Thow.*

Approach
From the CIC hut head up and left below the soaring tower of the Douglas Boulder and into the mouth of Observatory Gully.

The Route
Take to the slabs on the right and go up these easily to a large grassy area left of Douglas Gully (which rises up to the notch behind the Douglas Boulder – going up this lets you in for a hard little chimney out of the gap). Either go up to the top left-hand corner of the grassy area to gain a ledge starting slightly higher and follow this rightwards (path) all the way to the ridge, or (slightly harder) go up a squarish groove at the top of the grassy area, just left of a vertical face. Where the groove peters out go up right on ledges (traces of path) and zigzag up to the crest of the ridge above the exit from Douglas Gap.

Go easily up the crest of the ridge and along a sharp section. At steeper rock beyond this walk up right on a good ledge to the right-hand side of the ridge, then zigzag back up left, following the numerous crampon scratches. Lots of easy crest follows until the ridge steepens again at the Little Tower. Start up this direct then move left slightly and climb enjoyable slabby grooves running back up right. (Do not be tempted to follow obvious ledges on the left-hand flank. This is a common mistake known as the 'false traverse'.)

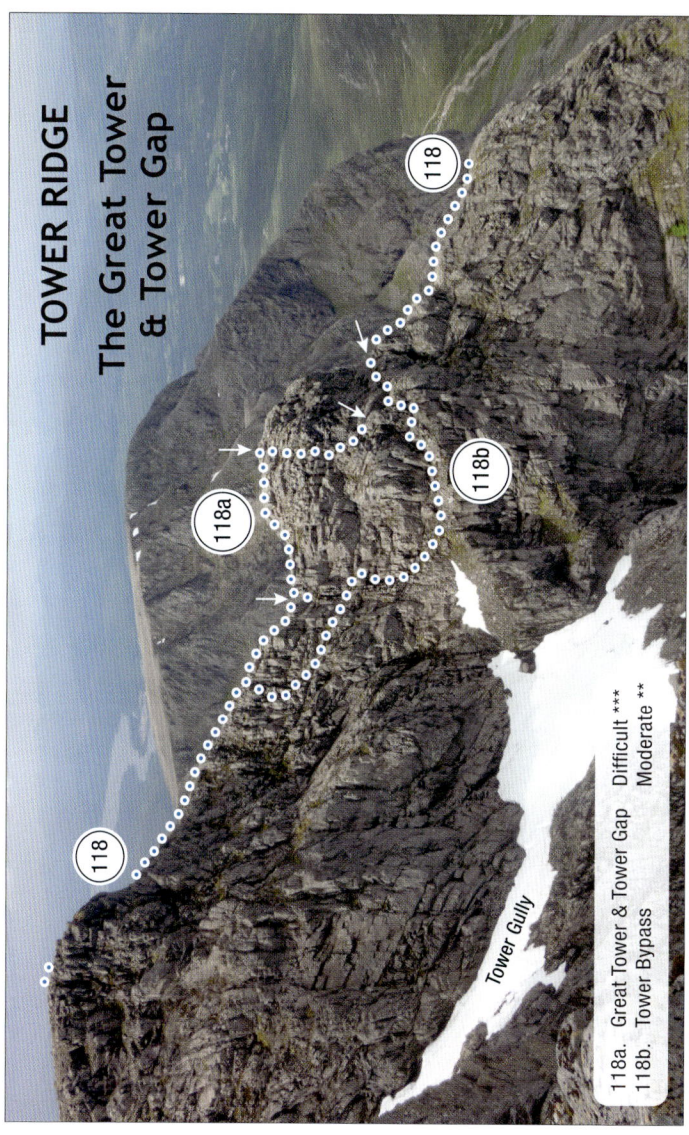

Descending into Tower Gap (Route 118a, Difficult).
Climber: Heather Morning. Photo: Noel Williams.

Keep to the crest until an easing where the Great Tower comes into view. Climb the easy first part of the Tower until it gets vertical. At this point the Eastern Traverse starts round a corner on the left. (Taking a lower ledge on the left below the Tower is another easy mistake.) Follow the Eastern Traverse horizontally leftwards – a contender for the most exposed walk in the country – to reach an alcove with a rift at the back. There are two options at this point, the first is harder and scarier than the second. See Diagram p249.

a) The Great Tower & Tower Gap   Difficult ***
Enter the rift and continue behind a huge jammed boulder. Emerge from the rift and climb steep exposed steps on big holds to the top of the Great Tower. Once beyond the summit the ridge descends and narrows dramatically. The route is now uncomfortably obvious. Descend awkwardly into Tower Gap (well protected) and climb the steep arête beyond. Breathe a sigh of relief and scramble pleasantly up an easier section of ridge.

b) Tower Bypass   Moderate **
The second option is easier but it is best avoided early in the summer when snow is still lying on the ledges. In good conditions it provides a way of bypassing Tower Gap and reduces the grade of the whole route to Moderate.

From the alcove after the Eastern Traverse, instead of entering the rift, descend scree leftwards through a narrow gap by a huge block. Turn right and ascend slightly, before descending to a broad scree terrace. (This can be followed into Tower Gully, although snow lies here well into the summer.) Go along the terrace for about 35m to a mossy groove. This lies below Tower Gap (which isn't obvious from below). Climb the groove for about 12m, and go round to the right of a triangular block. Join a slanting grassy weakness and follow this a long way up left until able to regain the ridge.

Both routes join some distance above Tower Gap. Continue up the ridge and arrive at a steep wall. Then traverse horizontally right and ascend a gritty scoop to the plateau.

The summit is a few hundred metres to the east, but the tops of Tower and Gardyloo Gullies necessitate a detour southwards. If there is still snow beware of big cornices at the top of the gullies.

119 Observatory Ridge   Very Difficult   ***
Alt 700m   Ht Gain +450m   (NN 168 716)   Map p236   Diag p247
A superb route, mainly sustained Grade 3 scrambling, but with a couple of harder pitches low down. Arguably the best of the Ben Nevis ridges.

Approach
From the CIC hut go up below the Douglas Boulder as for Tower Ridge but carry on up the scree of Observatory Gully to the slabs on the left of the narrows. These run up to the First Platform below the foot of Observatory Ridge proper. Right of centre is a steep smooth slab with a stepped weakness going up left from below its foot.

Above the main difficulties on Observatory Ridge (Route 119, Very Difficult). Climber: Noel Williams. Photo: Iain Thow.

MEALL AN T-SUIDHE

The Route
Go up the left slanting weakness and at its top move right to follow the crest up to the right end of the First Platform. Carry on up the crest via a V groove, exiting left at its top, then move right and up to the foot of a very well scratched steep groove. The First Platform can also be easily reached from the left, in which case a line of weakness leads up rightwards to the ledge below the scratched steep groove. Either climb this awkwardly, or (easier) walk 6m left on a grass ledge, go up 5m and hand traverse right on good holds to the top of the groove.

Continue steeply to a big ledge below an overhang, move up right into the foot of a groove, then right again into an easier one. Arrive at a nest of boulders below a steep polished crack with a jammed flake. Climb this, move up right and avoid steep rock by a groove in the right flank of the ridge which leads to easy ground. At the next steepening move right to climb a polished groove, finishing with a long step left across a steep slab to arrive suddenly at easy ground beyond the main climbing.

You haven't finished yet, however! Over 250m of excellent scrambling remains, some of it quite tricky. Detailed description is superfluous, just follow the crest, although in places easier variations can be found, usually on the right. A final exposed slab (avoidable on the left) brings you to the plateau about 200m east of the summit.

MEALL AN T-SUIDHE 711m

OS Landranger 41   (NN 139 730)   Map p233

Ben Nevis's puppy, only half the height of the main peak, is home to a couple of minor scrambles that are convenient for an evening or short day. Be careful not to dislodge rocks onto the busy Mountain Track below.

120 Central South-West Buttress   Grade 1/2
Alt 300m   Ht Gain +350m   (NN 137 719)   Map p233   Diag p254

Fairly easy angled scrambling up linked outcrops, with lots of choice of route.

Approach
From either the car park at Achintee (122 729) or the bridge by the Youth Hostel (128 717) go up the main Ben Nevis path. From where the two paths join carry on up past the next zigzag, then at the second stream there is a small buttress next to the path just left of the stream.

The Route
Climb the small buttress, then grass and minor outcrops above. The stream on the right is passable in a drought. Arrive thankfully at more sustained rock just left of the stream. Climb this on spikes, then more walking leads to steeper rock. Gain a niche between two prows, move awkwardly right and climb the right-hand rib. This section is easily avoided on the left. Above there are Grade 1 options by the easiest line, with possible Grade 2 outcrops.

GLEN NEVIS

121 Right-hand South-West Buttress   Grade 1 or 3
Alt 350m   Ht Gain +300m   (NN 136 720)   Map p233   Diag p254

Broken and heathery, but worth doing if you've already done Central Buttress.

Approach
From either the car park at Achintee (122 729) or the bridge by the Youth Hostel (128 717) go up the main Ben Nevis path. From where the two paths join carry on up past two zigzags to a stream just before a footbridge.

The Route
Either walk up left through the birches, or in dry weather go up the stream bed (Grade 3). The latter starts with easy steps, then goes up a mossy slot. This is quite hard but there are good footholds in the stream bed. These are covered in wet weather, making it much harder. After whichever start, carry on up left onto the main buttress. This is heathery but scattered with broken granite outcrops. Link these up as desired, with all difficulties easily avoidable.

GLEN NEVIS

OS Landranger 41

Although these three routes are technically on the flanks of Ben Nevis they feel much more like they belong to the glen rather than the mountain. They are better treated as evening or short day outings rather than being part of a longer day on the hill. For all of them the main attraction is the stunning setting of Upper Glen Nevis rather than the scrambling itself, although both Meall Cumhann and Scimitar Ridge have very enjoyable sections.

122 Surgeon's Rib   Grade 2
Alt 400m   Ht Gain +500m   (NN 146 703)   Map p233

A good general line but the scrambling is barely worth the long pull up a steep hillside.

Approach
The shortest approach is to hop or paddle across the river Nevis opposite the old graveyard at 137 702, easy in low water. Alternatively follow the path on the east bank from the bridge by the Youth Hostel (128 717) or the car park at the Lower Falls (145 683). About 300m south of the graveyard a stone wall runs up the hillside towards the deep cleft of Surgeon's Gully. Go up steeply left of the wall, with good views into the gully in places until you finally arrive thankfully at rock.

The Route
Ignore the lower wall off left and start at the right-hand side of the main band. Zigzag up heather, bearing up left into the centre of the crag, then go back up right below steeper rock to a large terrace. On the steep rock above start on the right and go up to pass left behind a flake. Go up slabby grooves

On one of the few sections of rock on Surgeon's Rib (Route 122, Grade 2). Scrambler: Iain Thow. Photo: Noel Williams.

behind this to the top of the steep band. Lots more heathery walking leads to boulders, which can be clambered over or spurned, then more consistent rock follows. Pass right of a pointed flake, up broken rock, then climb the right edge of slabs. Above is a large perched flake, climbed by either edge to easy ground. More heather leads to a broad stepped band, climbed centrally to finish up a left slanting ramp. The ridge now levels out before curving up towards the summit of Càrn Dearg, mainly walking but with the odd outcrop and a scenic narrowing. From this broad top an easy shoulder runs up to Ben Nevis itself, or an intricate descent can be made down the south shoulder to Polldubh, with care needed to avoid the numerous crags on the way.

123 Scimitar Ridge   Moderate   *
Alt 120m   Ht Gain +90m   (NN 156 685)   Map p233

A good evening route, short and close to the road in the beautiful setting of Glen Nevis. The first 10m is quite hard, and many will want a rope. It can be avoided to the right, but this misses much of the best part of the route.

Approach
Park at the small pull-in at NN 156 684, on the right about 200m after the road goes up and swings left about 1km above the Lower Falls. Walk back along the road for two passing places to pick up a small path leading up right to the toe of the ridge.

The Route
The lowest rocks are very steep but have positive holds. Climb the groove in the centre for 3m to a good flake handhold on the left. Swing left on this to a small foot ledge. Step delicately up left to reach a heathery ledge running left from the overhang. Go left on this and up a slabby crack to a niche. There is a metal spike for a belay below another steep wall.

Swing up left on a good flake onto the rib above and go up this. An easy ridge follows, then at the next rock step go up and right to climb a quartz vein. At the step after this do exactly the same! Carry on easily, via a lovely rough slab on the right and a big easy angled slab. Cross the grassy runnel on the left and climb the ridge crest to the minor summit of Mam Beag.

Off right at a lower level than the main start is a well-used slab with converging cracks. This can be climbed direct at Moderate or avoided on the right. A polished line of grooves zigzags up to the crest above to join the main route high up.

MEALL CUMHANN 698M

OS Landranger 41   (NN 178 696)   Map p258

It may be tiny compared with its neighbours, but Meall Cumhann is a splendid little hill, extremely rocky and with a tremendous setting athwart the throat of Glen Nevis. Very accessible from the car park at the top of the glen so a good route for an evening.

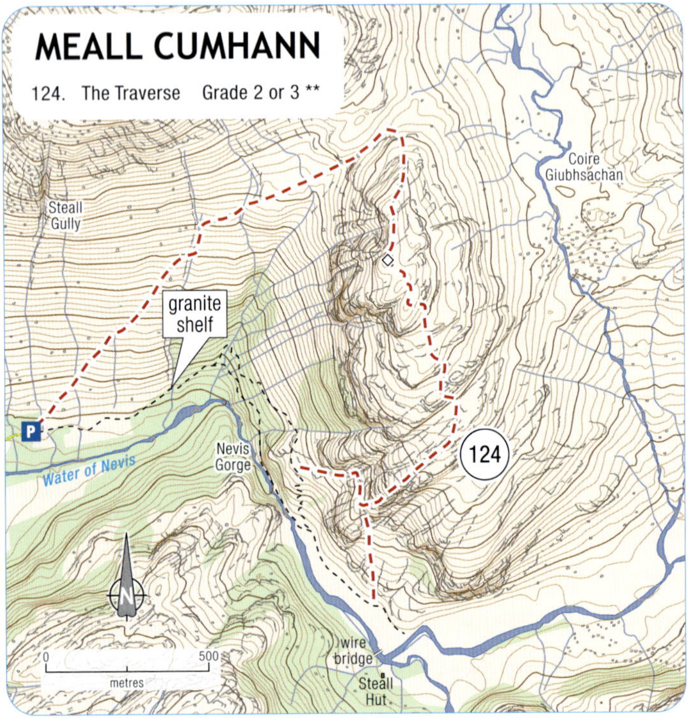

MEALL CUMHANN

124. The Traverse   Grade 2 or 3 **

124 Traverse of Meall Cumhann   Grade 2 or 3   **
Alt 350m   Ht Gain +250m   (NN 177 688)   Map p258

A good mixed ability route, with lots of variation possible on excellent schist in a setting that is hard to beat.

Approach
From the car park at the head of Glen Nevis there are two approaches. If you haven't been here before then take the main path through the Nevis Gorge. It gets quite busy at times but since it's one of the best short walks in Britain that's not surprising. Just before the path forks right towards the wire bridge go steeply back up leftwards on grass to a square-cut col above the large buttress known as Meadow Walls. Turn right and go a short way up the left side of the crest up to a huge block.

Alternatively leave the main path some 600m from the start. This point is about 140m after the path crosses a stream by a shelf cut in red granite. (If you reach another stream you've gone too far.) A small path, not at all obvious at first, climbs off leftwards through birches. The views of the gorge are excellent but lack the intimacy with the water of the lower path. At the high point (cairn) leave the path and, facing uphill, slant rightwards past the classic arête of Edgehog on the right-hand side of Wave Buttress. Ascend some distance before crossing a tiny stream. Head right below more cliffs and ascend a grassy recess to reach a small shoulder with views down to Steall Falls. Go up by a rock wall on the left side of the crest to a huge block.

The Route
Clamber onto the block and up a flaky groove behind it. Wind up more outcrops at Grade 1 or 2, keeping roughly to the nose of the ridge. Climb a steeper wall left of centre to easy ground. Above this is another very steep wall. Either climb a groove just right of this with a hard start (Grade 3) or avoid it on the right. Continue up a long easy whaleback crest.

Beyond a slight dip a steep rock band crosses the slope, with an easy central groove and a harder left arête. At the top there are lovely rough slabs on the right. Above this is another steep tier, avoidable on the right, but not as hard as it looks. There are lots of possibilities, but a line based on a quartz vein just right of the grassy central groove is excellent (Grade 2/3). There is a scrappy minor crag on the way to the summit. The walk northwards along the top of the cliff is a very scenic stroll, with a quick descent leftwards from Bealach Cumhann beyond back to the car park.

The Mamores

Just across Glen Nevis from the Ben, this chain of shapely peaks linked by high ridges gives some of the finest hillwalking in Scotland. A couple of ridge sections sharpen down to rocky arêtes, while a few subsidiary buttresses also run to scrambling. The Ring of Steall is one of Scotland's great classic hill rounds.

MULLACH NAN COIREAN 939m

OS Landranger 41   (NN 122 662)   Map p260

A granite mountain with four broad ridges at the western end of the Mamores. Although quite rocky on its eastern flank there are no significant crags, but on the north side of the ridge, between the two eastern summits is the following enjoyable little ridge.

125 Gendarme Ridge   Grade 3   *
Alt 850m   Ht Gain +60m   (NN 135 655)   Map p260

A fun diversion from the main Mamores ridge, short but quite alpine feeling. It is easily included in a round of Coire Dearg or after doing the next scramble on Stob Bàn (Route 126).

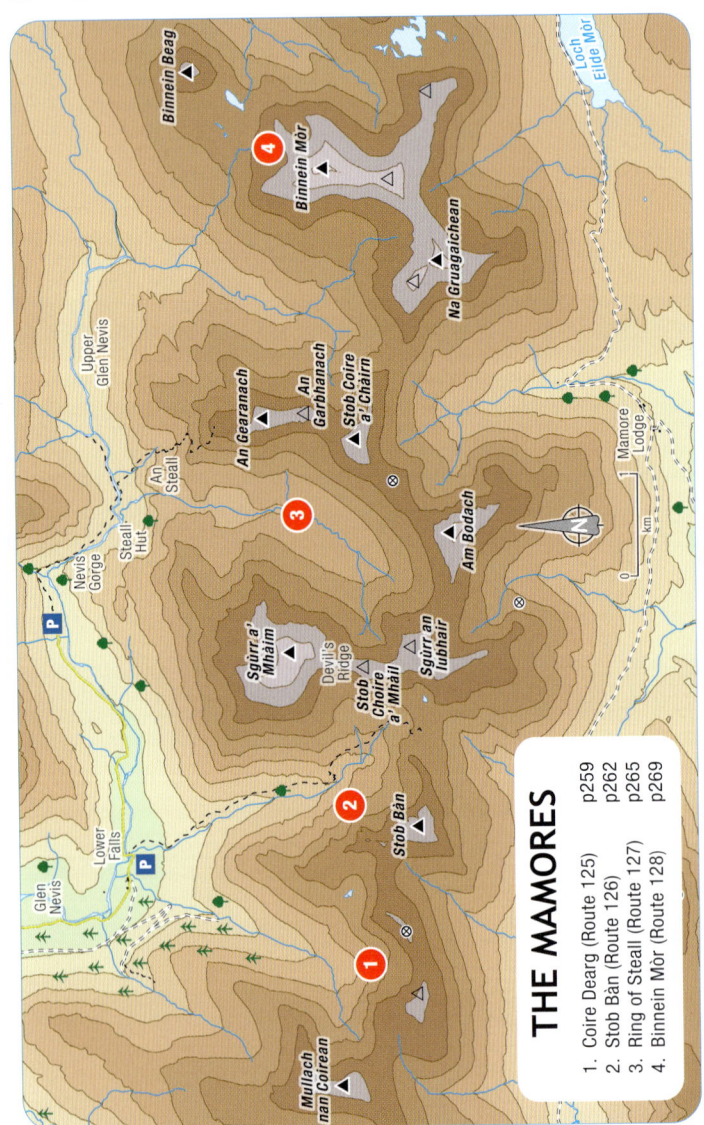

MULLACH NAN COIREAN

The Gendarme at the top of Gendarme Ridge (Route 125).
Scrambler: Noel Williams. Photo: Lucy Williams.

Approach
Few will approach from below, although an ascent of Coire Dearg is a pleasant option which offers fine views of Ben Nevis. When doing a clockwise round of Coire Dearg, cross the minor summit 1km west of Stob Ban, where the ridge narrows and becomes rockier. Descend to the next col (NN 1362 6553), where the prominent gendarme off to the right is a dead giveaway.

If coming from the west then cross the broad summit 1km south-east of Mullach nan Coirean and descend to a col where the ridge narrows. Continue for 150m to a higher col (NN 1362 6553) just before a minor summit. The gendarme is clearly visible just to the left. Either way descend the scree gully between the gendarme and the main ridge.

The Route
Start just right of the gully (looking out) at a grass ledge at the foot of the first continuous rocks. Go up right then back left to reach a ledge below a jutting rock finger. Either go up right of this or climb the pointed boulder left of it and step off the top. Walk left and go back to the crest by big juggy steps. The next step can be tackled direct at Moderate but is much easier coming in from the right. A delightful easy ridge then goes up to the first pinnacle, passed on the left, then the gendarme itself (passed on the right). The gendarme can be climbed at an airy Difficult.

STOB BÀN 999m

OS Landranger 41   (NN 147 655)   Map p260

A pointed summit with four well defined ridges and a large but broken north-east face with three separate buttresses. The scramble lies on North Buttress which is situated below the tiny northern top (c900m) of the mountain. The spur which drops from this top is excellent in both summer and winter.

126 North Buttress, East Ridge   Grade 3   **
Alt 650m   Ht Gain +300m   (NN 149 662)   Map p260   Diag p263

A long and varied route with some airy positions and a couple of well-separated hard sections.

Approach
From the car park just before the Lower Falls in Glen Nevis (145 683) go out onto the road, then turn right and go round a bend. Before reaching the Lower Falls turn right off the road and follow the path southwards up towards Coire a' Mhusgain for 2.4km. Leave the main the path where it climbs steeply leftwards in a series of zigzags. Instead continue straight ahead on a fainter path just above the gorge – scenic, exposed and with a little minor scrambling. Once above the gorge cross the stream at a levelling (can be tricky). Go up a ridge between two streams and pass a tiny waterfall. Reach a grass shelf and head right (north west) for some 300m to a pleasant viewpoint (150 662) at the foot of the ridge.

264 MAMORES

The arête on the East Ridge of North Buttress, Stob Bàn (Route 126, Grade 3). Scrambler: Charles Overstall. Photo: Noel Williams.

The Route
The lowest rocks are vegetated so walk up right to a narrow cleaner ridge and climb this. At its top go horizontally left onto the main buttress and up this and grass to steeper rock. Follow a diagonal line below vertical rock from the bottom right to top left, with an exposed step down at one point. Go up to a tower of huge blocks and up right of this. Either bridge up the gap behind the top block and into a groove behind it (Moderate) or go up the stepped gully just right. Climb the next wall by a niche and go up to easy ground. Avoid the next steep prow on its left, returning to the crest by a short traverse just below a small rowan.

At the next tier climb the obvious central groove to reach a grassy minor summit. Climb the next rock band by a grassy groove just right of a vertical wide black crack, then go up left to spikes on the crest above the crack. Step right into a niche and squeeze behind a flake right again to reach easy ground. Climb the next tier by a spiky groove left of centre, then follow a sharp rib and its more broken continuation. Climb a left slanting ramp, then continue up left to a level section of ridge.

At the large overhanging pinnacle go left and climb the side on big cracks and flakes, quite airy at the top. A short knife edge leads to another steepening, climbed by a slabby right to left groove. Another knife edge then leads to walking ground and the junction with the main north ridge of the hill.

SGÙRR A' MHÀIM 1099m

OS Landranger 41 (NN 165 667) Map p260

A distinctive wedge-shaped peak with three main ridges and a couple of subsidiary ones, the most famous and best of which is the Devil's Ridge which links it to the main spine of the Mamores. This is a good day out on its own, but is often combined with the three Munros to the east in the circuit described below.

127 Ring of Steall Grade 1 **
Alt 650m (NN 172 675) Map p260 Diag p266

A superb day including several sharp ridges, but with only minor scrambling. A complete version of the Ring starts and finishes at Steall Hut beyond the Nevis Gorge. In which case by far the best option is to do an anticlockwise circuit, as the exit from Coire nan Cnàmh is difficult to find from above and is definitely not recommended for descent. Even then the descent at the end into Coire Chadha Chaoruinn requires careful route-finding.

The clockwise circuit is perhaps more popular because it is less of a navigational challenge. However, it misses out the scenic north-east side of Sgùrr a' Mhàim by descending the north-west shoulder to finish at the Lower Falls. Unless two vehicles are used this option will entail a walk of 2.7km along the road either at the start or finish.

RING OF STEALL

Approach
Either way round starts from the car park at the top of Glen Nevis and follows the track through Nevis Gorge to cross the three-wire bridge at Steall.

a) Anticlockwise Route

From Steall Hut beyond the wire bridge go up right (west) then back left through trees to get into the shallow north-facing corrie at around NN 175 680. At the top left of this is a patch of boulders just below the start of the main cliffs with a dark slab up left and a cleaner rib on the right. From the boulders take an unlikely-looking straight deer path slanting left up a ledge. When this opens out to grass go up 10m and pick up the continuation of the deer path along a narrower rock ledge (quite exposed by walking standards). This goes up and over a minor crest, then descends a groove to reach a wider grass ramp slanting up left below steep rock. Follow this to the crest of the ridge (NN 177 679).

Traverse south-west into Coire nan Cnamh, with the impressive spur of Sròn Coire nan Cnamh ahead. On the right flank of this, in the upper left corner of the corrie, is a steep wall of folded quartzite. Go up right of this until it becomes easy to clamber up left onto the top of it, then follow the crest above it on easy rock and scree. A grassy ramp leads up left from its top to the ridge of Sròn Coire nan Cnamh above its steepest section. Go up the narrow ridge and where it steepens make an airy step right across the bottom of a slab, then go up right then left to regain the crest. Continue up the ridge over a minor top then follow the north-east ridge steeply but easily to the summit of Sgùrr a' Mhàim. This summit can also be reached without scrambling by continuing up westwards from Steall Hut to a notch at NN 172 682 (behind Creag nan Eun) and ascending steep grass between outcrops to join the north-east ridge at a level section overlooking Coire nan Cnàmh.

Now for the Devil's Ridge. A good path descends the south ridge to a low point, with a short slab on the far side. At a higher notch either keep to the crest (intimidating rather than hard) or dodge it on the right. An enjoyably narrow ridge walk follows over Stob Choire a' Mhàil. Then ascend scree to Sgùrr an Iubhair (1001m) before following a broader ridge eastwards to the Munro of Am Bodach. The descent north from this is steep and holds snow quite late, which can make it quite tricky in Spring. Cross a minor top before reaching the third Munro, Stob Coire a' Chàirn. The descent north from this is steep too, best tackled by retracing your steps slightly from the cairn before descending to a deep col, the lowest point of the round. Go up the shoulder northwards to An Garbhanach with the ground becoming rougher and more scrambly. The fine rocky crest beyond the summit is perhaps the best bit of the round, eventually becoming a grassy ridge leading to the final Munro, An Gearanach. Descend the north ridge until it drops away steeply, then take a path down the north-west shoulder to a flattening at 630m (NN 1844 6772). Make an important right turn here (easy to miss) and join a stalkers path which zigzags down Coire Chadha Chaoruinn to the floor of Glen Nevis. Pass below Steall Falls to rejoin the outward route at the wire bridge.

Looking southwards along the Devil's Ridge on an anticlockwise circuit of the Ring of Steall (Route 127, Grade 1). Photo: Jamie Hageman.

b) Clockwise Route

From Steall Hut follow a path to the bottom of the spectacular waterfall called An Steall (*The Cataract*). Cross the stream and after 300m take a stalkers path which zigzags up Coire Chadha Chaoruinn. Before the headwall go right to reach the north-west shoulder at 630m and go up this to the summit of An Gearanach. An easy ridge then leads to scrambling over the rocky spine of An Garbhanach. Descend broken, craggy ground to the col beyond. Go steeply up to Stob Coire a' Chàirn, then turn right and cross a minor top before rising steeply again to Am Bodach. Descend its west ridge and carry on up to the summit of Sgùrr an Iubhair (1001m). Descend scree north-westwards and continue along a pleasant ridge to the summit of Stob Choire a' Mhàil. The ridge then narrows and descends to a notch. Keeping to the crest here is intimidating, but it can be bypassed easily on the left. More easy scrambling leads down slabby rock to a low point before the ridge rises easily to the summit of Sgùrr a' Mhàim. The best way down from here is to follow the north-west ridge to a cairn at around 980m then bear left and descend the relentlessly steep north-west shoulder direct to the Lower Falls.

BINNEIN MÒR 1128m

OS Landranger 41 (NN 212 664) Map p260

The highest of the Mamores is a distinctive peak from most directions, with four good sharp ridges, oddly three of which point between North and East. Only the middle one, named Sròn a' Gharbh-Choire, provides scrambling.

128 North-East Ridge   Grade 1 or 2   *
Alt 850m   Ht Gain +300m   (NN 217 669)   Map p260

Rarely an objective in itself but easily the most exciting way up Binnein Mòr and the obvious way if taking in Binnein Beag first.

Approach

The broad saddle at the foot of the ridge can either be reached up grass slopes from upper Glen Nevis, with a problematic river crossing in wet weather, or by good stalkers paths from Kinlochleven. From the north edge of the village a choice of paths lead up to the traversing landrover track from Mamore Lodge to Loch Eilde Mòr. At 208 634 a well-used stalkers path slants up to the broad Coire an Lochain. Keep left of the lochan, then from the col beyond zigzag down steeply to the Allt Coire a' Bhinnein. Cross this and traverse along to the saddle between Binnein Mòr and Binnein Beag.

The Route

From the saddle go up the first steepening, passing some rather underwhelming outcrops. The ridge levels out then steepens again, much rockier this time. The route is obvious, just follow the crest incorporating whichever craglets take your fancy. Some are quite steep but all are easily avoidable. Finish along the narrowing arête right to the summit.

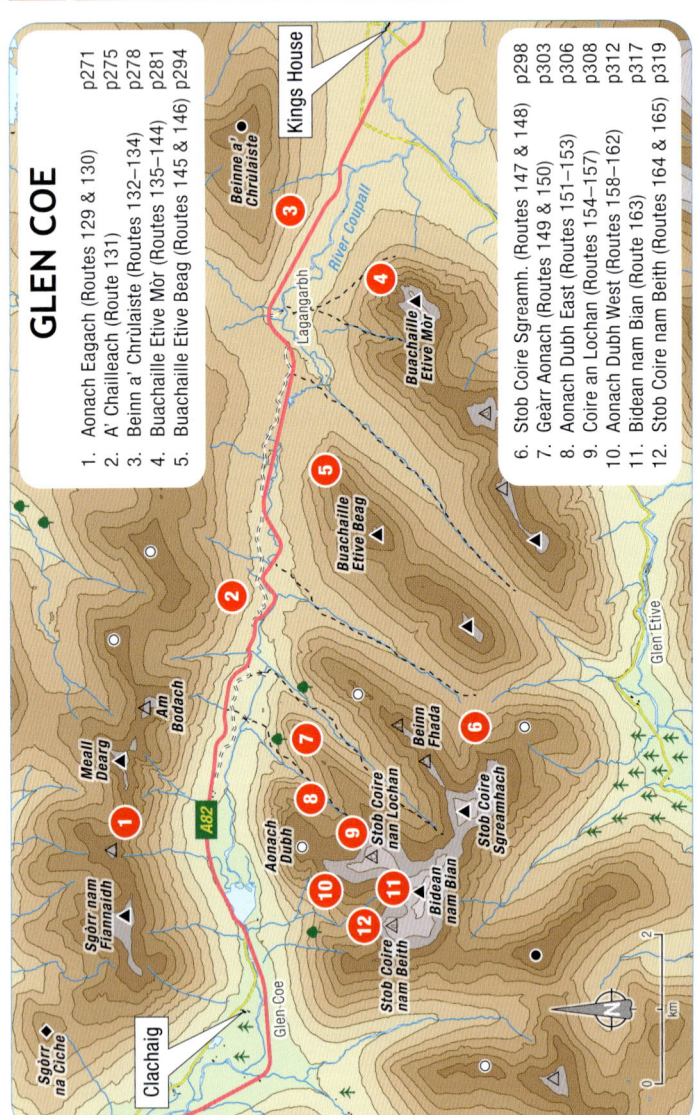

GLEN COE

Few areas can boast the sheer number and variety of scrambles that Glen Coe has and within Scotland only the Cuillin can top it. Well trodden and familiar they may be but Buachaille Etive Mòr and Bidean nam Bian are dramatic, complex and the proud possessors of acres of excellent rock. Generations of hill folk have cut their scrambling teeth on Curved Ridge and the Aonach Eagach and there are plenty of harder routes to graduate to once hooked. Buttresses, slabs, ridges and easy lines winding through impressive ground can all be found here. The compactness of the area and the good paths make access easy, and on Bidean in particular it is simple to link scrambles together to make challenging routes to the summits.

Glen Coe North

The north side of the Glen mainly consists of one long ridge, with the arête of the Aonach Eagach as its central section and the bulky mass of Beinn a' Chrùlaiste guarding its eastern end.

AONACH EAGACH 967m

OS Landranger 41 (NN 141 583) Map p270

The 'Notched Ridge' linking the two Munros of Sgòrr nam Fiannaidh and Meall Dearg is probably Scotland's most famous scramble, its traverse a lifetime objective for many hillgoers. It will rarely disappoint.

129 Aonach Eagach Traverse   Grade 2   ***
Alt 950m   (NN 155 583)   Map p270

Although never particularly hard technically the ridge is often wildly exposed and is notoriously difficult to escape from. It is often underestimated so allow plenty of time. Most people traverse it from East to West to take advantage of the higher starting point, as described here, although it is perhaps slightly easier in the opposite direction as the hardest sections are then ascended rather than descended.

Approach
From the small parking bay at NN 174 567 (larger car park 300m west) follow the built path steeply uphill. Once you reach the first rock some scrappy vegetated scrambling can be contrived on the shoulder above, or either fork left to zigzag up and dodge the steepest part of the shoulder or fork right to avoid it altogether. Continue up the easier angled spur to the summit of Am Bodach. Anyone starting up the South Face of A' Chailleach also joins the route here after traversing the summit of Sròn Garbh.

The Route
Follow the ridge westwards, easy at first, to a steep descent, probably the

GLEN COE

A quiet day on the Aonach Eagach. Photo: Iain Thow.

A rather busier day on the Aonach Eagach. Photo: Noel Williams.

crux of the route. If you're going to have second thoughts, have them here! The well-trodden line starts down the crest, then briefly descends the right flank (looking out) before crossing back left to climb down past a large square block, easiest furthest left. The next obstacle is a rather slippery slab descending the left side of the ridge, then looser rock on the right takes you down to the top of a large stone shoot. An easy ridge leads up to the Munro summit of Meall Dearg, with a possible escape northwards, although this leaves you a long way from your start.

There are now no sensible escapes on either side of the ridge until the end of the scrambling, so you are committed. The route is usually obvious – just follow the ridge! Pleasant walking and easy scrambling leads down to the start of the 'Notched Ridge' proper, which starts with a steepish chimney, then easier scrambling across a minor top leads to a walking section. Go down on the crest and an easy angled chimney/groove to cross a polished minor pinnacle and go up red steps and a narrow crest. A down-and-up leads to the first of the two central tops and a real 'wow' moment as you see the ridge ahead. A surprisingly easy descent leads to a knife edge, then go up to sharp pinnacles on the most exposed part of the ridge. Either tackle these direct or immediately to the right, a path lower down is very loose and no easier. Steep but easy rock just right of the arête now leads to the second central summit. A series of short but awkward and exposed descents on the crest take you down to a narrow notch, where you can either climb a spiky wall or easier rock further right. An easy narrow ridge ends the scrambling, although a few outcrops can be found on the ascent to Stob Coire Leith. Walking takes you to Sgorr nam Fiannaidh, the second Munro summit.

If you are happy with scree, rubble and steep grass then a descent due south is a fast way off from here and minimizes road walking back to the start (but misses out the pub). Alternatively keep to the broadening ridge towards the Pap of Glencoe (a fine viewpoint if you have time to include it, with some easy scrambling available) and veer off left as you approach the col below it to join the Glencoe side road. The path down beside Clachaig Gully used in days of yore is now horrendously loose and well worth avoiding.

130 Clachaig Rib   Grade 3
Alt 120m   Ht Gain +50m   (NN 131 569)   Map p270

Minor but enjoyable scrambling, surprisingly neglected considering its location only a few minutes from the pub doorway. A route to snatch during a brief break in bad weather or to squeeze in before a visit to said hostelry. Also known as Pink Rib, but this creates confusion with the scramble of the same name further up the glen.

Approach
Clachaig Gully is obvious, just above the pub, and right of it is a vertical curved wall (Banana Buttress), then right again are more broken rocks. On the lower left part of these is a prominent holly tree, just right of a steep wall. This is easily reached from the Clachaig in about five minutes.

The Route
Go left under the holly and up the left side of the buttress, then move left and up more broken rocks. Above this is an excellent rib of pink rhyolite, with two more clean steps above, finishing next to the Clachaig's TV aerials.

A' CHAILLEACH 901m

OS Landranger 41   (NN 189 579)   Map p270

An infrequently visited summit on the broad ridge leading east from the Aonach Eagach.

131 South Face   Grade 3   **
Alt 300m   Ht Gain +500m   (NN 183 565)   Map p270   Diag p276

A long chain of outcrops which link to give a fine route up the hill and an excellent half day. Also a useful preliminary to the Aonach Eagach, though most parties prefer to approach the latter directly so as to maximise their time on the ridge. The final tower looks intimidating but turns out to be no harder than many of the lower sections.

Approach
Parking has become a problem since road improvements have blocked off the most useful space, leaving a dangerous walk on a vergeless roadside to reach the previously most used start. It is safer now to approach along the old road, either from the parking place at the foot of the Lairig Eilde (187 652), hopping across the river, or from NN 195 564.

The Route
Just above the old road where it passes above The Study is an old climbing hut, The Drey. Go up past this on the left and follow a line of slabby outcrops of knobbly pink rhyolite. Where they finish go up left to a steeper face. Walk left under a long horizontal overhang and a steep wall, then climb the groove left of these on big steps. On the next outcrop climb a vague groove in the centre past a perched boulder, finishing with a hard step up using good handholds.

  Minor outcrops now lead to a vertical wall on the right. Climb the left edge of this on comforting square-cut holds. Scramble up the right-hand edge of a mossy outcrop and go up more broken ground to a steep black buttress. This is probably the crux of the route and in the wet is best avoided, but if dry start in the centre and go up to climb an awkward right-slanting ramp. At its top follow a ledge leftwards and up a thankfully easy corner to the top of the outcrop.

  At the next steep wall walk up leftwards until left of a perched block, then climb up rightwards past it. The steeper ground at the top has excellent positive holds. Walk up right and scramble up a rather scrappy ramp, heading rightwards for the obvious steep orange headwall, which looks an unlikely proposition but turns out to be much easier than it looks. Climb the right-

276 GLEN COE

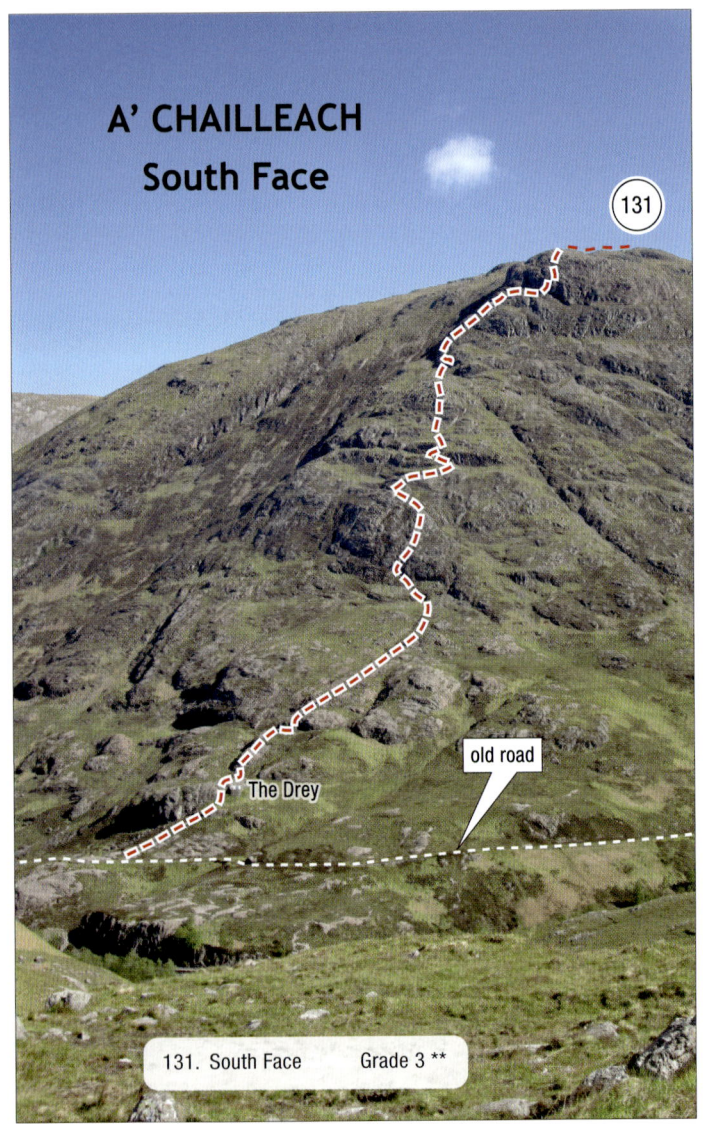

*On the black buttress, South Face of A' Chailleach (Route 131, Grade 3).
Scrambler: George Archibald. Photo: Noel Williams.*

hand of three right-slanting grooves, with a perfect juggy crack for security. At the top go right in an airy position past two perched blocks before going up easily to heather. Finishing straight up from here is fine, but it is better to follow the rough orange rhyolite up rightwards to the top. The summit of A' Chailleach is up to the right, or traversing up and left takes you to Sròn Garbh and the start of the Aonach Eagach in about 2km.

BEINN A' CHRÙLAISTE 857m

OS Landranger 41   (NN 246 567)   Map p270

A whale of a hill untypical of Glen Coe, but with terrific views over Rannoch Moor and straight across to the Buachaille. The line of ragged buttresses on the south flank provide several scrambles.

132 Summit Buttress   Grade 2   **
Alt 400m   Ht Gain + 150m   (NN 233 562)   Map p270   Diag p279

An easily accessible route which leads to the subsidiary summit of Stob Beinn a' Chrùlaiste, good either for an evening or to provide excitement on the way up the hill. The steeper buttress further left, below the apparent summit of the Stob catches the eye but although the main slab is brief fun at Grade 3, the approach and finish involve scarily steep heather pulling above big drops.

Approach
The two most prominent buttresses on the face of the Stob are the aforementioned steep buttress on the left and the well-named Split Buttress further right with its diagonal heathery groove. Summit Buttress lies halfway between these two, just right of a deep gully. It is easily though steeply reached from the West Highland Way.

The Route
The gully below the cliff proper offers some slabby scrambling as an introduction. At the main cliff start up a rib just right of the gully, then at steeper rock move right into the centre of the buttress. At first the rock is mossy but rough, and interspersed with heather, but soon it becomes cleaner and surprisingly sustained. There are plenty of choices of route, and it would be possible to get the difficulty down to Grade 1, but this would involve missing out most of the best bits of the route. Eventually the angle eases and the rock becomes more broken before arriving at easy ground close to the top of the Stob.

133 Split Buttress   Grade 1 or 2
Alt 400m   Ht Gain + 150m   (NN 234 562)   Map p270   Diag p279

Not in the same league as Summit Buttress, looser, less sustained and less defined, but worth doing if you have already done the former.

Approach
The buttress is near the east end of the cliffs descending from Stob Beinn a'

*On the upper section of Split Buttress (Route 133, Grade 2).
Scrambler: Lucy Williams. Photo: Noel Williams.*

Chrùlaiste, made distinctive by the heathery groove that splits the buttress. Like the previous route it is easily though steeply reached from the West Highland Way.

The Route
The basic idea is to climb the left-hand half of the buttress until it thins out, then transfer to the right-hand half. There is a clean initial slab low down, then vegetated ground intervenes before the rock reappears. This is quite shattered in places, generally better on the right. Where the buttress thins near the top go right across the heathery groove to the steeper final section of the right-hand buttress. This makes a good finish, easiest by going up right from the centre. Grade 2 variations can be found by transferring to the right-hand half lower down, where it is steeper, and by tackling the top section direct.

134 Pink Rib   Grade 1   *
Alt 400m   Ht Gain +100m   (NN 239 560)   Map p270

Easy but fun scrambling on a prominent dyke of excellent pink rock. Unlike many routes here it is almost as much fun in descent.

Approach
Well right of the previous routes and obvious from its name, this route lies just east of the heathery break in the south facing cliffs. Like the previous routes it is easily reached from the West Highland Way.

The Route
Start below and right of a small waterfall. Avoid a steep wall at the bottom on the right then go up the rib. The route is unmistakeable, on rock all the way, virtually walking in places but with three steeper sections. Escapable virtually everywhere, but why would you want to?

The Buachailles

The south side of the Glen consists of three extensive mountains, with the eastern two, Buachaille Etive Mòr and Buachaille Etive Beag, being long ridges consisting of several peaks. The former in particular hosts some of the best scrambles in the country. Good paths make the routes very accessible and it is easy to string routes together to make a superb long scrambling day.

BUACHAILLE ETIVE MÒR 1022m

OS Landranger 41   (NN 223 543)   Map p270

The dominant peak of the east end of Glen Coe, and one of the best scrambling peaks in Scotland. The soaring arrowhead of the North-East face is made up of converging ridges of excellent rough rhyolite, a mountaineer's dream.

BUACHAILLE ETIVE MÒR Stob Dearg, South-East Face

135. South Buttress — Grade 3 *
136. Chasm to Crowberry Traverse — Moderate

135 South Buttress Grade 3 **
Alt 400m   Ht Gain +350m   (NN 227 536)   Map p270   Diag p282

Although the buttress is broken up into three sections, the individual sections are sustained. Excellent holds make the route intimidating rather than hard.

Approach
Two prominent deep gullies cut the southern end of the Buachaille's North-East face, the right-hand one being the well known rock climb of The Chasm. This route climbs the three tiered buttress between the gullies. There are several parking places on the road below (take care not to block passing places), from where you can head up directly to the buttress. The lowest wall slants up leftwards, with a horizontal ledge 3m up.

The Route
Clamber up onto the left-hand end of the ledge and climb the wall above on good holds. This eases quickly and broken rock leads to another short wall, climbed left of centre. Carry on up left to the skyline. Here a steeper wall rises from the depths on the right and its left edge is brief fun.

Walking now leads up to another steep tier, split into three by mossy gullies. Head up to the right-hand buttress and start up easy rocks. Climb the left edge of two steep walls to a rock platform. From the centre of this follow flakes up right airily to a slabby shelf. Go right around the edge and up a short groove to easy rock, arriving at the top of the tier by a pointy boulder.

Walk up to the next tier, which is intimidatingly steep. Start centrally at the biggest patch of pink rock. Climb easily at first, then more steeply. Eventually you are forced left at a more or less vertical headwall. A mossy chimney bypasses the steepest section, passing left of a giant flake crack. An easy ledge leads back right to the crest from the top of the chimney, but it is better to move right a few feet lower and make an exposed move right to arrive at the top of the flake crack. Easy rock on the right leads to the top. There is another easy minor tier above before the buttress runs out into the hillside.

136 Chasm to Crowberry Traverse Moderate
Alt 400m   Ht Gain +600m   (NN 228 537)   Map p270   Diag p282

Much of this is walking, albeit in dramatic situations amongst big cliffs. Some bits are excellent, but the crux is both hard and unpleasant.

Approach
From the road at 233 531 follow a sketchy path up the north bank of the stream issuing from the Chasm.

The Route
The first rock reached is easiest left to right but excellent holds allow it to be climbed anywhere. Walking and a couple of minor outcrops lead to a large vertical wall. Go up right using the upper of two right-slanting breaks. Continue right and go up a scree gully, using the rib right of it wherever possible. Carry on up right, passing below a large slanting overhang, then go

out right below a perched boulder. Enter the gully on the right (Lady's Gully Left Fork) and go up its right fork on sloping holds. Continue up the gully to be confronted by the crux.

The groove on the left is smooth, usually wet and harder than it looks so in dry conditions the slabs just right offer the best route, although still quite insecure. Slightly further right a grassy groove leads up to a rising traverse across the top of the slabs, no easier but with more square-cut holds so a better option in damp conditions. Either way, once above the slabs head right up a grassy gully to a scenic perch at the top of Eagle Buttress. Climb the easy ridge ahead to grass, then continue up more broken ground. Bear right to arrive at the top of Curved Ridge.

137 D Gully Buttress   Difficult   *
Alt 400m   Ht Gain +150m   (NN 228 544)   Map p270   Diag p285

A good line and good rock, but the direct route has one pitch much harder than the rest, forcing a deviation at this grade.

Approach
From Alltnafeadh (221 563) cross the river and fork left about 200m beyond Lagangarbh hut to slant up below the crags for 1.5km. Once beyond the prominent Waterslide Slab an eroded path zigzags up, mostly scree, heading for the foot of the main crags. D Gully is the first gully on the left as you reach the foot of the crags, with D Gully Buttress just to its left.

The Route
Start at the entrance to D Gully and go up left on a well-trodden easy crest for 100m or so. Climb a short vertical wall on big jugs, then take a groove up right. More easy crest leads to the foot of the much steeper 'Hell's Wall', which is Severe if tackled direct. It is much easier to sneak around left to a chimney. Climb the left side of this and work back up right to rejoin the crest. Clamber over a small pinnacle to another steepening, which is much the hardest part of the route if Hell's Wall is avoided, and briefly quite exposed. Go up right to mantelshelf into a slabby niche, then make an airy step up on the right arête to easier rock. Easy scrambling now leads to scree, from where you can walk right onto Curved Ridge.

138 Curved Ridge   Grade 3   ***
Alt 400m   Ht Gain +400m   (NN 227 545)   Map p270   Diag p285

A popular classic, well positioned and on good rock. Although the scrambling is a bit disjointed, the situation below the Rannoch Wall makes up for it. The latter part of the approach is notoriously confusing, and it is easy to start up D Gully Buttress by mistake.

Approach
As for the previous route past the Waterslide Slab and up the scree on its far side. When you reach the main rocks go up right to reach a small stream. Ascend left of this, then go up right to reach the lower reaches of Crowberry

GLEN COE 285

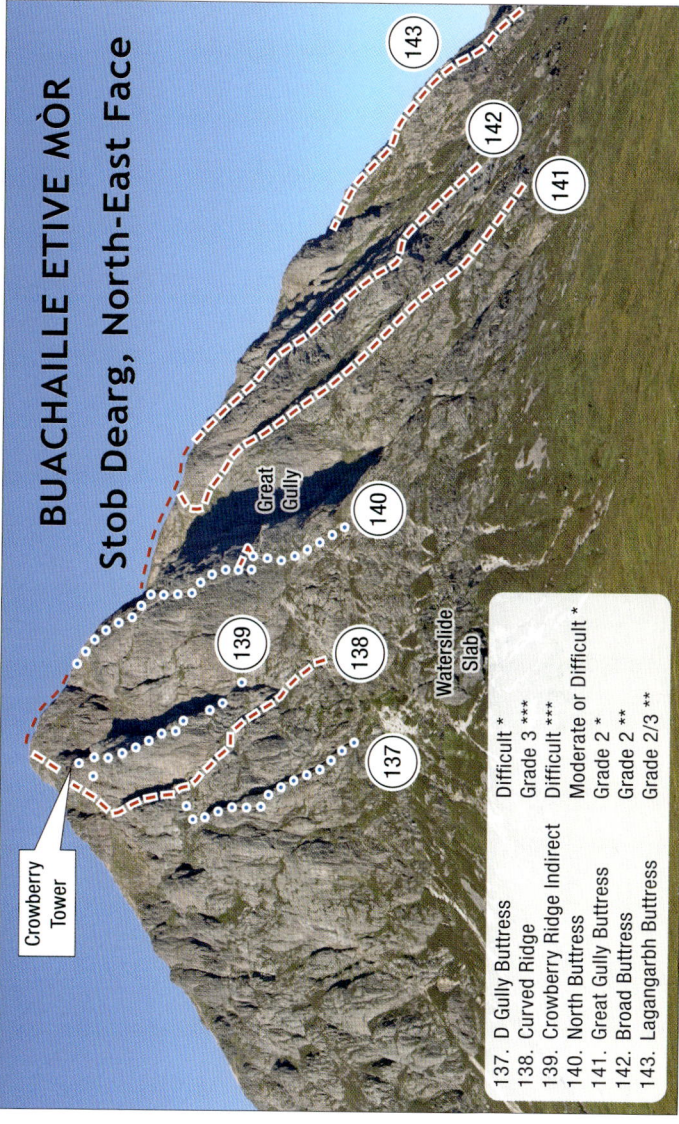

BUACHAILLE ETIVE MÒR
Stob Dearg, North-East Face

137. D Gully Buttress — Difficult *
138. Curved Ridge — Grade 3 ***
139. Crowberry Ridge Indirect — Difficult ***
140. North Buttress — Moderate or Difficult *
141. Great Gully Buttress — Grade 2 *
142. Broad Buttress — Grade 2 **
143. Lagangarbh Buttress — Grade 2/3 **

286 GLEN COE

On the crux of Curved Ridge (Route 138, Grade 3).
Climber: Jamie Hageman. Photo: Iain Thow.

Gully. Zigzag up more broken rock and scree to the foot of the prominent steep face below Crowberry Ridge. Curved Ridge starts up the slim ridge to the left, with a minor rib separating it from the main face.

The Route
Go up the crest to a large platform, then follow either the crest or a groove just right to another easing. The ridge now splits, with the best scrambling on the left-hand buttress, well marked by crampon scratches. Go up steeply right to left on big holds, then move left again to climb a steep polished right-slanting groove (crux). More arête leads to another easing, then the ridge breaks up into a series of outcrops, still enjoyable, climbed either direct or more easily on the left.

Arrive at a cairn, with Crowberry Tower ahead. Here you can go up the scree gully behind the Tower to reach the notch of Crowberry Gap, but it is much better to include Crowberry Tower, which is no harder, although much more exposed. Take a small path right close below the wall of the Tower to reach the top of the easy part of Crowberry Ridge. A more direct version following the arête just right of the gully leading to the Gap is Difficult, with the crux at a steep corner two thirds of the way up.

Climb the crest, or occasionally just left, to the top of the Tower and a superb view. Go back down the way you came for 10m then go round left (looking out), where an awkward descent on good holds leads to Crowberry Gap. Big steps lead up leftwards to easy ground, or more scrambling can be found by a short airy traverse right, linking outcrops to the summit.

 139 Crowberry Ridge Indirect   Difficult   ***
Alt 400m   Ht Gain +350m   (NN 227 545)   Map p270   Diag p285&290
A serious and exposed route up one of the best features of the hill, with lots of easy airy scrambling high up but a much harder lower section. This finds an intricate way through steep ground, with a hard and exposed crux. Not a route to be underestimated (or confused with the Direct which is Severe).

Approach
As for the previous route to the bay below the big steep face where Curved Ridge goes up left. Go up right to easy ground below and right of the main face to reach a V-groove with a slabby right wall.

The Route
Go right up the slab to broken ground overlooking Crowberry Gully (the First Platform). Climb a juggy crack a little left of the right end of the Platform to reach another good ledge (Pinnacle Ledge). Go round right to arrive in a bay on the left edge of Crowberry Gully. Go up left towards a subsidiary gully (Naismith's Route) but just before this take a traverse line left. This is exposed but on excellent holds, hardest at the end. At the crest descend slightly to reach a good ledge running left across the outer face (Upper Ledge). Climb an obvious groove until it bulges, then make an awkward move right to a good jug and easier ground. Breathe a sigh of relief! Carry on up the crest on

139. Crowberry Ridge Indirect — Difficult ***

much easier slabs, then follow easier steps to reach the traverse line coming in from the top of Curved Ridge.

Climb the crest, or occasionally just left, to the top of the Tower, a spectacular place. Return 10m down the way you came then go round left (looking out) to descend awkwardly into Crowberry Gap. From the Gap either scramble up and right above the void then link outcrops direct to the summit, or go up easy steps on the left and finish up easier ground.

140 North Buttress   Grade 3, Moderate or Difficult   *
Alt 400m   Ht Gain + 550m   (NN 226 546)   Map p270   Diag p285&290

Very impressive from a distance but mainly consisting of short hard sections separated by broken ground, on markedly poorer rock than many of the Buachaille's other scrambles. Quite a serious route but much easier than it looks from the road!

Approach
Take the path past Lagangarbh as for the previous routes. North Buttress is the large broad central buttress dropping directly from the summit. It is easily identified from below by virtue of two boulders prominent on the skyline as you approach. Leave the path and go up broken ground past the two boulders to reach a band of much steeper rock crossing the buttress.

The Route
A central chimney fault is the general line of the route. Taken direct this is a tough Difficult, but some weaving about is usual and gets the grade down to Moderate or even Grade 3. The initial steep wall can be climbed at Moderate or dodged by walking right then back left. Continue up the chimney crack and its left wall to easier ground, then head up to a continuation of the crack, here made up of two grooves. Climb either of them to a nest of jammed blocks in the right hand groove (crux of the easiest line). A little higher the chimney narrows and steepens, so unless looking for a hard time escape right up a smaller chimney, exiting left at the top. An easy ramp now leads up right, with harder direct versions at Moderate.

After more easy angled ground things steepen again, with the chimney line now a steep crack (Difficult). Traverse left at the foot of this to find easier scrambling leading back up right to more ledges. Easier angled rock with occasional scrambling now leads directly to the summit cairn.

141 Great Gully Buttress   Grade 2   *
Alt 450m   Ht Gain + 350m   (NN 226 547)   Map p270   Diag p285&290

One of the more shy and retiring buttresses on the face, fairly easy angled and vegetated in places, but still with excellent rock. Often used as a descent by climbers on the North Buttress routes, so the line is well marked.

Approach
From Alltnafeadh (221 563) cross the river and fork left about 200m beyond Lagangarbh hut to slant up below the crags. The first and lowest buttress, on

290 GLEN COE

BUACHAILLE ETIVE MÒR
North Face

- 140. North Buttress — Moderate or Difficult *
- 141. Great Gully Buttress — Grade 2 *
- 142. Broad Buttress — Grade 2 **
- 143. Lagangarbh Buttress — Grade 2/3 **
- 144. Creag na Tulaich — Grade 3 or Moderate **

the corner of the face, is Lagangarbh Buttress, then there is a more broken area, then the large Broad Buttress. Great Gully Buttress is the next buttress, about 1km from Lagangarbh, set back a little, bounded by the well named Narrow Gully on the right and the open Great Gully on the left.

The Route
Go up easily to the lowest steep wall, above a heather terrace with a big boulder. Climb the left-hand edge to vegetation. A rough path now zigzags up the buttress, passing numerous slabby outcrops, which can be added in or avoided as the mood takes you. Eventually a band of steep slabs crosses the ridge. Climb the right-hand of the two central grooves, quite awkward. A little higher another slabby band can be climbed by a mucky groove in the centre (or better but harder by one of the arêtes on either side). As the buttress narrows the rock improves, finishing with a rib of lovely clean slabs, which can be made as easy or as hard as you wish.

142 Broad Buttress   Grade 2   **
Alt 450m   Ht Gain +350m   (NN 226 549)   Map p270   Diag p285&290

As you might expect from the name, a buttress with lots of choice of route, on perfect rhyolite.

Approach
Follow the path from Alltnafeadh (220 562) past Lagangarbh, forking left about 200m beyond the hut, onto the well-used path slanting up below the main face. The first and lowest buttress, on the corner of the face, is Lagangarbh Buttress, then there is a more broken area, then the large Broad Buttress is next, with the well named Narrow Gully beyond.

The Route
An apron of slabs lies at the foot of the buttress, best climbed by its left-hand edge, which is rougher than the more water-washed centre. Avoid a vertical wall on the right, although the right arête of the wall has excellent holds at Moderate. Go up a pinkish rib right of the central groove, and when it breaks up transfer to the left side. Easy ground follows, gradually steepening to fine rough slabs. Ascend the right-hand side of a vertical wall by a staircase going up rightwards, then work back left to the crest. At a prominent slabby groove either climb the slab (harder than it looks) or the juggy left-hand arête. A long stretch of good rock follows, easier on the right, more exposed and on rougher rock on the left. Eventually arrive at a flattening where the scrambling ends.

From here walking leads up the spur to the summit, but an alternative route extends the scrambling by moving across to the buttresses further left. Descend slightly and cross Great Gully to reach an obvious narrow ramp slanting up left on the other side. This turns out to be a walk, but is exposed, sloping and often wet, so care is needed. The ramp passes behind a huge detached block to arrive at the top of Cuneiform Buttress, a superb viewpoint. Either continue left to join the easier angled upper section of North Buttress, or climb the final short step of Cuneiform Buttress, starting in a groove, then up the right arête. Walk right up scree below a steep wall until it relents, then climb its right edge on big holds. Go straight up on pink rock, a bit loose in places to arrive on North Buttress as it eases to walking not far below the summit.

143 Lagangarbh Buttress   Grade 2/3   **
Alt 450m   Ht Gain+300m   (NN 224 550)   Map p270   Diag p290

A sustained start on excellent rock leads to an easier section, then a fine finish. Although it finishes low on the mountain, it provides an entertaining direct route to the summit of the Buachaille from the car park at Alltnafeadh.

Approach
Follow the path from Alltnafeadh (220 562) past Lagangarbh, forking left about 200m beyond the hut, onto the well-used path slanting up below the main face. Lagangarbh Buttress is the first and lowest buttress, on the corner of the face.

The Route
A stream leads up through the heather to the foot of the buttress, and slabs in the stream bed provide a good introduction. They lead to more sustained slabby rock at the foot of the buttress proper. Start 10m left of the gully and climb slabby steps on superb rough rock. Where it steepens zigzag up to a heather slope below a vertical wall. Go right on a good ledge then take a rock staircase back up left to another heather ledge. Climb the next rock band by a right to left ramp, then work up left to the buttress crest. Go back up right and follow the centre of the buttress to easy bouldery ground. A steep wall crosses the buttress, climbed by its easy left edge, then more easy ground leads to another steep wall. This can be avoided on the right or climbed direct at Moderate (a delicate slab on small holds, then one steep haul on jugs).

Walking now leads up to the impressive upper buttress. Pass right of this up a shelf. At the top right edge of the sidewall are two corners. Either climb the right-hand one and traverse left across a slab to regain the crest, or, if feeling brave, traverse up left from the foot of the left-hand corner on good square holds. This latter variant is steep and exposed but much easier than it looks (Moderate). Either way leads to easy broken rock running up to the top of the buttress. About 250m of rough walking takes you to the summit.

144 Creag na Tulaich, North-East Spur   Grade 3 or Moderate   **
Alt 450m   Ht Gain+60m   (NN 219 551)   Map p270   Diag p290

A good evening route, quite hard at the top, although this can be dodged.

Approach
From Alltnafeadh (220 562) cross the bridge to Lagangarbh and follow the path to the narrows at the foot of Coire na Tulaich. The route is the lowest rock spur on the right of the path, forming the right side of the lower corrie, in three tiers. Start at a vertical wall with a straight central crack.

The slabs on the North-East Spur of Creag na Tulaich (Route 144, Moderate). Scrambler: Peter Duggan. Photo: Noel Williams.

The Route
Climb the left edge of the wall or the slab just left, then move up right to an airy traverse onto the front of the buttress. Easy slabs then lead to the top of the first tier. The second tier starts with two ribs separated by a bay with small trees. Start below the trees and gain the crest of the right-hand rib. Easy rough slabs run up to the foot of the third tier. More rough slabs lead to a steeper section, best started on the left and finished on the right, then go up to a large vertical wall, necessitating a move left to a minor gully. The finest finish climbs the left-hand side of the arête above, steep and exposed but on very good holds (Moderate). However, it is easier to cross the gully and move left onto slabs, then climb the rib just left of the gully to a very battered tree. Walk left below a steep wall and then work back up right to the top. The minor gully itself is not hard but is very loose, usually greasy and not recommended.

Other routes on Buachaille Etive Mòr

East Face of Creag na Tulaich   Moderate * or Grade 2 (218 550)
The left edge of the crag is bounded by a wet chimney corner. Right of this is a short vertical corner starting at a platform a couple of metres up (the taller corner just right is Arrowhead Groove, VD). Climb the short corner (or either arête) and carry on up steep but juggy rock, with lots of route choice. An easier route starts up the wet chimney corner on the left to a big platform, then climb a steep rib on the left end of the wall, with short walls above. It is also possible to connect both routes by slanting right up an exposed sloping shelf from the big platform to join the direct route. All these are on excellent rock.

Creag a' Bhancair Skyline   Grade 1 (217 551)
This is the gentler angled spur right of Creag na Tulaich, with the wildly overhanging Tunnel Wall falling away to its right. Climb a smooth central slab to start, then dodge steeper rock on the right to reach easier slabs and small outcrops. As the buttress narrows climb a steeper section by a right to left ramp, then easy slabs lead to walking.

On the Glen Etive flank, the East Spur of Stob na Doire has some minor outcrops that can be strung together, while a route can be made up the left edge of the Dalness Chasm, poor scrambling but with great views into the Chasm.

BUACHAILLE ETIVE BEAG 958m

OS Landranger 41   (NN 179 535)   Map p270

The lower of the two ridges that guard the east end of Glen Coe has a steep northern end with broken crags.

North-East Buttress of Creag nan Cabar (Route 146, Grade 3).
Scrambler: Peter Duggan. Photo: Noel Williams.

145 Stob nan Cabar, Alltnafeadh Buttress   Grade 2/3
Alt 450m   Ht Gain +350m   (NN 204 555)   Map p270   Diag p295

The northernmost summit of the ridge is Stob nan Cabar, below which the face drops away. The blunt spur falling eastwards into the foot of the Lairig Gartain has intermittent scrambling, quite serious in places. It is much better than it looks from below, with excellent rough rock and although slow to dry goes quite reasonably in the wet.

Approach
Start along the Lairig Gartain path (213 559), recently improved, until it starts to run alongside the River Coupall. Head directly up to the spur from here, arriving at a pair of diverging ribs below the main face.

The Route
The right side of the left-hand rib makes a good start, then walk up to and cross a wide grassy gully on the right to reach more sustained rocks. Climb a grey wall on good square holds, then minor outcrops and walking lead up left to a steep wall slanting up from left to right. Start about 6m below a rowan tree and well above a large mossy patch and traverse up left past a perched block to the skyline. Go up this on good holds. When the rock runs out walk up via craglets to a small boulder field below a large steep wall At its right end climb a pink rib then traverse right round the corner and up a steep groove. Follow an easy ramp up left, then work up and right to a crack (prominent from below). Follow this to heather, then go up to the skyline.

On the next crag take an obvious clean rib. This is Grade 3 if taken with a purist attitude, but much easier with minor variations. At a steep mossy wall go up steps rightwards and up the skyline to easy ground. One more craglet remains above, just below the summit of Creag nan Cabar, climbed by a brecciated slab on the right.

146 Creag nan Cabar, North-East Buttress   Grade 3   **
Alt 400m   Ht Gain +80m   (NN 198 558)   Map p270   Diag p295

Clean exposed scrambling with a definite crux, good for an evening trip or as the start of a longer traverse of Buachaille Etive Beag. The rock is quite smooth and although holds are large they are often sloping so this is a poor choice in the wet.

Approach
Low down on the right-hand side of the north face is a broad buttress consisting of a vertical cliff on the right, steep slabs in the centre and a more defined rib on the left. The route follows the rib, just right of a wide gully. There is a parking area on the other side of the road virtually opposite.

The Route
Below the left side of the cliff are some easy clean slabs to provide a warm up, then walk up to the main buttress, arriving just left of a substantial rowan tree. Zigzag up steeper slabs to heather, then go up left towards an overhang.

Slant up right below this to reach a large niche in the centre, then make steep exposed moves up right to easier rock (crux). The next steep section is climbed centrally on good holds, still quite exposed, then the angle eases. Another steeper band is climbed by a groove left of centre, then the rock peters out at a minor top around 530m. A few minor outcrops can be found higher up, but many people do the route as a brief foray and descend the gully just to the east, forking right down a grassy ramp where the gully steepens.

Bidean nam Bian Group

The highest peak in Glen Coe and a whole range in itself, with around a dozen peaks, two of which are Munros. Both the rhyolite crags at mid height and the higher andesite have plenty of scrambling. Although many of the routes are short they can often be linked together to make a full day.

STOB COIRE SGREAMHACH 1072m

OS Landranger 41   (NN 154 536)   Map p270

The culminating point of Bidean's easternmost ridge, Beinn Fhada, is a sharp peak which has now been given Munro status. The flanks of Beinn Fhada are extremely steep and rocky, and one route has been described here, with scope for several more. Eastwards again is the much steeper spur of Sròn na Lairig, a lovely outing in both summer and winter (when it is a long Grade II climb).

 147 Sròn na Lairig   Grade 2   **
Alt 600m   Ht Gain +300m   (NN 164 535)   Map p270   Diag p299

A long spur reaches down into the head of the Lairig Eilde between Bidean and Buachaille Etive Beag, making an excellent and popular scramble. Slabby at first, it breaks up into steeper towers, then becomes an easy narrow arête.

Approach
From the car park at NN 187 563 follow the Lairig Eilde path until just before its highest point, then go up right towards the obvious spur, aiming for the prominent large slab at its foot.

The Route
Start at the toe of the slab, at first on easy rock steps, then go left to climb the crest on good rough rock. Where the ridge becomes more defined go up a groove in the crest (or its left edge) and then continue up more easily to grass and boulders below a steep cliff. Go right to a clean scratched slab and from the foot of the scratches make a delicate step right into the top of a shallow groove (the groove direct starting lower down is Grade 3). Carry on direct to scree. Vegetated steps now lead up left to a large terrace.

In the centre of the steep tier above good steps lead up right then back left to grass. From here a rake leads back up right towards a huge block tower.

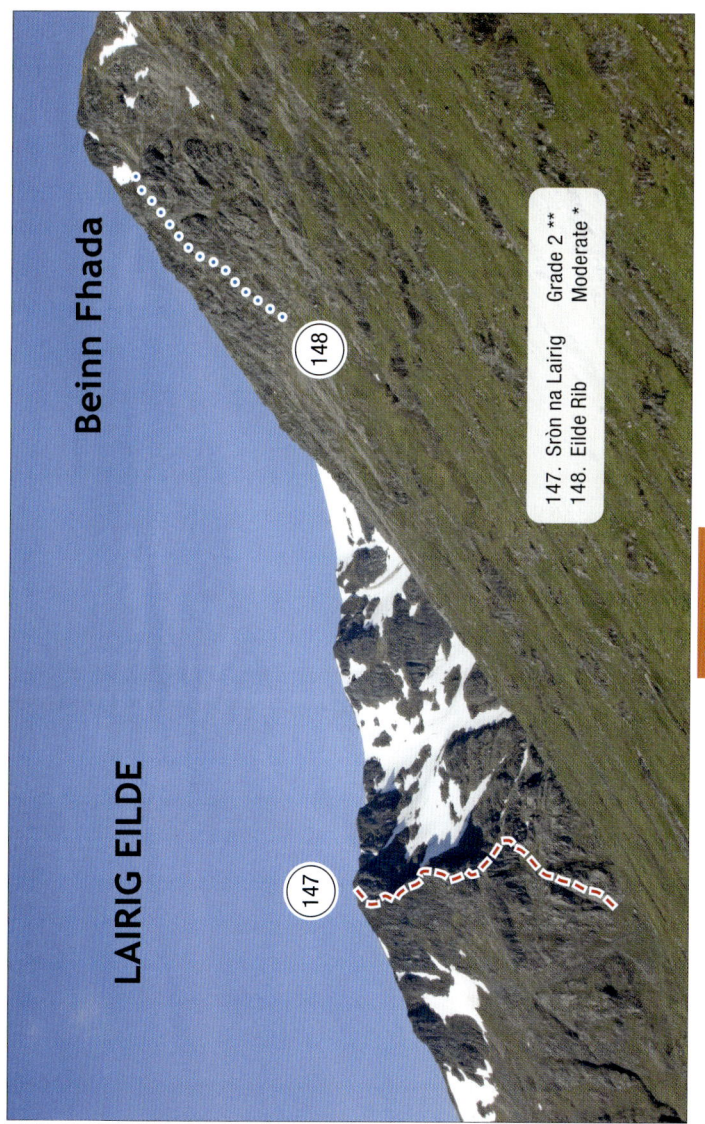

GLEN COE

Either go up easily behind this or go up more directly from halfway up the rake. The ground now eases and the route is obvious, just follow the ridge, narrow and airy in places. In spring snow lingers on some of the little cols, giving it a real Alpine feel. The largest tower can be climbed on its left arête or avoided by grassy steps further left. Eventually the arête runs into a grassy hillside, with a final upthrust above, usually avoided on one side or the other.

148 Eilde Rib   Grade 3   *
Alt 750m   Ht Gain +100m   (NN 167 545)   Map p270   Diag p299

A broad buttress with various lines, most of them quite hard. Even the easiest line is quite intimidating at times, but good holds appear at the right moments. There are several buttresses to the left which have possibilities, but they tend to be either too easy or have short hard sections out of character with the rest of the route.

Approach
Although this could be approached from below, most will include it as a diversion from the Beinn Fhada ridge (Stob Coire Sgreamhach's north-east ridge). From the col south-west of Beinn Fhada's far north top (169 547) traverse down southwards on the Lairig Eilde side. There is a useful deer track most of the way. Cross an open gully just above a short vertical pitch and pass below a steep rib dropping from the peak ahead. Continue the traverse for another 100m, now slightly uphill, below the lowest rocks, until below a steep triangular grey slab. Go up past this to a long shelf backed by a 5m wall crossing the buttress.

The Route
Above the triangular slab is an open mossy groove. Climb the rib right of this to grass, then the right-hand edge of the next wall on good holds. The main buttress is ahead, looking intimidating. Climb a square rib to reach lines of narrow slabs slanting up left. Go up to the second line and follow this, with an awkward step left at the bottom. The slabs lead to easy ground on the far side of the buttress, but halfway along a steep wall can be climbed direct. Above this head up to cracked blocks in the centre and climb these to easy ground. Further minor scrambling can be found above.

STOB COIRE NAN LOCHAN 1115m

OS Landranger 41   (NN 148 548)   Map p270

Bidean's twin peak, more prominent from the road than the main one, is a graceful curving ridge with two spurs running north-eastwards. Both subsidiary spurs are surrounded by steep cliffs with huge amounts of climbing and scrambling, while Stob Coire nan Lochan itself has a craggy north face which is more popular in winter than summer. The first two routes are approached from Coire Gabhail (Lost Valley), the others up Coire nan Lochan.

On the Zigzags (Route 149), with the Meeting of Three Waters in the distance. Scrambler: Joanne Schartz. Photo: Iain Thow.

GLEN COE

GEÀRR AONACH 690m

The middle one of the Glen Coe's 'Three Sisters' is a fine ridge with a prominent nose at its north-eastern tip which juts out dramatically into the main glen.

 149 The Zigzags   Grade 1   *
Alt 400m   Ht Gain +250m   (NN 168 560)   Map p270   Diag p301

Only just a scramble but impressive situations. Difficult to believe from below that something this easy goes up here! A good descent for those who know it but difficult to locate from above for those who don't.

Approach
From parking at 171 568 cross the bridge below the Meeting of Three Waters and follow the path up towards the Lost Valley. A little beyond the forest gate fork right up steep ledges, then once the ground flattens out go up right towards big cliffs. Follow a path running up left along the foot of the cliffs

The Route
Where a steep prow projects from the foot of the cliffs turn sharp right and slant up below a recent rockfall scar. This is still unstable so move quickly through debris below it, along the geological contact between the andesite and the rhyolite. At the outside edge of the face cut back up left, either by a blocky groove or a rather smooth slab just left. Ledges and short steps continue up left to a flattening, and you can continue left and up from here before cutting back right to the summit. It is better however, to make an awkward but not exposed move onto a ledge leading back up right, go up and left, then walk right on a good path which takes you round onto the front. Easy rock then leads to the top.

 150 The Nose   Grade 3   **
Alt 500m   Ht Gain +250m   (NN 167 560)   Map p270   Diag p301

An airy staircase on excellent rock, easier than it looks from below.

Approach
As for the previous route (note the recent rockfall and don't hang about!)

The Route
Follow the first leg of the Zigzags rightwards to where they cut back left, then continue rightwards onto the front face. Go up steeply on solid rock (easier the further right you go). The angle eases slightly before reaching a large sloping ledge below steep rock. Go up the crest to climb a short chimney left of a huge block. Carry on up gradually easing rock to a large heathery terrace. A little higher the track from the Zigzags comes in from the left, with a few minor outcrops higher up.

On Barn Wall Route (Route 151, Moderate).
Climber: Iain Thow. Photo: Noel Williams.

AONACH DUBH 892m – EAST FACE

OS Landranger 41 (NN 150 558) Map p270

This rounded summit is situated at the end of Stob Coire nan Lochan's northern ridge. It is surrounded on three sides by very steep ground. The East Face has some of the best climbing in Glen Coe with routes of all levels of difficulty. The three easier options described are situated slightly further up Coire nan Lochan from the main climbing area.

151 Barn Wall Route   Moderate   ***
Alt 500m   Ht Gain +150m   (NN 157 558)   Map p270   Diag p304

Steep and intimidating scrambling on good holds, with more ledges than is apparent from below. Low in the grade if the easiest variants are taken.

Approach
From the parking at NN 168 569 go south-west down to the bridge and follow the path up into Coire nan Lochan. Cross the stream at around 450m. On the far side the tallest part of the cliff is split by a large grassy terrace at half height with the well named Weeping Wall below. Further left the face is still high but leans back a little, this is Barn Wall.

The Route
Start at the highest point of the grass below the face. The first rock is steep but easily climbed by a right to left ramp (or harder direct at Moderate). Go up past a couple of ledges, then break through a steeper band by a left slanting weakness with big square holds to arrive at a terrace with a prominent birch tree. Go up right then back left to another ledge with smaller trees. Right of these work steeply rightwards up exposed rock to a big heather ledge leading up left (crux). Follow this up to its top left end below a gully leading up right. Going up this leads to easy rock and the top but it is better to go round the rib left of the gully and climb a steep juggy groove past a perched block. Slant up right on good holds with one steep move just right of a small prow (avoidable further right). Easy but still steep rocks lead to a sudden finish.

The summit ridge of Aonach Dubh is about 120m higher and easily reached, or for more scrambling cross a col and up an easy rib, then slant down left to reach the next route.

152 Far East Buttress, Right Edge   Grade 3   **
Alt 700m   Ht Gain +80m   (NN 155 556)   Map p270   Diag p304

A hardish start then easier but quite exposed higher up. Excellent clean rock helps imbue confidence. A good follow on to Barn Wall Route.

Approach
Cross the bridge at NN 167 566 and follow the path up the east side of Coire nan Lochan to the steepening at the head of the lower corrie. Far East Buttress is the furthest buttress up on the right. Alternatively descend left from the

*High on the Right Edge of Far East Buttress (Route 152, Grade 3).
Scrambler: Noel Williams. Photo: Iain Thow.*

top of Barn Wall Route as described above. On the right side of the main Far East Buttress is a bay with a steep narrow gully (Hole and corner Gully, Moderate). A wing of rock runs out right from the lower part of this, and the route starts at its lower right end.

The Route
Pull up steeply on big but awkwardly placed holds. The climbing soon eases and you carry on up leftwards to reach the vertical right edge of the main crag. Follow an exposed ledge round leftwards to reach a sloping ramp leading further left (possible escape). Either climb the arête above direct at Difficult or the easier rib a few metres left on good rough holds. Carry on just left of the main arête to the top.

153 Far East Buttress, Left Edge   Grade 2 or 3   **
Alt 700m   Ht Gain +90m   (NN 155 555)   Map p270   Diag p304

Three tiers of immaculate rhyolite with plenty of choice of line, quite steep and exposed on the top groove.

Approach
Approach as for the previous route but go to the far left side of the buttress. Some slabs just above the stream provide a Grade 1 introduction. The lower tier is cleanest on its left, start here.

The Route
Climb the left edge steeply (Grade 3) or slant in from further right at Grade 2. Carry on up rough rock to a large grass terrace. An easy short tier leads to another smaller terrace below a steeper final tier. The Grade 3 version starts at the lowest rock and climbs a steep groove just left of the nose before easy rock leads to the top. An easier version climbs steps on the left edge of the face above blocks, still steep, before zigzagging up right to the top. A scree gully leads down leftwards from the top towards the next two routes (which can also be approached directly up the main corrie).

COIRE NAN LOCHAN

At the head of the lower section of Coire nan Lochan – at a height almost 650m – the path splits to go either side of a prominent steep slabby wall. This guards the approach to the upper level of Coire nan Lochan, in which there are several lochans.

154 Lochan Approach Left-hand   Moderate or Grade 2
Alt 700m   Ht Gain +60m   (NN 154 553)   Map p270   Diag p309

The slabs on the left side of the buttress are much harder than those on the right.

Approach
The next two routes can be approached directly up the path from the bridge at NN 167 566. Alternatively slant down left from the top of Far East Buttress.

The Route
The slabs are guarded by a steeper band. They can be gained from the left at a scarily exposed Moderate, swinging onto the slab above the gulf then traversing delicately right before tiptoeing up right then left to an easing. This can be gained much more easily by coming in from the left higher up, just above a small overhang. Much easier slabs (Grade 2) then lead to the top.

155 Lochan Approach Right-hand   Grade 2
Alt 700m   Ht Gain +60m   (NN 154 553)   Map p270   Diag p309

Pleasant slabs that follow on naturally from either of the routes on Far East Buttress.

Approach
As for the previous route but go to the right side of the cliff.

The Route
Start at the bottom right corner either directly (steep) or just left (easier but often wet). Carry on up slabs with excellent friction but fewer positive holds than one would like. Cross a grass ramp running up left and climb steeper but more comforting slabs. Where they ease either carry on up or move left and finish up a steeper rib.

NORTH FACE 1115m

The next two routes are both situated beneath the very summit of Stob Coire nan Lochan. They are unlikely to be the sole objective of the day, but can easily form the finale to a string of other routes.

156 Summit Buttress, Left Flank   Grade 2
Alt 850m   Ht Gain +200m   (NN 151 552)   Map p270   Diag p309

A series of steps, with a tricky crux, then easing. Often greasy but a natural way to the tops after completing one of the lower scrambles.

Approach
The upper shelf of Coire nan Lochan is easily reached from the top of Lochan Approach; from any of the routes on the West Face of Aonach Dubh by crossing the broad shoulder between Aonach Dubh summit and Stob Coire nan Lochan; along Gearr Aonach after climbing the Zigzags, or directly up the corrie from the bridge at NN 167 566.

Summit Buttress lies directly under the summit of Stob Coire nan Lochan. On its left side is the curving gash of Boomerang Gully and on its right a prominent scree gully called Broad Gully. The route described climbs a more broken section of buttress to the left of Boomerang Gully. It leads fairly directly to the top of Stob Coire nan Lochan.

The Route
Climb the lowest rock by a groove right of centre, moving up right to spikes,

The crux on Dorsal Arête (Route 157, Moderate).
Climber: Nate Webb. Photo: Iain Thow.

then surmount the second tier on its shelving right side. Lots of craglets interspersed with boulders lead to a much steeper band crossing the buttress. Go right until above Boomerang Gully and climb a steep stepped pillar left of a slimy groove (crux). A shorter groove leads up right then work back left to the crest. This is easy to a narrowing. The whole steep band can be avoided on the left, coming back in at the narrowing. Above a short arête is scree, then climb a blocky buttress with a steep start. A mixture of mossy outcrops and loose broken ground then leads direct to the summit.

157 Dorsal Arête   Moderate   **
Alt 900m   Ht Gain +120m   (NN 148 551)   Map p270   Diag p309

Quite vegetated in places but the sharp section of the arête is extremely memorable.

Approach

As for the previous route to the upper shelf of Coire nan Lochan. Dorsal Arête is the slender ridge immediately right of Summit Buttress, and separated from it by the scree of Broad Gully. To its right is Forked Gully and further right again are the very much steeper South, Central and North Buttresses.

The Route

Start just right of Broad Gully and climb easy steps to big grass ledges. Carry on up numerous square steps to where the buttress narrows. Climb a groove left of a small pinnacle and go up a shattered crest. The arête now steepens considerably and the next (crux) section can be avoided using grass on the left (misses all the fun though). Go up steeply, take a deep breath and step across a gap. Make another steep move to the top of the next pinnacle and cross a knife edge to a col, where the easy variant comes in. A broken rib leads to the top, although a harder finish can be contrived by stepping airily left around the arête to a ledge and a juggy pull up.

AONACH DUBH 892m - WEST FACE

OS Landranger 41   (NN 150 558)   Map p270

This complex columnar face is very prominent from the Clachaig Inn, looking particularly good in evening sunlight, when all the detail stands out beautifully. Two prominent ledges divide the face into three tiers. The lowest one is vegetated, the middle one is steep and clean with several classic rock climbs, while the upper one is easier angled and broken into many ridges. The scrambles mostly sneak through the middle tier avoiding the steeper rock to enjoy the ridges higher up.

158 Dinner-time Buttress   Grade 1
Alt 450m   Ht Gain +120m   (NN 144 559)   Map p270   Diag p313

A steep and very direct route onto the hill, with only minor scrambling. Often used in descent.

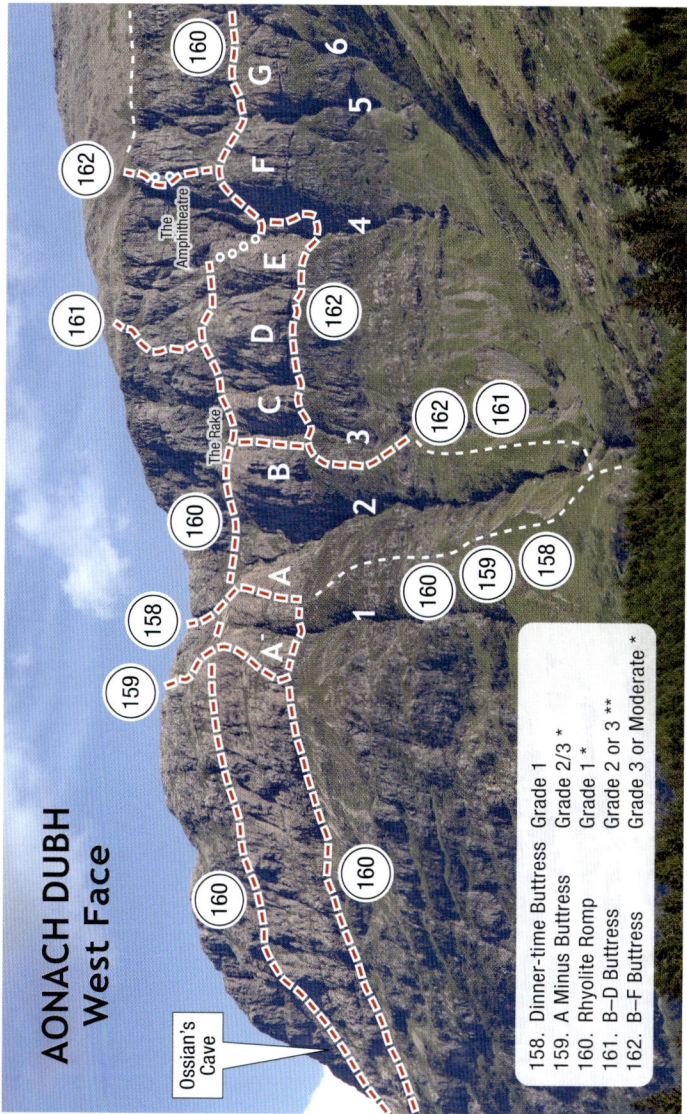

Approach
This is the buttress below the obvious col on the skyline of Aonach Dubh as seen from the Clachaig, between Gullies 1 and 2. Start up the path from the road bridge at Achtriochtain (137 565) until it starts to steepen. Cross the stream coming out of Coire nam Beith below the lowest waterfalls, then go steeply up the moraine crest between the two gullies. The first few minor outcrops can be bypassed by an eroded zigzag path, mainly on the right.

The Route
A slightly steeper step leads up to the traverse ledge at the foot of the main cliff, with much better rock above and loads of variations possible. The easiest line starts up a central groove then moves right of a steeper step. Well used tracks zigzag up to another steeper step, easiest by a slot in the centre. The ground now opens out into a wide bowl, with the easiest exit up to the left. The final section of the next route is only slightly further left and easy to incorporate (Grade 2/3).

159 A Minus Buttress   Grade 2/3   *
Alt 450m   Ht Gain +200m   (NN 147 559)   Map p270   Diag p313
A harder alternative to Dinnertime Buttress, in three sections, the last one being excellent.

Approach
As for the previous route to the traverse ledge at the foot of the main cliff. Walk left across Number 1 Gully and pass below a steep buttress to two small caves.

The Route
Just beyond the caves go up fairly steep broken ground past a small birch. Finish steeply between two blocks. Easy ground with two small outcrops and an easy rib leads to more sustained rock. Climb a clean rib on big sloping holds just right of a groove with a large jammed block. Easier slabs lead to grass below a superb final section. Tackle this direct via the central rib on immaculate rock with comforting pocket holds.

160 Rhyolite Romp   Grade 1   *
Alt 450m   (NN 146 558)   Map p270   Diag p313 & 315
Mostly walking along geological weaknesses with only minor scrambling, often on poor rock. The situations, however, are superb, excitingly exposed at times.

Approach
Go up Dinner-time Buttress (Route 158) to the traverse ledge at the foot of the main cliff, then turn left.

The Route
Walk left along the ledge below steep and sometimes overhanging rock. After almost 1km cross a major gully with Ossian's Cave visible above. Follow a

path up the spur on the far bank, with a short nasty descent into a vegetated gully and a delicate traverse out right to a small tree. Continue up a broad shelf below Ossian's Cave (the Difficult rock climb up to this is loose, vegetated and highly unpleasant). Cross the stream on the right as soon as feasible (keeping close to the cliffs leads to slick slabs, Grade 2). Zigzag up the spur then move out right to more open ground. Continue up right as the crags above diminish to arrive in the bowl above Dinner-time Buttress. Descend into this and traverse along the broad shelf above B, C and D Buttresses, known as The Rake.

Arrive at a projecting ridge above the gulp-inducing exposure of E Buttress. From the inner end of the ridge descend leftwards into the Amphitheatre either down a smooth slab or just to its right. Slant back up to the crest of F Buttress and an excellent view back to the classic rock climbs of Big Top, Trapeze and Heehaw. Keep traversing across the next gully and buttress, gradually becoming more open, until you arrive in Coire nam Beith.

 161 B–D Buttress   Grade 2 or 3   **
Alt 450m   Ht Gain +250m   (NN 145 557)   Map p270   Diag p313

Easy scrambling in a dramatic situation leads to an excellent finishing arête, which is harder but on superb sharp rock.

Approach
As for Dinner-time Buttress (Route 158) until the first steep section after crossing the stream. Go right here, cross the stream from Number Two Gully and go up steep grass on the lower part of B Buttress.

The Route
At the first rock band go to the right edge and step onto the bottom right-hand corner on big flat holds. Traverse left to easy rock and go up to grass. Pass left of a small rock band and join a path zigzagging up past a cracked boulder. Easy rock leads up to Middle Ledge at the foot of the main cliff. Start up the groove in the right side of B Buttress directly above you. Move right to the rib overlooking the gully on the right, which soon eases to a broad ramp with traces of path. When the rib reappears climb it, using a subsidiary groove in the crest at the steepest bit. Minor outcrops lead to the ledge known as The Rake.

Follow the Rake rightwards above C Buttress to the broad open crest above D Buttress, as for the Rhyolite Romp, but where this starts to descend slightly head directly up. On the right you can see a pinnacled ridge, the North Ridge of the Amphitheatre (Moderate), then left of this is a grassy gully and a broken area which becomes a more defined ridge higher up (Grade 2, quite loose). Left again is a cleaner steeper buttress which provides an excellent Grade 3 finish.

Go up left to a square cave above a small scree shoot dropping away left. Go into the cave and up left to grass. Go back right to the crest and climb it on big blocky holds of rough rhyolite. Zigzag around to find the best line, which is occasionally exposed but always on good holds. All too soon the rock runs out into grass, where the other options come in. A mossy loose tier is bypassed by a grass ramp up right before rough easy rock leads to the top of the rhyolite. Here a path leads left to go round into Coire nan Lochan and Routes 156 and 157 or alternatively an easy traverse goes right to Coire nam Beith and Routes 164 and 165.

162 B–F Buttress Grade 3 or Moderate *
Alt 450m   Ht Gain +250m   (NN 145 557)   Map p270   Diag p313

Exposed in parts, with a serious top section. Impressive rock scenery and grand situations abound although the scrambling itself is rather scrappy.

Approach
Start up the path from the road bridge at Achtriochtan (NN 137 565) until it starts to steepen. Cross the stream coming out of Coire nam Beith below the lowest waterfalls and go up the first steep section by the remains of a fence. Go right here, cross the stream from Number Two Gully and go up steep grass on the lower part of B Buttress to reach Middle Ledge.

The Route
Walk right across Number Three Gully and follow the exposed Middle Ledge across C, D and E Buttresses to the wide cleft of Number Four Gully. Looming above you on the left is the huge steep wall containing the famed rock climbs Trapeze & Big Top. Cross the gully, go past a pale groove and climb a stepped rib beyond it on good holds. Go up the left-hand of two chimneys, with piled blocks on the right wall. The rib ahead has a steep start on big holds but soon eases (the easier angled rib and gully to the left are both a lot looser). Grass and broken rock now run up to the broad ledge of The Rake. Go up right to the crest of F Buttress and an excellent view. Escape is possible here by traversing right into Coire nam Beith, as for the Rhyolite Romp (Route 160).

Directly above are two steep sharp rock ribs, the right one being Shrike Ridge (V Diff). Start up the left-hand rib and go up a short chimney. Carrying on up the rib direct starts as an excellent scramble on superb rock but finishes with a scary swing down from an exposed pinnacle on loose holds (Moderate). It is easier to slant up left from the short chimney and step into the grassy gully on the left. Go up this until level with the aforementioned pinnacle then move to the arête further left, climbed airily on big rough steps. From the top of this continue up past a steep block to a lovely V-groove (or the arêtes on either side). A final rough outcrop leads to easy ground and the traverse path mentioned for the previous route.

BIDEAN NAM BIAN 1141m

OS Landranger 41   (NN 142 542)   Map p270

The presiding summit of the range has fewer scrambling possibilities than its underlings, but the following route is worthwhile (just!)

*Negotiating the scary pinnacle on F Buttress (Route 162, Moderate).
Climber: Richard Merryfield. Photo: Noel Williams.*

GLEN COE

163 Diamond Edge   Grade 3
Alt 1050m   Ht Gain +70m   (NN 144 544)   Map p270

A good line but very mossy with lots of loose rock. A convenient diversion from a common route up Bidean but definitely comes with a health warning.

Approach
This route will never be anyone's main objective for the day, so by whatever means get yourself to the saddle between Stob Coire nan Lochan and the main summit of Bidean nam Bian. The ridge is obvious off to the right, gradually converging with the standard route.

The Route
Avoid the lower steps (a joke Diff) by traversing in across rubble to gain an easing of angle by a short slab. The easing turns out to be a narrow arête. Climb the steep step above it using a block on the left (crux). Above this follow the crest direct, never all that hard but quite loose and mossy.

STOB COIRE NAM BEITH 1107m

OS Landranger 41   (NN 139 545)   Map p270

Much more prominent from below than from a distance, Stob Coire nam Beith is a dramatic prow topping a fan of steep buttresses which provide two excellent scrambles with serious situations.

164 Number 1 Buttress   Grade 2 or 3   *
Alt 750m   Ht Gain +300m   (NN 142 549)   Map p270   Diag p320

Two well separated sections, the rock not being quite as good as on some parts of the hill.

Approach
From the bridge at the Clachaig road end (137 566) take the path up west of Allt Coire nam Beithach. High up in the corrie the path crosses the stream and a little higher (around 650m, tiny cairn) a small path goes up and left to run below the cliffs of Stob Coire nam Beith. At the left side of the face is a buttress set back from the others with a prominent chockstoned gully to its right (Arch Gully) and a big terrace at one third height. The lower tier is split by a straight deep chimney.

The Route
Start steeply on the right edge, just left of Arch Gully. Work left and up rough slabs (tricky if wet), then up the right edge of the central chimney to the terrace. Above the terrace is a steep wall, go up to the right end of this, almost in the gully. Work up left to climb a short chimney back to the crest. Climb this to grass then zigzag up small outcrops and ledges to a large scree patch.

The rock ahead is steep and although routes can be worked out on the wall up right they are serious, exposed and at least Moderate. A better scrambling

option is to climb the slabby rib above the left end of the scree patch. Crossing the bridge rock off left may prove irresistible (swing up from the left). The rib itself is of rough knobbly rock and leads to a grass ledge. Easy rock then runs up rightwards to the top, but a good finish at Grade 3 zigzags up the steeper squarish spur ahead, with an exposed climax.

165 Number 3 Buttress   Grade 3 or Very Difficult   **
Alt 750m   Ht Gain +350m   (NN 140 549)   Map p270   Diag p320

The buttress is an excellent line up the centre of the face, mostly on good rough rock, but the slabs at its foot are disproportionately hard, forcing scramblers to start from the left. If climbing the slabs direct note that there is little protection; good climbers have had epics here.

Approach
As for Number One Buttress until the traverse below the main face. Just after the path crosses a scree slope go up between this and the unappetising wet rock to its left to reach the prominent clean steep slabs that foot the buttress.

The Route
a) Direct Start
The slabs are hardish V Diff, starting on the right and moving up left.

Left of the slabs there is a short chimney, usually wet, with a squarish rib left again, just before the grassy foot of Central Chimney. Climb the rib, starting on the left, then above it move up right onto the main buttress above the hard part of the slabs. A steep intimidating prow is climbed leftwards on big jugs to reach easier rock (technical crux if avoiding the slabs).

Now zigzag up more broken rock left of the main steep face (usually wet but positive) until you reach an obvious slabby ramp slanting up right across the face. Follow this, with an exposed step around the front of the buttress. A few metres beyond this go back up left to a comforting ledge, then climb a short steep wall on its left to reach easy ground. Go up the left edge of the wall above before returning right to the crest as the angle eases.

Things now get much easier, with lots of lovely scrambling up the crest on superb rough rock, eventually leading to a bouldery flattening. The wall above is easy on its left, but it is hard to resist climbing the squat pinnacle on the right and stepping off its top onto the face. In this case a short ramp takes you up left to a steep wall with good holds. Either way leads to easy ground, where it is possible to traverse off left and descend to the upper corrie beyond Number One Buttress. Most will ignore this, however, and head rightwards up broken rock and minor outcrops to the summit of Stob Coire nam Beith.

APPIN

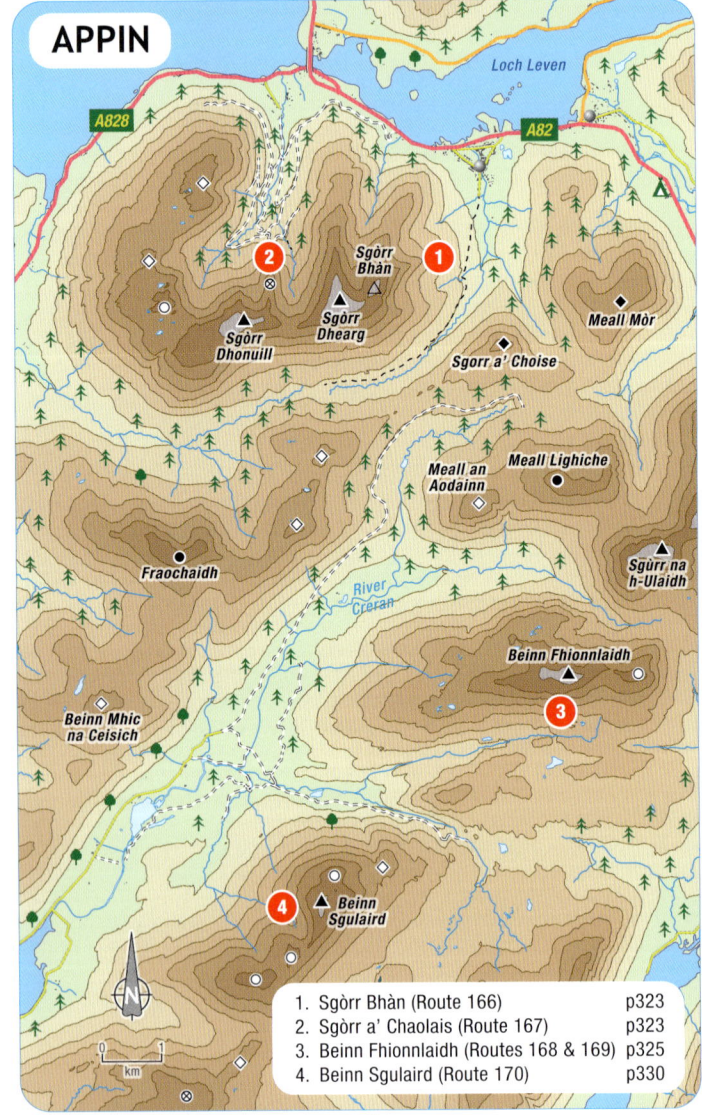

1. Sgòrr Bhàn (Route 166)   p323
2. Sgòrr a' Chaolais (Route 167)   p323
3. Beinn Fhionnlaidh (Routes 168 & 169)   p325
4. Beinn Sgulaird (Route 170)   p330

APPIN

West of Glen Coe and south of the Ballachulish Bridge the peaks feel less massed together and the closeness of the coast gives a more open feel. Some excellent easy ridge scrambles lead up to the summits while there is a more serious route on Beinn Fhionnlaidh.

BEINN A' BHEITHIR 1024m

OS Landranger 41   (NN 057 558)   Map p322

The twin summits of Sgòrr Dhearg and Sgòrr Dhonuill are a popular round from Ballachulish, with the corrie variants more popular than the ridges, rather oddly. The following two scrambles both go up subsidiary ridges, one on each peak.

166 Sgòrr Bhan, North-East Ridge   Grade 1   *
Alt 600m   Ht Gain+300m   (NN 069 565)   Map p322

Only just a scramble, but a great line, nothing like as tricky as it looks from below.

Approach
Park in Ballachulish village (there is no parking on the side road heading south past the school). Walk up the road past the school until it becomes a path and goes out into open country. The north-east ridge is obvious up to the right. Cross the first couple of minor streams and head up steepening grass and heather towards it.

The Route
At about the 600m level the ridge narrows, steepens and becomes rocky. By now a clear path has developed, which largely zigzags around the rock outcrops, though most of these can be tackled direct without much difficulty. Incut holds make things easier than they look, and all too soon you arrive at the junction with the north ridge of Sgòrr Bhan. Turn left up to the summit.

167 Sgòrr Dhonuill, Sgòrr a' Chaolais   Grade 2   *
Alt 600m   Ht Gain+350m   (NN 045 564)   Map p322

Sometimes called the Dragon's Tooth and also known as the 'Fairy Peak' because it appears prominent from below when Sgòrr Dhonuill is in cloud, but apparently disappears when the higher summit is clear behind it. The ridge starts steeply, with some optional scrambling, then the narrow arête behind is mostly grassy, but contains minor pinnacles and one much harder descent. It is sometimes used as a descent route because then the only hard section is climbed upwards, but in this case finding the best way off from the steep section can be a problem, with direct routes taking you through thick forestry plantations.

*Descending the crux buttress on Sgòrr a' Chaolais (Route 167, Grade 2).
Scrambler: Lucy Williams. Photo: Noel Williams.*

BEINN FHIONNLAIDH   325

Approach
There is a good car park at the top of Glenachulish road at NN 046 586. Carry on up the forestry road, fork left over the first bridge, then turn right on a smaller path (signed). Where this zigzags back left then meets another forestry road go slightly left to take a signed path up through the woods. Follow this out to open country and continue southwards along the top of the forestry. Once beyond the trees go right through a hole in the fence, cross the corrie and traverse right. The two big buttresses high up ahead are not the scramble. Avoid gaining too much height on the traverse and go round onto the north face of the spur. Once around the corner there is a large grassy scoop with heathery ribs on the far side.

The Route
The easiest way from here is to take a sheep track slanting up across the scoop to the far skyline above the ribs. Alternatively, either of the ribs makes a good start, with the right-hand one being better, quite steep and airy where it narrows at the top, on big spiky holds. The three routes rejoin at the top of the ribs, where you bear up left, mostly walking but with some minor outcrops available, to arrive at the top of Sgòrr a' Chaolais, a great viewpoint.

Beyond the summit the ridge narrows and is grassy at first, then you cross a small tower on flaky holds, avoidable on the left. The next tower is much bigger, with a hard descent, avoidable by an unobvious traverse left about a third of the way up the tower. The descent is very steep but the holds are big and positive, although sometimes further apart than you might wish. After this the ridge continues easily over boulders and a broken arête to reach the main ridge about 50m below the summit of Sgòrr Dhonuill.

A little more scrambling can be found by moving left for 100m from where the path steepens just below the summit. Climb any of several blocky ribs to arrive at the summit from the south. This is quite pleasant, but misses out the best bit of the main ridge.

BEINN FHIONNLAIDH 959m

OS Landranger 50   (NN 095 498)   Map p322

A long steep-sided ridge with a lot of rather broken rock on both flanks.

168 South Face   Grade 2 or 3   *
Alt 550m   Ht Gain +200m   (NN 093 493)   Map p322   Diag p326
Sunny open scrambling on well separated outcrops.

Approach
Park at the head of Glen Creran (NN 035 489) and take the private road to Glenure. Fork left 100m before the house, then turn left just beyond the farm buildings. 50m after crossing the first bridge take a track up right through the forest. This becomes a sketchy path traversing well above the left side of the stream which continues to Loch na h-Uraich. Continue slanting slightly up for

APPIN

BEINN FHIONNLAIDH
South Face

168. South Face — Grade 2 or 3 *

Eas nan Clach Reamhar

another kilometre to the foot of a gully with a thin waterfall (Eas nan Clach Reamhar) and a short gorge and boulder fan below it.

The general line slants up right from above the short gorge, just left of a band of pink rock. A longer and rougher approach is also possible from Glenure farm, following the track up Glenure until beyond the fine small peak of An Grianan. Cross pathless moorland west of Lochan na Fola to the foot of the gully (or climb An Grianan first via its steep west ridge).

The Route
Walk up the east bank of the stream until above the gorge, then zigzag up a small craglet and walk up the right side of a smaller gully to reach rocks left of the foot of the pink band. Either go up a right slanting grassy groove or take harder rocks on its left (Grade 3). On the main buttress above zigzag up ramps and short walls, occasionally exposed but always with an easier option handy. The buttress gradually curves over and becomes more broken before reaching an easy groove.

Go up a little then cross scree on the right to a small buttress. Climb this either by its left edge (Grade 2) or centrally (Grade 3), then walk up left and ascend rocks just right of a small stream. At steeper rocks traverse right across scree and climb a broken buttress then a steep wall with left to right quartz veins. Easy but rough ground leads up to the summit.

169 North-West Slabs   Grade 3
Alt 700m   Ht Gain +150m   (NN 087 500)   Map p322

Quartzite slabs with lots of small positive holds, a bit disjointed but with a good middle section.

Approach
As for the above route as far as the top of the forest. About 50m beyond this a small path slants up left, heading up onto Leac Bharrain and the west ridge of Beinn Fhionnlaidh. Follow this to around 550m, then traverse left past Lochan Coire Laogh into an open corrie with a triangular slabby left headwall.

The Route
Start at the far left of the triangle and go up easy slabs to scree. Go right to more sustained slabs, with a striking corner line on their right. Climb the left edge of these on small sharp holds to a ledge at 30m, then slant up right on bigger holds to the arete. Go up this in a good position. Above is walking topped by a steep wall, so traverse right across scree to quartz ribs on the right skyline. Scramble up these to scree, then climb the right edge of the steep wall on positive but occasionally suspect holds (easily avoided on the right). Easy rock continues to the top of the face, with a nicely perched minor top off to the left. The main summit is about 60m higher, south then east.

North-West Slabs, Beinn Fhionnlaidh (Route 169, Grade 3).
Scrambler: Paddy Earle. Photo: Iain Thow.

APPIN

BEINN SGULAIRD 937m

OS Landranger 50   (NN 053 461)   Map p322

A straggling steep-sided mountain with a lot of rock, although little of it runs to consistent scrambling. The east ridge has short Grade 1 slabs starting at NN 058 462, while some scrambling can be got out of the north-east ridge, especially if you keep left, just scraping into Grade 2 on the top buttress. In descent the rib to the top of Stob Gaibhre (NN 064 466) from the lochan is an excellent but brief Grade 2.

Below the saddle between Meall Garbh and the main summit on the west side are some clean buttresses which provide good short scrambles with lots of variations (NN 051 454). Left of these, on the south-west flank of the main peak is the climbing ground of Sgulaird Slabs, and left again a succession of rough slabs can be linked up to provide a long route to the summit.

170 South-West Slabs   Grade 2/3
Alt 650m   Ht Gain +250m   (NN 049 459)   Map p322   Diag p329

Excellent granite slabs, but sadly parts are just too steep for scrambling, forcing detours onto more broken ground.

Approach

Park at the head of Glen Creran (NN 035 489) and take the private road to Glenure. Fork left 100m before the house, then turn right just beyond the farm buildings to cross the bridge above the main house. Turn right and follow an estate road round until past the first large stream, then take a hydro road up to a small dam. Cross below this and head directly up alongside a fence to reach a surprisingly deep gorge. Cross this and head up steeply rightwards to reach the left side of the south-west corrie, with the climbing slabs ahead. Left of the main slabs are three small streams, and left of the left-hand one is a scree tongue that goes higher up the hillside than the others. Start at the top of this.

The Route

Climb slabs just left of the stream, then steeper rock starting with an awkward mantel onto a jammed boulder. The fine slab off left is just too steep, so carry on up the rib, then go up left to the top of the slab. Slanting rightwards up the slab just below its steepest part is a scary Moderate. Clamber up boulders, then go left and up a small padding slab, then left again to the right edge of a much bigger slab. Again this is slightly too steep for scrambling (perhaps V Diff) so go up its right edge. Where it starts to break up the angle eases slightly, allowing the slab to be climbed more directly. A succession of small slabs lead up and left, gradually becoming more broken but staying rocky all the way to the summit cairn.

BEINN SGULAIRD 331

*South-West Slabs, Beinn Sgulaird (Route 170, Grade 2/3).
Scrambler: Noel Williams. Photo: Iain Thow.*

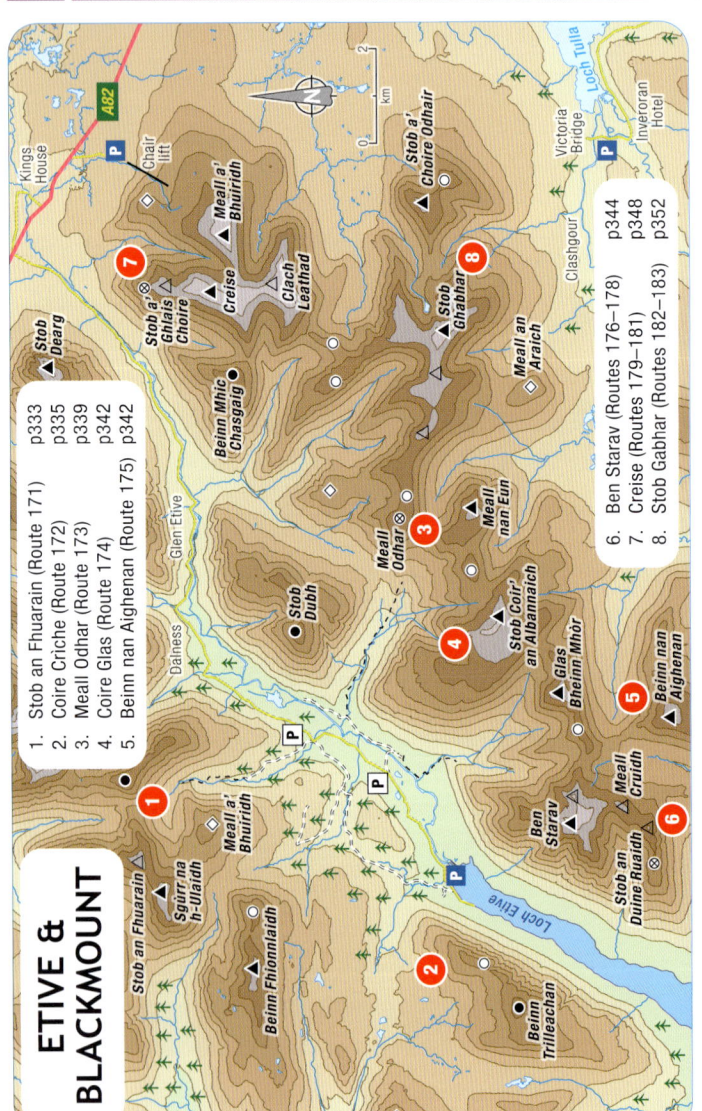

ETIVE & BLACKMOUNT

South-east of Glen Etive lies a forest of densely packed peaks including 13 Munros. Fine ridge walks abound, although all are walks rather than scrambles. Leading up to these, however, are plenty of rocky buttresses and slabs which make interesting ways up onto the ridges.

Also usually accessed from Glen Etive are two slabby scrambles which offer unusual approaches to a Munro and a Corbett.

Glen Etive West

Glen Etive is a very scenic glen which is accessed by a 20km-long single-track road. It starts from the A82 near the Kings House and ends by Loch Etive. The first two routes both lie in quiet corners on the west side of the glen.

STOB AN FHUARAIN 968m

OS Landranger 41   (NN 112 517)   Map p332

This Munro Top has a long northern ridge, Aonach Dubh a' Ghlinne, which is a prominent feature when viewed end on from Glen Coe. At the very end of the hill's shorter eastern ridge, a knuckle of good rock gives some brief fun.

171 Bealach Fhionnghaill Buttress   Grade 2
Alt 400m   Ht Gain +150m   (NN 132 519)   Map p332   Diag p334

Better than it looks from below, with a scenic start up the stream and a nice airy finish.

Approach
Although this route can be reached from Glen Coe it is easier to take the path up from Invercharnan bridge (NN 144 485) in Glen Etive. Go up through the forest into Gleann Charnan and continue up the right-hand side of the glen to reach the stream coming down from Bealach Fhionnghaill.

The Route
Start up the stream, avoiding a vertical fall by a short wall on the left. Carry on upstream to reach a long red wall on the left side of a small gorge. Climb this and walk left to the right-hand foot of the main buttress. Go up a rib on positive holds to heather, then a mix of short ribs and more heather follows, with the right-hand sides of the ribs having much better holds than the left. Arrive at steeper rocks with a vertical black wall up left. Go up a wet ramp to the foot of this then up and right on heathery slabs to arrive suddenly at the top of the face. The slabs can be approached more directly up a short rib, then moving airily left past two quartz blobs (Moderate). Above the main face are some playground slabs, which can be made quite hard if desired. The ridge continues up leftwards to the top of Stob an Fhuarain with Sgùrr na h-Ulaidh beyond, or alternatively the Bealach Fhionnghaill is just off right.

BEINN TRILLEACHAN 839m

OS Landranger 50 (NN 087 439) Map p332

Trilleachan is well known for the climbing ground of the Etive Slabs, but there is a great deal more rock scattered around the hill. The east flank above Loch Etive is very steep and vegetated apart from the Slabs themselves, while the north and west sides are easier angled. The two most continuous rocky areas are at Leacann na Sguaibe (NN 077 446), fairly steep, and in Coire Crìche, which gives quite a sustained scramble. Most of the rest is walking angle.

172 Coire Crìche Slabs   Moderate   **
Alt 400m   Ht Gain +200m   (NN 097 458)   Map p332   Diag p336

A scramblers version of the Etive Slabs, with clean slab padding separated by vegetation. Quite serious at times, and some parts seep for a while, so pick a dry spell.

Approach
From parking at the head of Loch Etive (NN 111 453) go up the edge of the forest on a boggy path until the fence makes a sharp turn right. Head up leftwards, left of the Allt Crìche, then continue further left towards a sweep of clean slabs, left of a wide shallow gully.

The Route
Pad easily up the right-hand side of the first slab, then go left to another slab. Go up this briefly then traverse up left on the lower of two pegmatite veins. Continue up the left edge of the slabs, taking care at a brief steepening. Go up piled blocks and a short rib above, then make a delicate traverse right (about 6m above a small rowan tree) to the foot of a heather tongue with a rock overlap to its right. Use the heather to break through the steeper section, then take to slabs on the left. Climb these to more heather and pull up the right side of a large prone flake. A short easier slab brings you out below a larger slab, with a prominent thin boulder lying on it. It is possible to pad up delicately right of the boulder but this is much harder than the rest of the route, so it is more consistent to cross the narrow slab on the left at a slight easing of angle and climb its left edge. Above the slab go right along the rim of a crevasse, make a steeper move and go up an easy slab. Above this a huge slab soon eases and a line of walking angle slabs leads up right all the way to the ridge, briefly interrupted by a short steep wall climbed on the left at a recess with good holds.

Glen Etive East - The Starav Range

This group of five Munros can all be collected in one long day, but a plethora of granite slabs means that some superlative scrambling can be had on each individual summit.

ETIVE & BLACKMOUNT

BEINN TRILLEACHAN
Coire Crìche

172. Coire Crìche Slabs   Moderate **

BEINN TRILLEACHAN 337

On easier slabs to the right (west) of Route 172. (NN 0939 4566)
Scrambler: Martine Cooper. Photo: Alan Moore.

MEALL ODHAR 879m

OS Landranger 50   (NN 190 465)   Map p332

Strictly speaking this little frequented summit lies at the western-most end of the Stob Ghabhar massif and should be included with that mountain. However it is described separately here because the scramble is much more conveniently approached from Glen Etive. It could be done as part of a cross country traverse of Stob Ghabhar starting in Etive and finishing at Victoria Bridge. Various other contrived combinations are possible including as part of a round of Coire nan Cnamh in which case this could include the north-west shoulder of Meall nan Eun. Slabby scrambling on the latter offers some amusement, though it is quite vegetated and lacking in line.

173 Epiphany Arête   Grade 2
Alt 700m   Ht Gain +60m   (NN188 462)   Map p332   Diag p338

The route consists of slabby ribs of excellent granite with avoidable steeper sections and is well worth doing if passing. The slabs on the north flank of Meall Tarsuinn provide an alternative approach, and the route can also be used as a follow on to the Coire Glas Headwall on Stob Coir' an Albannaich – the next route described.

Approach

From Coileitir in Glen Etive (NN 136 468) cross the bridge and turn left to the mouth of Glen Ceitlin. Take the path up the north bank of the stream until it peters out then head up boggy slopes to the saddle between Meall nan Eun and Meall Odhar. From here the buttress is obvious, on the south flank of Meall Odhar just above. Epiphany Arete takes the line of ribs on the right-hand edge of the face, just left of the deep gully.

The Route

The foot of the gully has a steep left wall, the top forming a shallow rib. Start just left of this and pull up left to grass. Climb the left-hand rib above on rough granite with good holds. Where it steepens move left into a groove, go up it for a few metres then move right up a slanting crack to regain the crest. Go up to heather, with a steeper ridge ahead. Walk right to climb the right-hand of two stepped right-slanting ramps, close to the edge of the gully. At steeper rock work up left, then back right to the crest. Gain the next rib from the left, above its steep start, then at its top work up left across right-slanting grooves. The angle soon eases, although some of the slabs are quite smooth, before the cliff breaks up into boulders, with the summit ridge of Meall Odhar not far away.

An alternative route takes the centre of the face, with much dodging about on grass low down but a good finish up quite sustained slabs (also Grade 2).

ETIVE & BLACKMOUNT

STOB COIR' AN ALBANNAICH
Coire Glas

174. Coire Glas Headwall — Grade 3 or Moderate **

STOB COIR' AN ALBANNAICH 341

*Coire Glas Headwall, Stob Coir' an Albannaich (Route 174, Grade 3).
Scrambler: Iain Thow. Photo: Noel Williams.*

ETIVE & BLACKMOUNT

STOB COIR' AN ALBANNAICH 1044m

OS Landranger 50   (NN 170 443)   Map p332

A mountain with two contrasting faces, steep but grassy on the south and west, but with a glacially scoured north and east. There is a long sweep of very easy slabs starting at NN 173 462 at the head of Glen Ceitlein and running up almost to the col south-west of Meall Tarsuinn, with shorter steeper slabs below the shoulder at NN 174 444. These make a great way onto the hill, but better still is the route described below.

174 Coire Glas Headwall   Grade 3 or Moderate   **
Alt 650m   Ht Gain +150m   (NN 162 452)   Map p332   Diag p340

Sustained slabs at a reasonable standard on excellent granite.

Approach
Cross the bridge over the River Etive at Coileitir (NN 136 468) and turn north to go round into Glen Ceitlein. A possible short cut in dry weather is to ford the Etive at NN 145 476 or (for the bold) to jump the river at the mouth of the gorge just to the south. Either way, follow the path up the north bank of the stream to reach the stream issuing from Coire Glas. Go up the gorge into the corrie (Grade 2 and an entertaining outing in its own right). The slabs are just left of the deep gully at the head of the corrie.

The Route
Start at the bottom right, although blocks on the left provide a good option too. Go up slabs, moving left at first, the go back right to a slightly steeper section. Go back up left, then up right to climb a nicely positioned arête. Above this the line peters out into broken craglets, but up right are steeper slabs (Moderate) with an easier finish.

BEINN NAN AIGHENAN 957m

OS Landranger 50   (NN 148 405)   Map p332

Although usually combined with Starav and Glas Bheinn Mhòr in a round from Glen Etive this is quite an independent peak with a remote feel, dominating the head of Glen Kinglass.

175 North-East Face   Grade 2/3   *
Alt 550m   Ht Gain +350m   (NN 149 411)   Map p332   Diag p343

A long slabby route which starts well but peters out higher up. Those used to slab padding may find it easy for the grade, but one section is quite serious.

Approach
From the bridge at Coileitir (NN 136 468) take the path southwards to the bridge over the Allt nam Meirleach, then the smaller path up the west bank of the stream to the saddle between Ben Starav and Glas Bheinn Mhòr. Slant

down on a small path to reach the col north of Beinn nan Aighenan. From the col descend eastwards down a steep broad gully to get below difficult slabs, then traverse along south-east below the face. Fifty metres beyond the first substantial stream is a short slabby rib, with more slabs above.

The Route
Ascend the short rib then go up left to climb the next slabs. Above these go up left again to reach bigger slabs. Zigzag up these, quite sustained, finishing with an avoidable smooth slab above a grass ledge. On the left a short rib just right of a stream leads to grass, then go up a left-slanting band of slabs, which gradually becomes the crest of the main spur. Follow this, quite grassy but with lots of small craglets providing interest. At about 800m there are steeper slabs on the right flank and the left edge of these provides an exposed variation. Above this the angle eases and the outcrops get less frequent, arriving at the ridge a little east of the summit.

Other options nearby
Aighenan's north ridge has some nice short outcrops on its right flank, while if returning via Glas Bheinn Mhòr then the shoulder running up to Meall nan Tri Tighearnan from the south has enjoyable Grade 1/2 slabs in its top half. The Glas Bheinn Chaol ridge running up to this summit from the north (which provides an alternative approach to the col below Starav) also has some fun easy outcrops on its left flank at around 400m. The nearby Corbett Beinn Ceitlein has a two buttresses just below its main summit, Stob Dubh. The left one is a pleasant short Grade 2, easily reached by traversing in from the col to the east. The right-hand one leading to the summit consists of loose quartzite blocks held together by moss and is well worth avoiding. The best scramble on the hill is below the minor summit of An Grianan (191 504, not named on the Landranger map). At the left end of its south-east face is a line of granite steps, an enjoyable Grade 2 which ends just below the summit.

BEN STARAV 1078m

OS Landranger 50   (NN 125 427)   Map p332

The dominant peak of upper Loch Etive, with several enjoyably narrow ridges and half a dozen wild rough corries. The north-east ridge out to Stob Coire Dheirg is a sharp rocky spine (Grade 1) and can be approached via slabs in Coire an Fhir Leith to its north and the north ridge of Stob Coire Dheirg. The scrambling is fairly minor but the scenery is superb. The best scrambles are on the south face of Stob an Duine Ruaidh, which can be enjoyably approached by the route below.

176 Leac nam Fionn   Grade 2
Alt 350m   Ht Gain +600m   (NN 106 413)   Map p332
Unimpressive from a distance, but there are nearly 300m of granite slabs

scattered up the spur, with some individual sections reaching 50m. Many parts are walking angle and all sections are avoidable, but much fun can still be had.

Approach
Cross the bridge over the River Etive at Coileitir (NN 136 468) then follow the path south along the riverbank and along the east bank of the loch. As you approach Rubha Doire Làrach about 3km down the lochshore slant up to cross the Allt Coire na Laràch and gain the broad spur running up to Stob an Duine Ruaidh. Go up this to the first slabs.

The Route
Start with easy slabs, climb the left edge of a steep wall, then walk right to climb a longer slab just right of its very smooth central streak. Walking and more easy slabs lead to a more concentrated belt of rock. Sadly the clean slab off right is just too steep, so keep to the main crest with a short arête off right worth including. Climb bigger slabs centrally, then when the angle eases walk left to another excellent slab and go up its right edge. Eventually this eases to walking angle, with the west summit of Stob an Duine Ruaidh not far above.

177 Red Man's Rib   Grade 2
Alt 600m   Ht Gain +300m   (NN 125 406)   Map p332   Diag p346

A long route on excellent rock on a very remote feeling face, finishing on a nice pointy summit.

Approach
From the top of the last route go over the 822m west summit of Stob an Duine Ruaidh to the col beyond. Slant down right to a minor flattening on a subsidiary shoulder. Traverse along to a big scree gully with a steep crag on the far side. Descend the near side of the gully on a small deer path, cross the gully when it gets less steep and slant down a minor spur below some clean steep slabs. Follow a deer track below these to the next deep gully, roughly opposite a prominent slabby crag on the other side of the upper corrie (Coire a' Charadh). The scramble starts here, at a clean white slab on the far side of the gully. It can also be approached as for the following route, which involves less ascent but is longer and the scramble is less obvious from this direction. It follows the right edge of the gully whose stream joins the main one right at the mouth of Coire a' Charadh.

The Route
Pad up the slab and link together outcrops up the right side of the gully. As the ground opens out follow slabs diverging slightly right from the gully. The best scrambling ends at a long vertical wall, which can be inched up along a narrow left slanting crack (Moderate) or avoided. Easy slabs follow, breaking up into boulders and minor craglets and finishing right at the summit cairn.

BEN STARAV 347

Slabathon, Stob an Duine Ruaidh (Route 178, Grade 3).
Scrambler: Noel Williams. Photo: Iain Thow.

ETIVE & BLACKMOUNT

178 Slabathon Grade 3 **
Alt 500m   Ht Gain +400m   (NN 127 406)   Map p332   Diag p346

Superb clean slabs for 200m or so, then more broken outcrops, which would be worth another star if the line was more direct. Lots of wet streaks after rain, so pick a dry spell.

Approach
From Coileitir (NN 136 468) take the path up the Allt nam Meirleach as for Beinn nan Aighenan (Route 175) to reach the saddle between Starav and Glas Bheinn Mhòr. On the other side slant down right then traverse along to reach the saddle at the head of Coire a' Charadh. The face is just down west from this, but it is worth making a detour over the 654m top to get a good view of the route. Slant down to reach the second tongue of slabs from the right, which doesn't come quite as far down as the rightmost one, above a prominent pointed boulder.

The Route
Climb the slabby tongue, almost walking, then bear left once it broadens out. Go leftwards up grass to reach a left slanting rib, then ascend this and the wider slab above. More grass leads to steeper slabs, which are slightly too hard for scrambling, so go up left along the foot of these until it is feasible to zigzag up steeper steps, working generally left towards the skyline (several possible lines). Carry on up rougher slabs and steps, culminating in a steep flake crack to reach easier angled ground. Now climb a much easier slabby rib to reach the top of the main section.

It is possible to walk up to the summit from here but moving left every so often gets another 150m of scrambling. Slant left up slabby outcrops to more boulders then move left again to reach left slanting ribs. Climb these (occasionally exposed and with some loose rock) to reach yet more boulders. These lead to the summit, but a better finish can be found by walking left to climb an excellently positioned steep rib right on the skyline. The summit is now less than 50m away, 400m above the start.

The Black Mount

This cluster of peaks fringing the sweeping basin of Rannoch Moor provides a set of very accessible scrambles, several of them quite long. High roads provide handy start points.

CREISE 1068m

OS Landranger 41   (NN 237 501)   Map p332

A broad ridge with a steep east face which throws down spurs of varying degrees of steepness. The three scrambles described can easily be done in one trip if the southern one is descended, or alternatively any of them makes a good start to the round of the two Munros of Creise and Meall a' Bhuiridh.

179 Sròn na Creise   Grade 3   **
Alt 400m   Ht Gain + 450m   (NN 240 528)   Map p332   Diag p349

A blunt spur scattered with outcrops of excellent rock which link together neatly to provide a long but not sustained scramble. Exposed in places and quite tricky in others but not both at the same time. Harder but still reasonable in the wet.

Approach
The route can be approached by fording the River Etive if it is low, but if planning to continue round the two Munros it is better to start at the White Corries ski car park (NN 266 524) and traverse round the foot of Creag Dhubh on a boggy path to pick up the bottom of the spur. Walk up it steeply until it becomes rocky at a pink rib.

The Route
Climb slabs centrally, with good rough holds where they steepen. Walk up left to a big flat-topped boulder and climb a clean rib above it, starting on the right at left-slanting steps (hard to start but soon easing). At the top of the steps continue up slabs to steeper rock. Go into a niche and exit either left (delicate) or right (steeper but juggy), then continue easily to a col below a pink buttress. Climb this direct, delicate to start, then on better holds. Zigzag up outcrops left of a scree gully then cross the gully about 10m below a deep slot on the other side. The traverse onto the buttress on the far side is probably the crux of the route. Start at a big square flat hold by a block and step up using a good jug, then traverse airily right to easier rock on the crest of the buttress. Romp enjoyably up rough holds on the crest. There is one more outcrop above, started by an awkward steep groove, before arriving at the rocky top of the Sròn. Walking leads over the top of Stob a' Ghlaise Choire to the Munro summit, but veering left before the former takes you to the top of the following route, with an easy descent on its far side.

180 Inglis Clark Arête   Grade 3   *
Alt 700m   Ht Gain + 120m   (NN 242 521)   Map p332   Diag p349

More of a climb than the two nearby routes but always on good holds and no harder than the Sròn. Mainly Grade 2 except for one airy step up and a hard move above a big ledge.

Approach
Start at the ski car park (NN 266 524) and traverse under Creag Dhubh as for the previous route but then either slog up the slopes east of the northeast ridge of Stob a' Ghlais Choire to the 700m level where the ridge starts to become defined or (better) do either of the other two routes and reach the same point by reaching then descending the broken slopes and scree south-east of the Arête.

The Route
The ridge starts with broken rock a little above a stream junction then

*North-East Spur, Stob a' Ghlais Choire (Route 181, Grade 2).
Scrambler: Lucy Williams. Photo: Noel Williams.*

becomes a better-defined slabby rib, climbed either by a central groove or by slabs on either side. Where the rib becomes grassy move up right and ascend fairly easy rock on the skyline to a grass terrace below steeper rock. Go up steps just right of the nose, move left onto the crest, then follow a ramp up left to the edge. Make an exposed step up on the exact arête then work up right. Climb a steep groove on good holds, then easier rock leads to the vertical upper wall. Bypass this by an awkward slabby mantelshelf into the groove on the right, hard but safe. The wider groove on the left is no easier and much more exposed.

181 Stob a' Ghlais Choire, North-East Spur   Grade 1 or 2   *
Alt 500m   Ht Gain +200m   (NN 247 523)   Map p332   Diag p349

Much of this is walking up rock slabs but the rock is excellent and there are a few steeper sections. It makes a fun descent for the competent.

Approach
From the ski car park (NN 266 524) traverse right below Creag Dhubh (boggy path) and cross the Allt Cam Ghlinne about 100m above the scenic falls at NN 248 526. Keep ahead up to the foot of the spur, which is the left-hand and much longer of two masses of rock, steepening at the bottom.

The Route
Start at the bottom left above easy angled quartzite slabs and take a left to right ramp onto the buttress. Head right up easy angled slabs and follow the broad spur on clean rock. Most of this is walking, but with the odd move where hands are needed. At a little over half height it steepens briefly and splits into two rock spurs separated by grass. The left-hand one is Grade 2, the right-hand Grade 1. The spurs merge and more rough easy rock leads to the top of the ridge. Either walk up 120m or so of scree to the summit of Stob a' Ghlais Choire or traverse right across the top of broken rock spurs to drop down south-east of Inglis Clark Arête (Route 180) to reach its start.

STOB GHABHAR 1090m

OS Landranger 50   (NN 230 455)   Map p332

A complex peak with at least half a dozen spurs separated by little visited corries. Much of the rock is quite broken but outcrops can easily be linked together to form longer routes. Two obvious routes are described but there are many more options. See also Route 173 on Meall Odhar which can be used to approach the mountain from the west.

182 Aonach Eagach, South-East Nose   Grade 3   *
Alt 400m   Ht Gain +300m   (NN 248 443)   Map p332

A route in three well separated parts. First a stepped waterfall, then cracked ribs and grooves up a blunt spur (quite hard), topped off by an easy narrow ridge.

STOB GHABHAR

Approach
From the car park at the west end of Loch Tulla (NN 270 418) go north across Victoria Bridge then turn left alongside the Abhainn Shira. Turn right by the tiny former schoolhouse at Clashgour to follow a well used stalkers path up alongside Allt Toaig, then fork left at the 300m contour to cross the stream and go up to the prominent waterfall of An Steallair.

The Route
Go up a short groove left of the lowest fall, continuing up between two branches of the stream to a rowan tree. Go right to zigzag up a steeper wall on positive holds. Follow slabs up rightwards and climb a short wall next to a fence post (hard to start if wet). The last and largest fall has to be avoided by a path on the right. At the top follow the path alongside the stream for another 100m before heading up right across tussocky ground towards the cliffs of the South-East Nose. Aim for a pale rib at the bottom right above a scree patch.

Start on the right-hand side of the rib and traverse left onto it as soon as feasible. Go up to a ledge below steeper rock. Move slightly right and zigzag up to grass, then either pull up left onto the crest at big spikes and climb a short groove above or go up right and ascend an easier weakness. The ground now eases and after a couple of minor outcrops the best route traverses well left to a pinkish slab seamed with cracks. Go leftwards up this to its apex, where it abuts against a steeper band and a higher slab. It is possible to escape left here onto easier slabs and up these. Better though is to move 3m right and climb a prominent crack on excellent holds (the thinner crack directly above the apex of the lower slab is quite a lot harder). Even this right-hand crack is quite sustained and exposed though. Where it peters out go up left to easier ground, where minor outcrops soon lead to walking. Continue up the spur to the Aonach Eagach itself, which is an enjoyably narrow arête, barely scrambling but still fun.

 183 Lochan Buttress   Grade 2 or 3   *
Alt 700m   Ht Gain +300m   (NN 234 458)   Map p332   Diag p354
Better and more sustained than it looks from a distance. Outcrops and a streamlet lead to a steep crux and a final sharp arête.

Approach
As for the previous route up the Allt Toaig, but stay on the stalkers path to the saddle at the head of the corrie and up to a minor levelling at about 760m. Descend westwards to reach the lochan, with the route starting at its south-west corner. The levelling can also be reached from the top of the south-east nose of the Aonach Eagach using a not-very-obvious deer path, but failing to find the path would leave you traversing awkward rough ground with many small cliffs. A scrappy but enjoyable scramble can be made up this ground, starting up the right-hand side of the slabs at NN 242 455.

The Route
From the lowest rocks at the south-west corner of the lochan climb a rib, possibly dodging left at the steepest bit. Slabs on the left lead to walking, then minor craglets take you to the bed of a tiny stream that rather oddly runs down the crest of the spur. Follow this for further than you expect on surprisingly good holds, going up through a steeper wall until it becomes scree. Move up left to a cliff with a prominent quartz blob. Pull steeply onto the quartz and up the groove above (loose), or climb the harder but cleaner rib to the left. Another slabby outcrop up right leads to more open ground, where many easy slablets run up right towards a prominent tower, getting steeper as you approach it. This is very much the crux and is briefly quite exposed, avoidable by walking round the tower on the left.

There is a large overhung niche centrally at 10m. Work up right into this, steep but on good holds. Tiptoe airily right round the edge to arrive suddenly at easy ground. Go up left to the crest and climb a groove, then easier steps above. The avoiding detour comes in here. Carry on up to clamber along a superb knife edge and cross a minor pinnacle. A final tower can either be climbed on big loose spikes or avoided, reaching easy ground almost at the summit of Stob Gabhar, 400m above the lochan. The final arête can be enjoyed on its own by a short detour left from the north-west ridge, a short steep gully taking you to the start of the knife edge.

The Cruachan Range

A long and fairly sharp east-west ridge with several peaks and a sprawl of spurs on both sides, Cruachan dominates western Argyll. The southern horseshoe around the top of the reservoir is a classic loop and the eastern 'Dalmally Horseshoe' is popular too. With a bit of ingenuity the two scrambles described can be incorporated into these two loops, but either is a worthwhile objective in its own right.

BEN CRUACHAN 1126m

OS Landranger 50   (NN 070 305)   Map p356

The presiding peak of the range has a nice sharp summit, with a little easy scrambling on its East Ridge, but the best scramble is on its slightly smaller twin just to the west, Stob Dearg (also known as the Taynuilt Peak).

184 Stob Dearg, North Ridge   Grade 1
Alt 700m   Ht Gain +350m   (NN 063 314)   Map p356

Slabby outcrops in a great wild setting. The scrambling doesn't amount to much but the atmosphere is wonderful, with a real sense of remoteness.

Approach
There is very limited parking opposite Brander Lodge at a gate (NN 036 294).

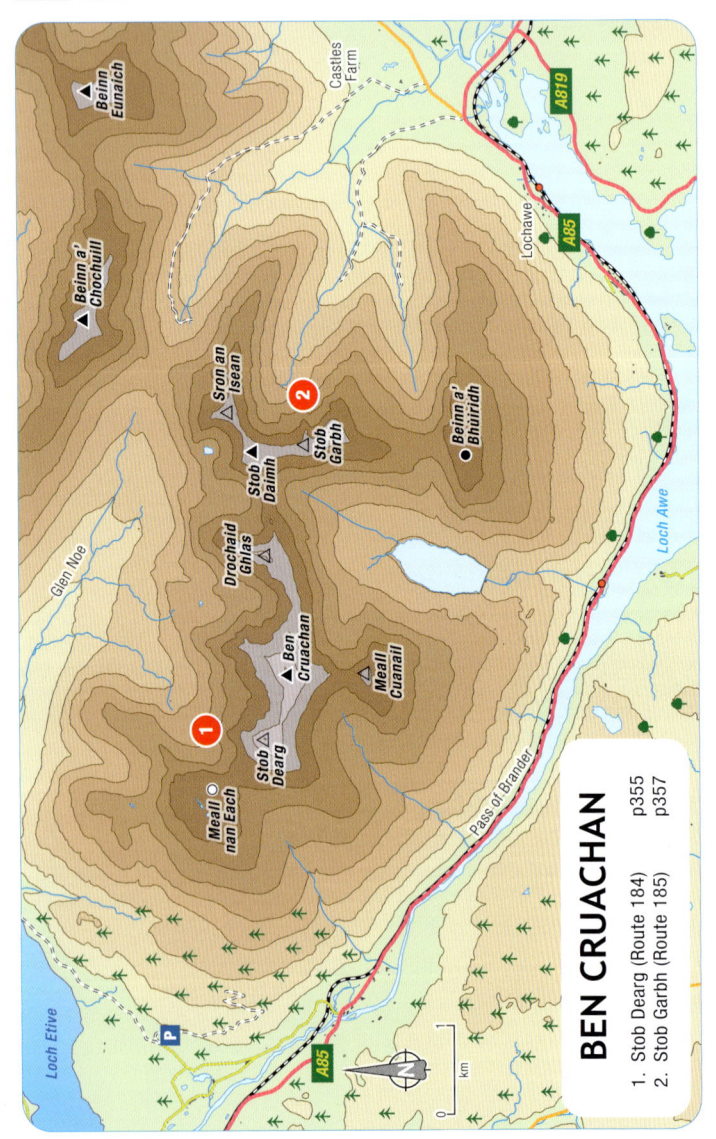

Go under the railway at a bridge for a stream 100m east and head up the stream bank. Where the ground steepens radically go up the east bank of the Allt Gruiniche on a sketchy path leading out to open country. Continue up steeply at first, then more gently to reach the saddle between Meall nan Each and Stob Dearg. Cross this and descend from the higher (south-east) part of the saddle to slant down below slabby cliffs. Once past the slabs go up right to reach the foot of the ridge.

The saddle can also be reached by following the normal approach for Cruachan past the reservoir to the col north of Meall Cuanail. A long traverse with some up and down leads round the south flank of Stob Dearg. This allows the scramble to fit into the southern horseshoe but is a bit of a convoluted approach.

The Route
The ridge is broad at first, with the best rock on the left-hand side, where the drop to the left adds spice. Clamber up granite slabs and boulders, steepening near the top. Difficulties can be found if required, particularly some nice balancy slabs.

STOB DAIMH 998m

OS Landranger 50   (NN 094 308)   Map p356

Cruachan's second peak (mis-spelled on OS maps for years) has a pair of minor summits either side of it. The southern of these has a subsidiary ridge which gives some scrambling.

185 Stob Garbh, North-East Ridge   Grade 1
Alt 750m   Ht Gain +250m   (NN 099 303)   Map p356

A blunt ridge with some nice positions but the scrambling is not as good as it looks from a distance.

Approach
Park on the side road at the Stronmilchan turning, where the B8077 leaves the main A85 (132 283). Follow the farm track in a north-westerly direction, slanting up left at the first junction past a quarry. Continue to a bridge over the Allt Coire Ghlais, cross this and carry on up the track into Coire Chreachainn. Once the track ends carry on up past a vertical fall, then at a more complex cascade go up left to the foot of the buttress.

The Route
The initial face is steep and vegetated, so go right below it and up a grassy scoop. Work up left on vegetated steps and ledges to reach the crest above the steep part. The ridge narrows as the angle eases, then steepens again. Dodge the steepest part on the right then follow the crest, crossing an easy narrow arête with a small tower before rough slopes lead up to the summit of Stob Garbh.

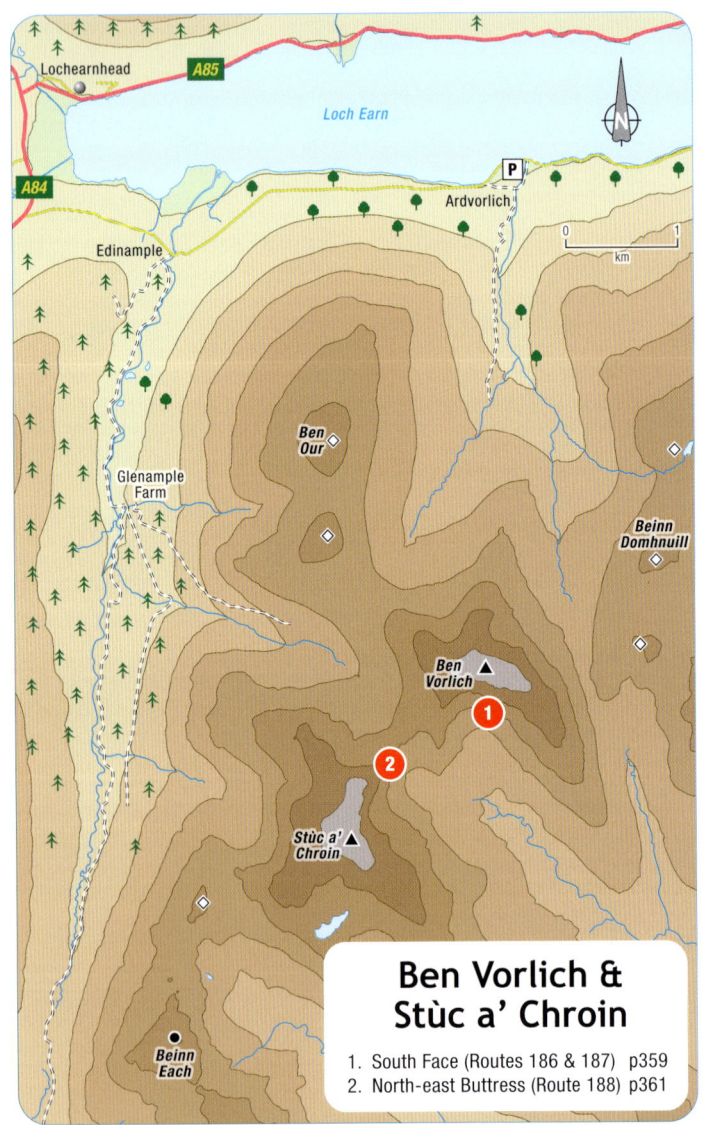

SOUTHERN HIGHLANDS

This is a large area but the mica schist of which most of it is composed tends to produce scatters of small outcrops rather than continuous cliffs. The one glorious exception is The Cobbler, where frost shattering during the ice ages has left a trio of jagged peaks whose traverse is one of the classic Scottish hill days. The hills around the Cobbler provide a few more scrambles, while there are minor routes spread across the region. Also included here are routes on Colonsay and Islay, isolated bits of fun which don't really fit anywhere else.

The Loch Earn Hills

The twin hills of Ben Vorlich and Stùc a' Chroin are prominent from many places in the Central Belt and they are usually climbed together to make an enjoyable round with superb views. Starts at Loch Lubnaig, Callander and Glen Artney are possible, but to include the scrambles it is best to begin from the south side of Loch Earn at either Ardvorlich or Edinample.

BEN VORLICH 986m

OS Landranger 57   (NN 629 189)   Map p358

Ben Vorlich itself has a few minor outcrops on the south-west ridge, while the south face has several ribs of clean though rather broken rock. They fit in well if doing Stùc a' Chroin first.

186 South Face, Central Rib   Grade 2
Alt 700m   Ht Gain + 150m   (NN 628 186)   Map p358   Diag p360

Good rock, but steep sections force avoiding action in places.

Approach
The bealach between Ben Vorlich and Stùc a' Chroin can be reached by starting along a track on the east side of the Ardvorlich Burn (NN 633 232). Fork right past buildings, cross a bridge and turn left onto a track up the west side of Glen Vorlich. Fork right away from the Ardvorlich Burn, and eventually cross the Allt a' Choire Bhuidhe. Then, at about 530m, follow a small path which slants up the west side of the north ridge just below its steepest part. Once over the saddle keep traversing to reach Bealach an Dubh Choirein.

A more direct route comes up from Edinample (NN 601 223). There is very limited parking but the Falls of Edinample just below the road are superb. Follow the track up the glen until it crosses the river, then go along the east bank of the river before following signs to rejoin the track beyond Glenample Farm. Turn right and after 100m turn left up a small path (waymarked but not obvious) to join a higher forestry track. Follow this into Coire Fhuadaraich with Bealach an Dubh Choirein at its head.

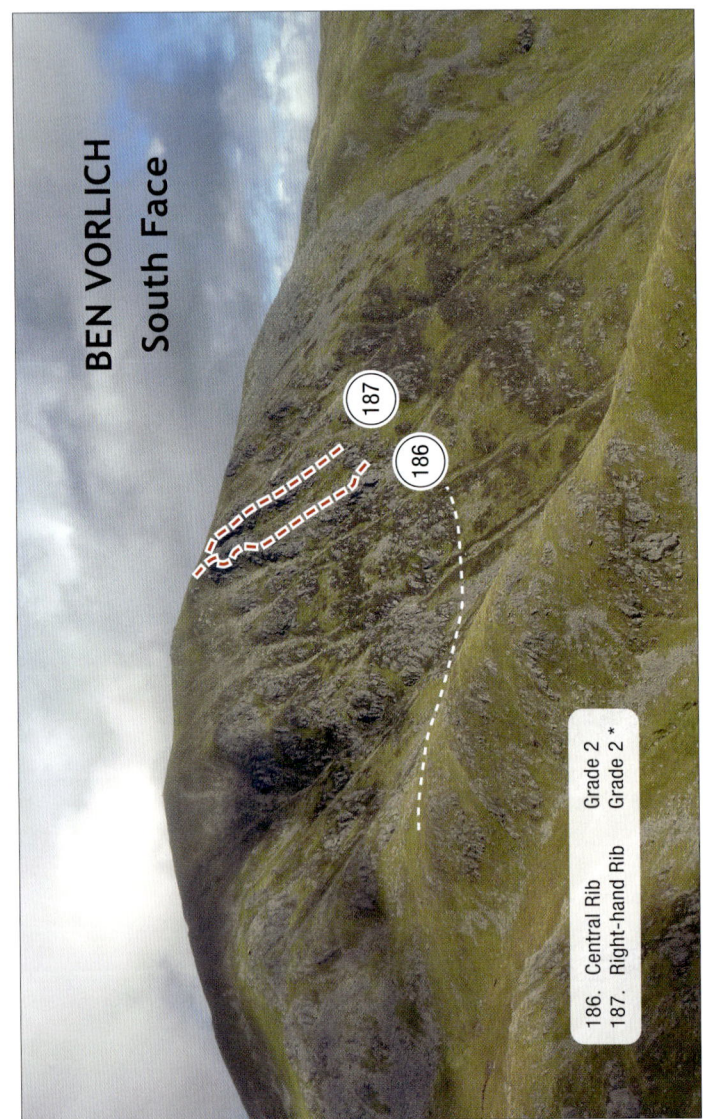

If climbing Stùc a' Chroin first then from its summit slant down west of the north top to the minor col at NN 615 181. From here a path goes steeply down right to pass under the crags and reach the bealach.

From the bealach go up the first bump then cut down right to the foot of the rocky part of the face. Go rightwards up scree and broken ground to the most continuous rib on the face, right of centre.

The Route
The obvious direct start (V Diff?) is avoided on the right to gain the rib above the first buttress. Go up left to the crest and up boulders. Climb a steeper wall on good holds, then carry on up the crest to a steep tower. Move up the left side, at first by a steep grassy groove, then moving left to avoid steeper rock and climbing a grassy chimney. Return to the crest above this for an easy finish.

187 South Face, Right-hand Rib   Grade 2   *
Alt 700m   Ht Gain +150m   (NN 629 186)   Map p358   Diag p360

Some nice sharp arête sections with a couple of steeper towers, mostly on good rock but with the odd loose flake.

Approach
As for the previous route but continue to the rightmost rib.

The Route
The rib has a steep tower near the top and splits into two below it. The right-hand branch has some good scrambling but includes sections of V Diff climbing on suspect rock which will force most scramblers off the ridge. The left-hand branch is quite bouldery at first, then coalesces into a more defined rib. Follow this to arrive below the steep tower, which is avoided on the left. Some excellent ridge follows, with a steeper wall overcome by either the central groove (harder than it looks) or an energetic pull on the big flake to its right.

STÙC A' CHROIN 975m

OS Landranger 57   (NN 617 174)   Map p358

Usually combined with Ben Vorlich in an excellent hill day, into which this scramble can easily be incorporated.

188 North-East Buttress   Grade 1 or 2
Alt 800m   Ht Gain +100m   (NN 620 181)   Map p358

Good positions but quite grassy, much easier than it looks.

Approach
If planning to include this scramble it is best to climb Ben Vorlich first, either by the obvious north ridge path up Glen Vorlich or by the more complicated route from Glen Ample described above. From the lip of Coire Fhuadaraich

*North-East Buttress, Stùc a' Chroin (Route 188, Grade 1 or 2).
Scrambler: Dave Edley. Photo: Noel Williams.*

(NN 611 192) you can either go straight up to the Vorlich/Stùc a' Chroin col or climb Ben Vorlich first via its north-west Ridge. From the summit of Ben Vorlich a clear path runs down to the Bealach an Dubh Choirein.

The Route
Just above the col a clean slab off left is sadly too steep for scrambling, although its right edge can be sneaked up. The main scrambling begins at a boulder slope below intimidating steep rock. Go up the left-hand of two boulder fans to reach a zigzag path. Where this traverses off right head up grass to overhanging rock. Traverse horizontally left on good holds to boulders above the first section of cliff. Boulders and grass ledges lead up to more steep rock, which forces you rightwards round the crest into a grassy gully. Go up this briefly, then escape right up more boulders, before working back up left to an airy perch on the crest. More boulders lead to a final upthrust, avoidable on the left. A Grade 2 direct finish involves steep pulls through a niche on the right, dodging right of a vertical wall and finishing with a pull up on the absolute crest.

In poor weather, this north top has been mistaken for the summit, which is about 400m south and about 50m higher.

The Arrochar Alps

A tight group of steep rocky peaks squeezed in between Loch Long, Loch Lomond and Loch Fyne, these superb hills are justly popular. For many Glaswegians in particular they have provided a great introduction to hillwalking, scrambling and climbing.

THE COBBLER 884m

OS Landranger 56   (NN 259 058)   Map p364

One of the few mainland hills that requires scrambling just to reach the summit, the Cobbler is undoubtedly one of Scotland's best-loved peaks. The distinctive triple prong is easily recognisable from a distance and the views from it are terrific. Whether enjoying the excellent rock and winter climbing, completing the classic ridge traverse or just bagging the summit, satisfaction is guaranteed.

189 South–North Traverse   Grade 3, Moderate or Difficult   ***
Alt 750m   (NN 261 057)   Map p364

The classic day out, with several possible variants. Although the actual scrambling isn't as good as on some of the other major traverses the situations and scenery are superb. Mica schist gets very slippery in the wet. The various parts of the route are often done separately and are described with this in mind.

Approach
There is a large car park just west of Arrochar, testimony to the mountain's

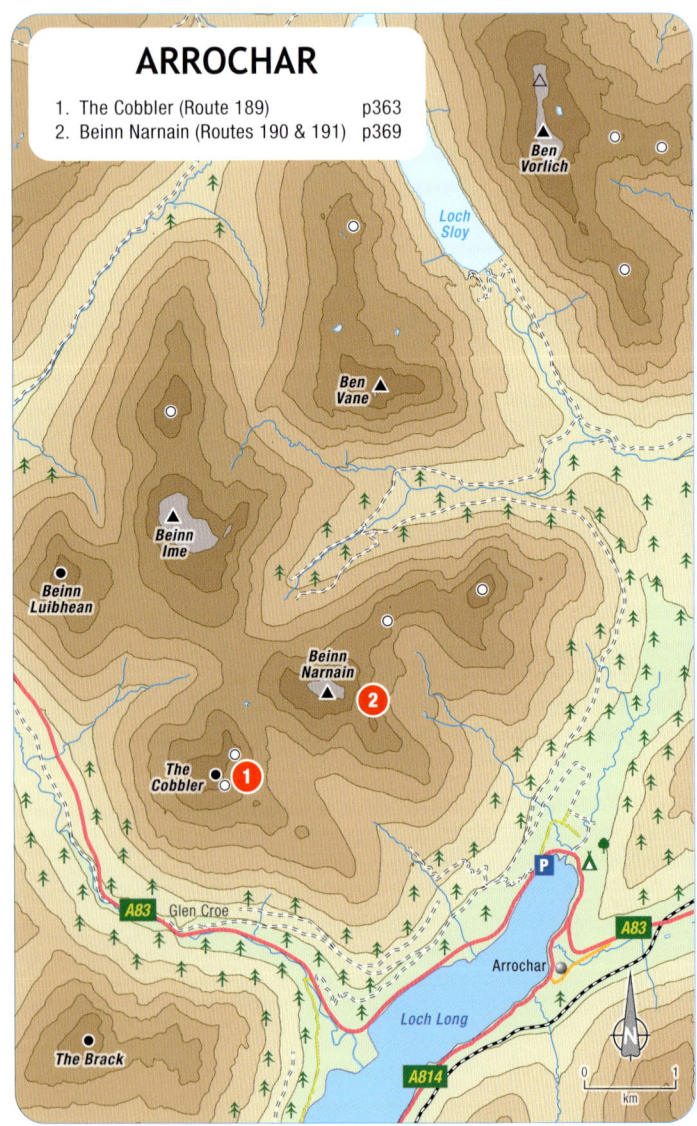

enduring popularity – this is one route you won't have to yourself. A good path leads up to the Narnain Boulders at 470m. Soon after this fork left and cross the Allt a' Bhalachain. Follow the built path until beyond a steep slabby crag on the left at about 600m, then traverse up left to the col on the south-east ridge at about 680m. It is also possible to leave the path below the Narnain Boulders and go up to join the south-east ridge lower down. Either way, follow the ridge up to the lowest rocks of the South Peak.

The Route

a) South Peak, South-East Ridge   Grade 3   *
This is the easiest way up the peak, so be prepared to reverse it. The first section is avoidable on the left, and in descent always is. Slant up right on shelves to a steepening on the exact arête. Step round the edge and make an exposed pull up (Moderate), then go up a groove to easy ground. Carry on up the crest and over big boulders to a col. The easy variation comes in from the left here. Above the col either go up airily right then left or pull steeply up right from a short groove just left. Carry on up bouldery steps (path on left) to another col. Climb a left-slanting crack (crux, worth Moderate if damp), then an easier crack and a bouldery step lead to the top. Either return the way you came or descend the following route.

b) South Peak, North-West Face   Difficult   **   Diag p367
In descent, go a few metres down westwards before descending a short steep crack to a ledge. Go down right to a grass bay, then cut back left down an exposed slabby ramp, with an awkward off balance move halfway down. Reach a grass ledge with relief and follow it right to another tricky move down to the col.

In ascent (easier, as usual), make a tricky move up right from the col, follow the ledge right till it ends, then go leftwards up the slabby ramp to the grass niche (awkward move left in the middle). Go up right briefly then either thug up the steep crack or climb onto a boulder just left and pull airily onto the summit (the latter is not an option for the short).

c) Central Peak, South-East Arête   Moderate or Difficult   **
From the South Peak/Central Peak col go up to and climb either of two steep cracks (left one jamming, right one easy to start then a thrutch, neither being soft touches for Difficult). They are easily avoidable on the left, reducing the grade to Moderate. Where the routes rejoin go right and up a grassy groove to regain the crest. A narrow arête leads to an exposed delicate slab which leads enjoyably to the summit. Descend by the next route to reach the cairn.

d) Central Peak, Doorway Route   Grade 3   **   Diag p368
If ascending from the cairned summit climb into the nearest hole in the summit tor from the left. Go through it and along the ledge on the far side. A short slab leads to a niche, then clamber onto a boulder and step left onto the summit.

189d. Centre Peak, Doorway Route — Grade 3 **

SOUTHERN HIGHLANDS

In descent, face back the way you have come, go down right awkwardly into the niche, then go down a slab, along the ledge and through the hole to the cairned summit.

e) North Peak
This isn't really scrambling but is well worth doing for the lovely airy views. Follow the path down from the cairned summit to the col, well left of the ridge line. Some scrappy scrambling can be contrived by keeping to the ridge initially, but the lower part is a dead end. A good path leads up left of the crest to finish up easy slabs onto the North Peak. Dare you stand on the wildly exposed end? To descend either retrace your steps to the built path which reaches the North Peak/Centre Peak col from the Arrochar side or follow the broad ridge north-west to pick up the path down to the Narnain col. Both Beinn Ime and Beinn Narnain are easily reached from here.

BEINN NARNAIN 926m

OS Landranger 56   **(NN 272 066)**   **Map p364**

Quite a rocky hill but the crags lack continuity. Close to the summit is the distinctive Spearhead Block which has several easy climbs which ambitious scramblers may enjoy.

190 Spearhead Arête   Difficult   **
Alt 900m   *Ht Gain +40m*   (NN 274 066)   *Map p364*   *Diag p370*

Steep and exposed for the grade but on good positive holds.

Approach
A good add-on to the Cobbler Traverse, gained by walking up the west ridge of Narnain from the col between it and the Cobbler (some minor scrambling can be found on the way up). Pass over the summit and the Spearhead soon comes into view. Descend either side and head for the lowest rocks on the east end. From Arrochar climb the east ridge of Narnain over Cruach nam Miseag to reach the Spearhead just before the summit.

Route
a) Right-hand
Start at the left corner of the lowest rocks and go up easily to a grass ledge, then up a short groove to another ledge on the left. It is now possible to pull awkwardly up right onto the very steep front and climb sharp jugs until forced left to the top of the Spearhead.

b) Left-hand
Alternatively, from the ledge pull up left to a boulder on the left arête (easy escape possible on left), then step up right onto the face and climb this to the top of the Spearhead, more insecure but less steep.

From the Spearhead move up on more sharp jugs to an exposed pull up on the arête, then easier ground leads to the top. The top of the Spearhead

can also be gained from well to the right, starting up a greasy groove just above the mouth of the right-hand gully (Moderate, but much less good).

191 Restricted Crack   Moderate   *
Alt 900m   Ht Gain +30m   (NN 274 066)   Map p364   Diag p370
A steepish crack with a couple of awkward moves. Easy for the grade although the start requires some commitment.

Approach
The crack at the left end of the south face of the Spearhead Block.

Route
Oomph into the crack then surmount two boulders to a big ledge. Climb a steep left slanting crack to a nice perch, then follow the much easier crackline above.

Further right the vertical cleft of Jamblock Chimney is V Diff, with an awkward exit through a hole at the top, for the slim and speleologically inclined only.

Other Routes in the Arrochar Alps
Some of the other Arrochar peaks have minor scrambling, the best being the east ridge of Ben Vane, which has innumerable optional slabby outcrops, some quite delicate and serious. The north ridge of Beinn an Lochain and the north-east ridge of Ben Ime both have short steep sections and narrow arêtes where hands are useful (Grade 1). On The Brack, *Edge Route* on the Split Pinnacle is fun. This well-named feature is about 100m below and 250 metres east of the summit (NN 247 030). Start on the south-east corner of the long side and follow the arête (Grade 3). The step off the pinnacle to regain the hillside is distinctly exciting. The nearby *Inglis Clark Ridge* (Moderate) is steep grass with short vertical walls and wins no prizes. For the mildly barmy, the landslip on the east ridge of Ben Donich at NN 233 044 can be descended by jumping from block to block. Note that the last jump is further than you want it to be, but by that stage you're completely committed.

Other Routes in the Southern Highlands
On Beinn Laoigh (NN 266 262), the left-hand rim of Coire Gaothach can provide some minor Grade 1 scrambling if followed direct, but on the South Rib to its right you mostly end up forced onto steep vegetation by short vertical rock steps. Both routes are excellent in winter. Just to the north the prominent quartz rib on the north-east shoulder of Beinn Udlaidh gives some rather artificial but fun scrambling in two sections (NN 283 348). A few slabby outcrops low down on the north-west ridge of Beinn Chaluim are fun (NN 379 328), while Beinn Achaladair's north ridge (NN 346 437) is a good line with some outcrops at the top, again better in winter. However, the prominent line on Meall Buidhe to its left, the winter climb of *Echo Edge*, is

very loose and grassy, though a good line (NN 354 436), while the two buttresses on the east side of Gleann Meran (NN 398 453) are similarly steep and vegetated. Probably the best easy scrambling in Breadalbane is on the traverse of the Tarmachans (NN 585 390), where both the narrow summit of Meall Garbh and the descent from Beinn nan Eachan can feel quite exposed.

Stretching the boundaries slightly, the south ridge of Beinn Duirinish above Bonawe (NN 021 347) has some nice granite slabs, reached by more broken vegetated ground.

Colonsay & Islay

These two islands are both accessed from the ferry port at Kennacraig at the north end of Kintyre, so visits to them can easily be combined.

COLONSAY

OS Landranger 61

Colonsay is a delightful island well worth spending some time on, with a rugged coast, lots of small rough hills and a surprisingly remote feel. The obvious highlights are the ruins of the mediaeval priory on the tidal island of Oronsay and the superb sandy beach of Kiloran Bay. Ferries run from Oban and Kennacraig, the latter calling at Port Askaig on Islay, enabling a combined trip to both islands and also Jura.

From a scrambling point of view Carnan Eoin (NR 409 985), the island's highest point, has a nice south-west ridge above Kiloran Bay with some schisty steps (Grade 1/2), and if killing time waiting for the ferry then the boulders at NR 391 937 are worth a look (just below the monument). Swing onto the lower one from the right, climb it and step across the gulf to climb the second on sharp quartz ripples (Grade 3). By far the best scramble on the island, however, is the following.

192 Beinn nan Caorach West Ridge   Grade 2   *
Alt 50m   Ht Gain + 60m   (NR 363 939)

A blunt ridge of juggy quartzite.

Approach
Take the road from Scalasaig straight across to the west coast. As you arrive at the coast crags appear on the right, first the buttresses of Sliabh Riabhach, set back a little, then across a small valley the furthest west prow is Beinn nan Caorach, with the blunt crest obvious.

The Route
A steep juggy wall low down on the left provides an optional start, then go over a hump to the buttress proper. Climb just left of the crest on big but occasionally loose holds. Near the top a grassy groove splits the crest into an easy right-hand line or a set of short and steep but positive walls on the left. The scale of the view is completely out of proportion to the size of the hill.

SOUTHERN HIGHLANDS

ISLAY

OS Landranger 60

Islay is one of the largest of the Inner Hebrides, roughly 40 by 30km, and also one of the most fertile, with a much higher proportion of farmland than its neighbours, often reminiscent of Galloway or parts of Ulster. Its eastern part has several knobbly quartzite hills upon which some scrambling can be contrived, but this is not continuous and is best enjoyed as brief incidents in a hill day. By far the best scramble on the island is on the south-west peninsula of the Oa. This is rimmed by shaggy sea cliffs, up to 150m high in places, largely very loose but making a superb coastal walk. About 2km east of the Mull of Oa itself is the promontory fort of Dun Athad, and running seawards from this is a baby Alpine arête.

193 Dun Athad   Grade 1 or 2   *
Alt Sea Level   Ht Gain +200m   (NR 284 405)

Not worth a visit from afar for its own sake, but atmospheric and well worth doing if on the island. The star is for the excellent situations more than the scrambling itself.

Approach

The Mull of Oa is a bird reserve, with a car park at NR 281 422. Take the well signed path out to the monument on the Mull, commemorating the loss of the American troopships Otranto and Tuscania at the end of World War I (one torpedoed, the other wrecked in a storm). Several hundred troops died. From the monument follow the coast eastwards on a good path. After crossing the stream and fence below Upper Killeyan Farm head right (bits of path) to pass inland of the projecting summit of Dun Athad fort and descend to the shore beyond it. Cut back westwards along the shore to reach the foot of the ridge. To reach this point from the west involves climbing a vertical wall of about Difficult (impossible to reach at most states of the tide), but the sea stacks in the bay just to the west are worth a look if the tide is out, one hollow, the other with a two-tiered arch. Immediately under the overhanging west face is a prehistoric settlement, now used for shelter by the many feral goats in the area.

The Route

The ridge is easy at first, then becomes an exposed crest. Cleaner steeper rock to the right is Grade 2. Follow the arête over two steeper steps, easiest on the right or Grade 2 on the crest direct. The many signs of traffic are created by goats not people! The fort is a splendid viewpoint, originally built in the Iron Age but occupied into mediaeval times. Leaving it involves crossing a moderately airy gap (by walking standards), take care in the wet on the steepish grass.

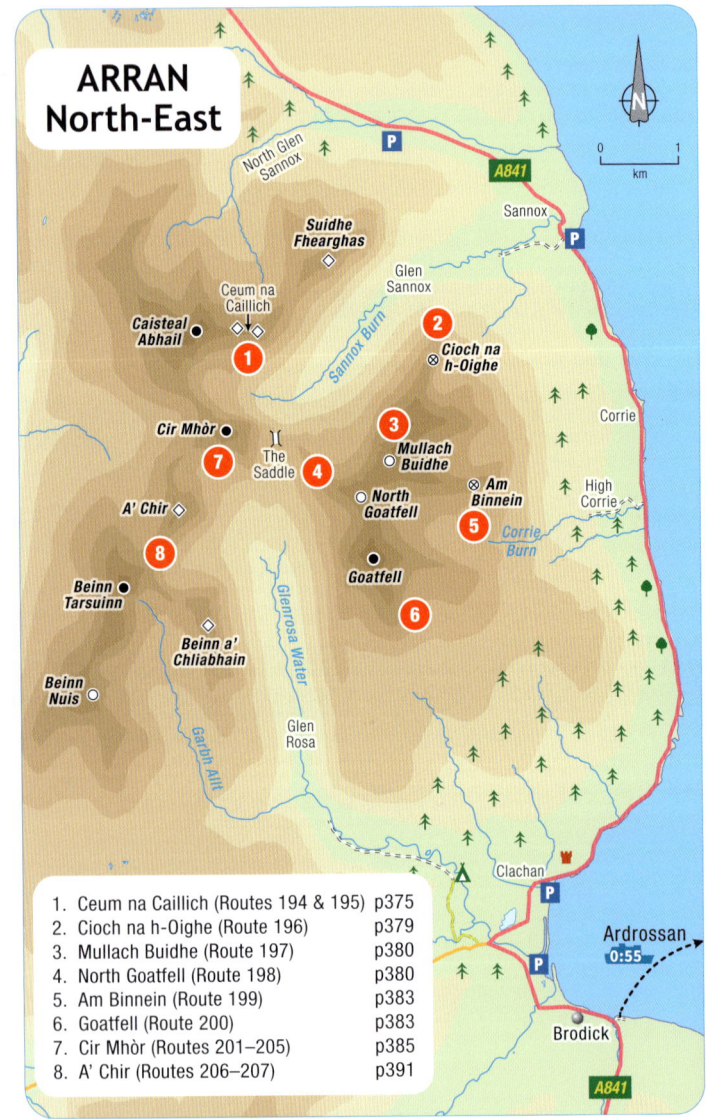

ARRAN North-East

1. Ceum na Caillich (Routes 194 & 195) p375
2. Cioch na h-Oighe (Route 196) p379
3. Mullach Buidhe (Route 197) p380
4. North Goatfell (Route 198) p380
5. Am Binnein (Route 199) p383
6. Goatfell (Route 200) p383
7. Cir Mhòr (Routes 201–205) p385
8. A' Chir (Routes 206–207) p391

ARRAN

The granite intrusion that forms the northern half of Arran has been ice-shattered into a twisted H of jagged ridges. Not only do parts of the ridges themselves provide excellent scrambling but there are myriads of rocky lines up to them of all standards, walking, scrambling and climbing on rough granite. Cir Mhòr in particular ranks with the best peaks in the country, but A' Chir, Goatfell and Caisteal Abhail are gems too. Even the more rounded Pirnmill Hills on the west coast have one fine scrambling ridge on Beinn Bharrain. The compactness of the area is another of its attractions, enabling a large number of routes to be accomplished in one trip.

The Rosa & Sannox Hills

The main group of hills on the island forms an H of ridges surrounding glens Rosa and Sannox, with scrambles both on the ridges and their flanks. They are described moving from north to south and a great day out can be had by linking several together. The two classic trips are the horseshoe rounds of the two main glens. The Glen Rosa Horseshoe combines Routes 207 and 198, and 206 and 202 can easily be included. The Glen Sannox Round starts up Route 196, descends 198, and eventually takes in 194, with 197 and 205 involving only minor detours.

CAISTEAL ABHAIL 847m

OS Landranger 69   (NR 967 443)   Map p374

A flat topped hill with summit rock tors and three enjoyable ridges, two easy and one spectacular, the traverse of the spike and gash of Ceum na Caillich (Witch's Step) being one of the island's classic outings.

194 Ceum na Caillich   Grade 1, 2 or V Diff   **
Alt 650m   (NR 977 443)   Map p374   Diag p376

Superb situations but only mediocre scrambling, and frustratingly hard if taken direct. Either direction is feasible, with more uphill scrambling on the east to west version, but this involves descending (or sensibly avoiding!) the crux. Those doing the round of Glen Sannox will do it in reverse, descending the easier scrambling to be faced with the short but decidedly tricky slab beyond the gash. More people take the avoiding route than tackle it direct, which is both hard and exposed. Protection is excellent however for those using a rope.

Approach
Going east to west it is usual to park at North Sannox Bridge (NR 993 468), from where a path leads up southwards and up to the summit of Suidhe Fhearghas ('Fergus's Seat'), from where Fergus Mac Erc, the first Scottish king,

Climbing the direct route up the east side of Ceum na Caillich (Witch's Step). (Route 194a, Very Difficult). Photo: H. MacRobert (SMC Image Archive).

is supposed to have surveyed his kingdom after coming across from Ireland in the early 6th Century. The view is certainly well worth the effort. From here an easy ridge runs south-west to a broad saddle before rising to the start of the rock.

Coming eastwards the scrambling starts right at the summit of Caisteal Abhail, which requires hands to reach.

The Route
East to West
The ridge rises easily at first towards the pointed summit overlooking the gash of Ceum na Caillich itself, then there is an exposed and awkward step onto the final summit block (which of course has to be reversed too). There are three commonly used descents. Direct is V Diff and most scramblers will avoid it, and there is a Grade 2 version down the north flank, but this is hard to find from above and better in ascent.

The best option is to return down the north-east ridge to the start of the rocks and take a clear path traversing the north flank with some Grade 1 scrambling. This descends a steep groove on good holds to reach the gully on the north side of the notch. From the notch zigzag right up broken slabs to reach the left skyline at a big slab. From here a path slants along the left side of the ridge, avoiding virtually all difficulties. It is much more fun to go up the big slab and follow the crest over three tops before descending to a col. A sharp crest then leads up to easy ground below the summit of Caisteal Abhail, reached by a short wall.

West to East
From Caisteal Abhail descend the summit tor and follow the ridge eastwards, either clambering over the minor tops or using the path on the right. Both ways lead to the same rather loose zigzag down slabs into the notch.
a) The direct route from here is V Diff – climb the short groove directly ahead then the tricky overhung slab on the left (wedging a limb in the crack on the right helps). No wonder the ancients wore hairy breeches! Continue direct more easily to finish up a groove and crack just left of the summit block, which is best reached round to the left.
b) The Grade 2 version involves descending the North Gully for about 30m, then traversing left on well used spikes to a grass ledge. Cracked slabs above develop into a path zigzagging up to the ridge just east of the summit.
c) The easiest option (Grade 1) is to go a further 10m down North Gully and climb a blocky groove. This leads to a path traversing across the north flank to reach grass slopes beyond all difficulties, from where the summit can be easily reached (except for the top block!).

195 Little Broomstick Ridge Grade 2 *
Alt 500m   Ht Gain +100m   (NR 977 442)   Map p374   Diag p376
The steep spur just right of the gully leading up to the gash of Ceum na Caillich from Glen Sannox is Broomstick Ridge (Diff), and just right of this is

its baby brother, with a steep face on its right halfway up. It provides varied scrambling on good granite, fairly escapable, with a purgatorial approach.

Approach
Either slog up the heather directly from Glen Sannox (parking NS 016 453) or slant down from the saddle south-west of Suidhe Fhearghas (NR 981 447) across pathless heather, losing about 70m of height and keeping below the lowest rocks. From this direction the steep face right of Little Broomstick Ridge is prominent. Neither way is all that pleasant.

The Route
From the lowest rocks go up easy slabs and heather, with the ridge gradually becoming more defined. At the first steep nose slant up left before traversing right to regain the ridge. Carry on up the slabby crest, with a mantel onto a perched block to reach a grass rake. Go right up this to the crest and up slabs. At the next steep nose start on the left and go up right to a groove, then up slabs. At another nose step right onto a flake and climb a wide crack. An easing slabby crest continues to the top, arriving on the main ridge a little east of the Ceum na Caillich summit.

GOATFELL 874m

OS Landranger 69   (NR 992 415)   Map p374

The highest hill on Arran and by far its most popular summit, Goatfell is a much more complex and rugged mountain than the casual tourists see. The broad north ridge runs over Mullach Buidhe to the scenic aiguille of Cioch na h-Oighe, with plenty of rock on both flanks – unfortunately most of it very loose and vegetated. The West Ridge of North Goatfell running down to the Saddle between Glens Rosa and Sannox has some optional scrambling, while there are interesting crags on the flanks of both southern ridges, including the huge Rosa Slabs and the excellent climbing ground of the South Slabs, home to the friction padding classics of Blank, Blankist and Pochmahone.

196 Cioch na h-Oighe   Grade 1   *
Alt 400m   Ht Gain +200m   (NR 000 444)   Map p374

Mostly walking amid heather fields but a little easy scrambling on the way up leads to a lovely summit and a fun sharp ridge. The star is more for the situations than the scrambling itself.

Approach
From the car park at the foot of Glen Sannox (NS 016 453) take the path up the south side of the glen for about 1km. Turn left on a smaller path up the east bank of the Allt a' Chapuill, crossing it as the ground flattens out to follow sketchier paths up to the steeper ground leading into Coire na Ciche. Below the lip of this a path slants right on a heathery shelf to reach the North Ridge. Direct versions above the shelf start well but peter out into acres of heather.

The Route
Once on the North Ridge follow the crest with occasional rocky steps. Near the top the path zigzags through more sustained rock (still easy, with a path off left). The summit itself is a splendid perch with a terrific view. Descend on the right, then from the col either clamber over awkward boulders on the crest or avoid them on the right. An easy narrow ridge follows, crossing two tops, before either a loose descent on the crest or a path further right leads to easy ground running up to Mullach Buidhe.

197 Bonus   Grade 2 or Moderate   **
Alt 700m   Ht Gain +60m   (NR 994 430)   Map p374

Although only short (about 70m) this blocky buttress provides a hugely enjoyable clamber well worth the short detour from the main ridge.

Approach
This would be purgatorial to approach from below, but for those coming from Cioch na h-Oighe the foot of the buttress is easily reached without loss of height by a short traverse across stony ground. Bonus is the first prominent buttress reached, running up to the North Summit of Mullach Buidhe.

The Route
Start at the toe of the buttress and climb the crest, bouldery at first, then up steeper wide cracks. At the steepest point a groove on the right avoids the difficulties. A purist approach using pockets and a wide crack is Moderate. The crest gradually eases as you gain height. At the top few scramblers will be able to resist slanting down the 20m to climb the next buttress to the south. This is steeper but on huge holds (Grade 2/3).

198 North Goatfell, West Ridge   Grade 1, 2 or 3
Alt 700m   Ht Gain +250m   (NR 985 425)   Map p374

Nobody would make this route their main aim of the day, but it provides a convenient way of adding interest to the steep ascent from the Saddle. A bit loose in places.

Approach
The Saddle (NR 979 429) is reachable easily by a good path up Glen Rosa, or from Glen Sannox with a finish up a rough and eroded groove.

The Route
A path runs up the ridge to 700m, at which point a big tower appears off to the left. The pinnacle at its foot can be clambered onto via the notch behind it (Grade 3). The path continues right of the big tower, but its crest can be gained above the steepest section at a flake crack. It provides an airy Grade 2. The path continues up a central groove, then another pinnacle can be traversed or avoided on the right. At the top of the ridge there is a rather loose slabby scramble left of the path. The summit of North Goatfell is just off to the right. Between this and the summit of Goatfell itself are three tors

*The pinnacle at the foot of the West Ridge, North Goatfell (Route 198, Grade 3)
Scrambler: Iain Thow. Photo: Nate Webb.*

Descending the West Ridge of North Goatfell (Route 198, Grade 1, 2 or 3). Photo: Noel Williams.

known as the Stacach. The first is enjoyably climbed by a groove on its right-hand corner or by slabs further right, the second is easy and the third usually avoided on the left, although the steep flakes on the front provide a rather dirty Grade 3.

 199 Am Binnein, South Face   Grade 2/3
Alt 500m   Ht Gain +120m   (NR 005 423)   Map p374

A broken face of slabs and boulders providing a string of varied problems on good granite. No real line but around 100m of rock with lots of options.

Approach
There is limited parking at High Corrie (NS 024 422), up the track just north of Corrieburn Bridge. Where the tarmac goes right a gravel track heads straight up the hill. A smaller path soon forks right, signed to Goatfell. Follow this up past the waterfalls as far as the lip of Coire Lan. Where a branch path forks left across the stream ignore both paths and head right towards Am Binnein. The face has two sections, the described route starting at the lowest slabs on the right-hand side of the right-hand one.

The Route
Pad up the slabs, then climb a fun corner on the left edge of the next slab, finishing on the arete. The slabs soon break up to boulders, then easy slabs lead up left to more sustained bigger boulders and flakes. These provide all sorts of possible variations, some of them quite technical but always with an easy option. They lead enjoyably to the cross just east of the summit of Am Binnein.

 200 Coire nam Meann Slabs   Grade 2 or 3
Alt 550m   Ht Gain +100m   (NR 995 410)   Map p374   Diag p384

A steep slabby spur, quite hard in places but with many possible escapes. A more interesting finish to the walk up from Brodick.

Approach
Follow the main tourist trail up from Brodick into Coire nam Meann. At around 500m head left to the broken cliffs on the left side of the corrie. This point can also be reached by following the path up from Corrie as for the previous route to the lip of Coire Lan. Turn left across the stream and go up to Meall Breac then traverse across to the slabs. There is a steep sided shallow gully high up in the middle of the most continuous part of the cliffs and the route goes up the rib left of this.

The Route
Gain the foot of the gully via introductory slabs and an easy angled left slanting rib. Climb the rib left of the gully, Grade 3 direct or Grade 2 with occasional detours, to reach boulders below a steeper blockier rib. Climb the right edge of this to the main South Ridge, again with easier detours available at Grade 2. There are a few more easy towers on the way to the summit.

200. Coire nam Meann Slabs Grade 2 or 3

CIR MHÒR 799m

OS Landranger 69   (NR 974 431)   Map p374

The heart of the Arran hills and it doesn't disappoint – one of the finest hills in Scotland. A pointed summit tops a huge shaggy north face and throws down a steep blunt southern pillar offering the island's best rock climbing. Sou'wester Slabs (VD) and South Ridge Direct (VS) are the deservedly popular classics. The north face is very vegetated and usually wet, but although the main faces on the south are too steep for scrambling several excellent scrambles find their way through them. They are generally clean, slabby and face the sun and can be linked together to produce a brilliant mountain day, much greater than the sum of its parts.

201 Cubic Ridge Indirect   Moderate
Alt 550m   Ht Gain +100m   (NR 971 428)   Map p374   Diag p386

A blocky buttress with some entertaining moves. Taken direct it is a hardish Diff, but the route described feels more like a scramble, albeit with the odd harder move.

Approach
Coming up Glen Rosa (limited parking at NS 000 376) Cir Mhòr is dominant ahead, with the Rosa Pinnacle central. Cubic Ridge is the separate buttress off to the left (not the steeper spur that joins the main crag near its top, which is Caliban's Creep, V Diff).

The Route
Follow heathery ramps up leftwards onto the buttress. Steep walls force you left to arrive at a cave in the gully that splits the lower part of the buttress. Go through the hole in the back then up right to the crest. Climb a groove in the centre, then short walls to a shark's fin. From the col behind this go up a bouldery ridge, then work right up ramps to the crest. More bouldery steps lead to a shelf below a vertical wall. This is Difficult but easily avoided by slabby boulders on the left. Easy rocks lead to the path up Cir Mhòr.

If coming from A' Chir to Cir Mhòr then a short detour rightwards from the path lets you include some fun slabs leading to the top of Cubic Ridge.

202 Cubic Gully Spur   Grade 3 or Moderate   **
Alt 500m   Ht Gain +250m   (NR 972 428)   Map p374   Diag p386

Not sustained and very escapable, but with some excellent padding on superb rock low down and a lot of variety higher up. A great way of reaching the best summit on the island.

Approach
As for the previous route. The line is the shallow slabby rib between Cubic Ridge and Caliban's Creep, just right of the main gully line. Either start at a yellowish fallen block just right of the gully, or alternatively start 100m

The right-hand start to Cubic Gully Spur (Route 202, Moderate).
Climber: Nate Webb. Photo: Iain Thow.

further right, up smooth padding slabs below the main south-west Face, traversing left after 50m to join the main route.

The Route
From the yellowish block an initial slab and heather lead to a sharp but low relief arête, then more broken ground leads to a big concave slab. Climb this and the next slab, then climb a crack on the left-hand sidewall (or the right edge, easier). An easier blocky ridge follows, heathery in places. At a steeper bluff go up left below twin cracks and climb the slabby left side of the ridge. Either climb the arête above direct past a spike (Moderate) or the easier right edge. Easy slabs above eventually peter out into the gully. Walk up until the ground opens out, and up right is a maze of blocks, slabs and chasms. Innumerable possible variations can be found through this, which continues up to the Rosa Pinnacle, with the summit beyond and up left.

203 Prospero's Prelude/Old East   Moderate   **
Alt 550m   Ht Gain +250m   (NR 974 427)   Map p374   Diag p386

Superb positions on mostly excellent rock. An unlikely looking outing at the grade, with a high intimidation factor and quite complex route finding.

Approach
As you approach up Glen Rosa the main tower running down from the Rosa Pinnacle, taken by the classic VS of South Ridge Direct, becomes more and more dominant. Below and right of this a less prominent spur runs up rightwards, steepening into the prow of Prospero's Peril. The lower part of this is the excellent Moderate of Prospero's Prelude, then an intricate line finds a way up left to the skyline of the main face and up to the summit.

The Route
From the lowest rock on the Prelude wind up slabs and small overlaps, then cross left below a larger overhang and up the arête to a stance. Either step right onto a slab and up a groove above (bordering on Difficult) or go up left and climb a wide crack in the arête. Either way leads to a lovely cracked crest, then blocks and ledges. A grittier slab (avoidable on the right) leads to more blocks and a zigzag of wide cracks. The crest becomes easier angled and blockier before petering out into Sub Rosa Gully.

It is possible to escape unpleasantly up the gully, but it is far better to head left up Old East, the break where the lower slabs abut against the vertical headwall. Go up left past a rockfall, with the steep crack of Minotaur prominent above. Climb sharp jugs at the top right corner of the slabs then move left along a ramp at the foot of the headwall. Keep going left across grass, veering away from the wall, then zigzag up ledges and use a short wide crack to gain the main arête of the buttress. Follow this to a wide bouldery rake below the Upper Pinnacle.

Walk left up the rake to reach more open hillside (direct routes are V Diff). When the wall on the right eases clamber rightwards up slabs and clefts to reach the top of the Rosa Pinnacle. Return down the top chimney and the crack below it, then cut right (looking out) to cross below the steep slab of the Rosetta Stone to a grassy col. The path now gains the summit round to the left, but it is more fun to go up a padding slab on the right edge of the summit mass and along a sharp arête to the top. There are also several easier variations between these two.

204 Lower South-East Slabs   Grade 2/3
Alt 400m   Ht Gain + 200m   (NR 976 425)   Map p374   Diag p386

Surprisingly good scrambling despite the heather, and easy to combine with other scrambles because of the low start.

Approach
As you walk up Glen Rosa (limited parking at NS 000 376) this is the rather heathery buttress low down on the right-hand part of Cir Mhòr, easily reached from the path to The Saddle. The lowest rocks are walking angle slabs off left, while up right are two parallel lines of slabs separated by a square cut groove. The right-hand one starts at a small steep face, and the described route starts up the left-hand one.

The Route
Boulders coalesce to easy slabs, then cross an overlap and pad up superb rough slabs and a knobbly groove. A blunt arête and a lumpy bulge lead to more slabs, with a parallel (more sustained) line of slabs off right across the main groove. Either line leads to heather, but above the left-hand one are easier angled spaced slabs which gradually merge into a more defined spur. This runs up to a heathery shoulder at about 600m, where walking leads up to join the main path up from the Saddle. Alternatively a sketchy path slants down left to the foot of Prospero's Prelude (Route 203).

205 East Shoulder   Grade 2
Alt 500m   Ht Gain + 300m   (NR 977 431)   Map p374   Diag p390

Rather vegetated scrambling but more enjoyable than the path. Briefly intimidating but not too exposed.

Approach
Reach the Saddle (NR 979 429) either by the built path up Glen Rosa or the similar path up Glen Sannox followed by a clamber up a loose right-slanting gully (or over Goatfell or Cioch na h-Oighe).
   From the Saddle take the smaller path up westwards to the start of the rocks, just left of a deep gully. Traverse right across the gully (slightly down) to reach a broad shoulder.

The Route
Zigzag up the shoulder on boulders, slabs and heather to a more open grass patch with more sustained rock above. Go right up either of two vegetated ramps, finishing on the upper one. Make a short traverse right across a slab, roughly level with a large pointed flake off right. The continuation looks problematical from here, but go up left and a deep slot appears on your right.

Thrutch rightwards through this to reach easy ground. Boulder problems add interest to a walk up to the top of the initial shoulder.

Grass leads up left to another steepening with the main path just off left. The path goes up and further left to go through the gap between the Rosa Pinnacle and the main peak and reach the summit from the south-west. Alternatively, for more scrambling ignore the path and zigzag directly up the shoulder on broken but quite steep rock using big flakes. Cross a minor peaklet to reach a grassy saddle with the path well off left and a broken gully ahead. Walk up to the right skyline of the final tower and clamber back left to a small notch (escape into the gully possible from here but unpleasant). An awkward wide crack goes straight up to reach an airy ramp going up right to boulders and the summit.

A' CHIR 745m

OS Landranger 69   (NR 966 422)   Map p374

Arguably the best ridge in Scotland south of Skye and the hardest summit to reach outside the Cuillin. The South Ridge consists of rough slanting slabs, narrow arêtes and rock tors, while the harder North Ridge involves an airy step across a gap and an exposed and technical descent. Unusually, the latter is much harder in ascent, so the ridge traverse is usually done south to north. The South East Face consists of steep overlapping slabs cut by deep gullies, giving the classic climbs of Pagoda Ridge (Severe) and Mosque (HVS), as well as the easier Boundary Ridge described below. The south end of the West Face has some pleasant slabs running up right, enjoyable but rather trivial.

206 Boundary Ridge   Difficult   *
Alt 450m   Ht Gain +100m   (NR 964 415)   Map p374   Diag p392

The slabby ridge that bounds the left-hand side of the South East Face. Much of this is Grade 3 scrambling, but the final crack is quite hard (although short and above a big ledge).

Approach
Follow the good track up Glen Rosa from NS 000 376 for about 5km until below the main Rosa Slabs up to your right. Head left here and follow the stream up into the rough and trackless Coire Daingean, The main slabs are obvious, up to the right at the head of the corrie, and Boundary Ridge is the furthest left, just right of the gully leading up to the Tarsuinn–A' Chir col. An alternative route in takes the track over Beinn a' Chliabhainn (a little Grade 1 scrambling in places) and from just before the lowest col beyond it take a deer track down right into the corrie and traverse round to the route.

The Route
Gain the ridge from the left at a notch 5m up (or climb a steep direct starting crack, much harder). Go up a slabby crest, with one awkward step at a steeper wall, until forced left into an easy groove. Climb this to an open area with

Boundary Ridge, A' Chir (Route 206, Difficult).
Climber: Nate Webb. Photo: Iain Thow.

blocks. Climb the right-hand of two wide cracks, then another (better) groove on the left edge, finishing up right to reach a grass shelf below a sharp arête. Climb wide cracks just right of the arête to a nest of boulders below a steep corner. The huge detached flake off left is worth a detour for the view. Traverse right along a ledge above a pool, then climb the slab above it on good pockets. Go up left and climb the Y-shaped crack, hard for the grade but both protectable and above a good ledge. Easy slabs lead to the ridge.

207 A' Chir Ridge Traverse   Moderate   ***
Alt 630m   (NR 963 415)   Map p374   Diag p395

One of the great outings of Scottish mountaineering, this is sustained, exposed and difficult to escape from. The rock and situations are superb. Easier south to north as described here, V Diff the other way round.

Approach
The usual way to approach this is up Glen Rosa (limited parking at NS 000 376) to the footbridge at 982 386. Turn left up the Garbh Allt and where the path flattens out fork right to go up over Cnoc Breac. Follow the ridge over Beinn a' Chliabhain with some minor Grade 1 scrambling and after the col beyond it take a path cutting right below Beinn Tarsuinn to the Bealach an Fhir-bhoga (NR 963 415). The longer approach going further up the Garbh Allt and crossing over Beinn Nuis and Beinn Tarsuinn is also excellent. The A' Chir traverse is also the obvious follow on to Boundary Ridge (Route 206) and indeed to the harder climbs to its right.

The Route
From the bealach the path runs left of the ridge line at first, with optional slabs up right (very scenic). At a wide gully zigzag up the left flank of the tower ahead, with lots of possible variations. The ridge narrows over a minor top, with an avoidable knife edge descent. At the next col traverse left onto slabs, then either keep slanting left easily to go up the first slab then left, or go up right to the crest via either of two flake cracks. All the options rejoin at the next col. Traverse left and through a hole, then go back right above it to the crest. An easy crack follows, with a path. Descend a steep step either on the crest by a spike or by a juggy corner on the right (looking out). Pass two minor tops, the first a nice detour, then climb the summit tor by an easy gully. The left-hand block is the highest, easiest by its south-east corner. The tall can belly flop on from the lower boulder, while those of more modest proportions need to do a delicate two step left and up which might well get a Severe grade if met on a 'proper' rock climb.

Descend on the crest until forced to make an exposed step down on the right (or a delicate but less airy descent in the centre). Drop down a steep juggy crack below this to reach a small gap. Step across the gap and soon after reach a cairn. The next section is much the hardest part of the traverse and many will use a rope. Do not continue along the ridge, which leads to *Le Mauvais Pas*. Instead descend the steep face on the right (east) using a good

*Descending the crux section on the A' Chir Ridge Traverse (Route 207).
1. The narrow ledge.   2. How not to do it!   3&4. The usual solution.*

flake crack to reach a narrow slanting ledge. This is descended (usually sitting down!) to a swing down a steep face. Most hang off the jug and drop to the good flat landing, ungainly but effective. This is V Diff in ascent. An alternative descent down the gully on the east side of the small gap is extremely loose and not recommended. The whole section is often abseiled.

From the col slant left up a shelf to an awkward step off a block onto a higher ledge. Zigzag back up to the crest, then follow it down over a succession of easy steps to reach easy ground at the head of Coire Buidhe. A path descends into Glen Rosa from here and another cuts left to the Cir Mhòr/Caisteal Abhail col, or you can follow an easy shoulder up Cir Mhòr.

Pirnmill Hills

This is the smaller group of more rounded hills in the north-west corner of the island, the traverse of the three highest tops making a lovely day out. Somewhat inconveniently the best scramble is on a subsidiary ridge of the central summit.

MULLACH BUIDHE 721m

OS Landranger 69   (NR 902 427)

The highest of a ridge of rounded granite hills above Pirnmill on the north-west coast, with a jagged blocky north-west ridge.

 208 North-West Ridge   Grade 2   **
Alt 450m   (NR 896 433)
Broken slabs and boulders followed by a succession of enjoyable rock towers.

Approach
Parking is available at the south end of Pirnmill (NR 872 441), just north of the bridge. Follow a lane (signed 'footpath') up between buildings to the edge of woodland. A signed path leads into these, going rightwards to the edge of the gorge of the Allt Gobhlach. Follow this up to open country at a gigantic step stile and carry on up the side of the gorge. Cross its left branch and carry on up to reach a new hydro track. Cross the stream and take a smaller path (not obvious at first) towards the left-hand of two ridges ahead, crowned by rock tors. Go up to it on a mixture of heather, grass and walking angle slabs.

The Route
Where the ground steepens go up the left-hand side on piles of boulders. At the top the prominent tor is started by a loose left then right zigzag, then either pull up left to the crest or go round right more easily. The ridge now narrows, only walking at first, then giving fun clambering over a series of towers until they peter out into the hillside. The summit is not far away up left. If going out to the south-west summit (Beinn Bharrain proper) there is also a brief easy scramble over the tor of Caisteal na h-Iolaire.

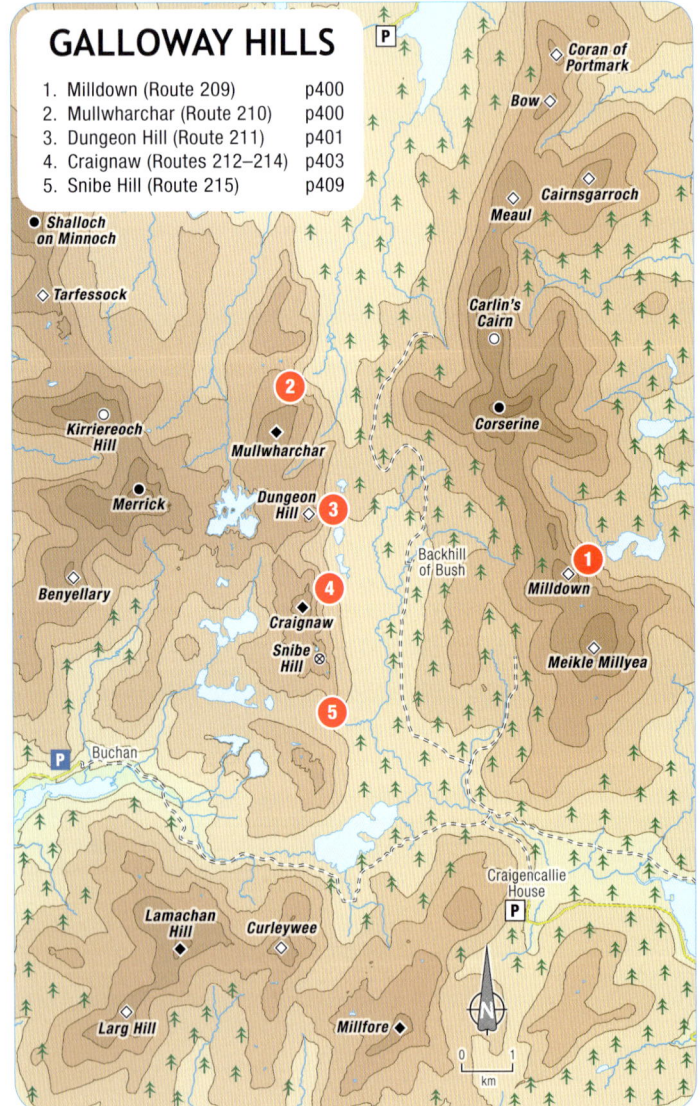

CENTRAL LOWLANDS & SOUTHERN UPLANDS

Although the vast bulk of the best scrambling in Scotland is to be found in the Highlands and Islands, there are a few exceptions, both in the Central Lowlands and particularly in Galloway.

Central Lowlands

Although none of these routes are of any great quality they do have the advantage of being close to where the majority of people in Scotland actually live and provide brief fun.

Minor scrambles in the Central Lowlands
Cirque Gully on Dumyat above Stirling is a surprisingly atmospheric Grade 1. From Blairlogie Meadow (NS 836 974) go right and after a few hundred metres work a way up through gorse to reach the defile of the Warlock's Glen, running up between the two summits of the hill. Where this narrows there are two deep gullies on the right, the deeper left slot being Cirque Gully. There are also a few scrambly outcrops higher up, while for the masochistic routes can be found in the gorse jungle lower down to the left of the Warlock's Glen – not worth the effort without napalm.

Even more accessible is the Gutted Haddie on Arthur's Seat in Edinburgh, the left slanting groove that runs up the west face between the two main summits (Grade 1). From the saddle south-east of Salisbury Crags go up grass right of the scree to gain the groove. Just left of the top a little technical interest can be found, notably a little rib with an overhanging start at Diff. Its ascent is almost certainly a breach of Holyrood Park's byelaws but it's probably Scotland's most climbed scramble, mostly by local children during the day or drunken students after dark (guilty m'lud).

The delightful coast path around the East Neuk of Fife offers one variation for scramblers, a coastal via ferrata around Kincraig Point about 2km west of Earlsferry (NT 465 997). The well used route runs below the cliffs, Grade 1 in either direction with the odd chain to help, with the cliff top path making a scenic return route. Not feasible at highest tides.

The Galloway Hills

Although the Southern Uplands contain a large amount of hill country, the vast bulk of this is grassy and rolling and what rock there is consists mostly of shattered greywacke which doesn't make great scrambling. The exception is the Galloway heartland in the south-west, where granite intrusions provide some better routes. Most of the lower ground here is commercial forestry and the access roads prove useful easy walk-ins. Once outside the trees, however, it is a different story, with few paths and some of the roughest ground in the country to traverse. Huge tussocks and deep bogs abound!

MILLDOWN 738m

OS Landranger 77   (NX 511 839)   Map p398

A grassy summit south of Corserine with a steep rocky east face. The subsidiary summit of Millfire just to the north has a similar scramble to the one described but much more vegetated and not nearly as good.

209 North-East Spur   Grade 2   *
Alt 450m   Ht Gain +300m   (NX 516 842)   Map p398

A blunt spur of rippled metamorphic outcrops deserving to be better known.

Approach
From the car park at Forrest Lodge (NX 553 862) follow Professor Hans Heiberg Road south-westwards, then about 1 km beyond Burnhead turn right onto Mary Watson Road. This takes you north of Loch Dungeon to the monument in the Hawse Burn (515 853), just short of the forest edge. Turn left, cross the bridge and stile, then traverse left towards the obvious rocky spur descending from the summit of Milldown, about 100m beyond the stone wall leading up to the face.

The Route
The lowest cliff is steep and vegetated so bypass it by grass on its right, moving left onto the crest when the angle eases. Short slabs and heather lead up to pass left of a big steep wall, then go up right to the crest of the main spur. Climb a lovely rough slab, then a steeper rib gained from the left. Move up right to another slabby crest, then easy outcrops lead to a flattening.

Where the ground steepens again scramble rightwards up a broad buttress to the skyline, finishing up a nice rippled slab. Across a small col is more sustained rock. Move left and climb a cracked slab, then go left again to swing onto and climb another slab and the rib above. Go right and up the skyline rib, which opens out to well-positioned easy slabs. On the left is another rib with a steep right wall, gain this (several possibilities) and follow it to the top of the main face. Carry on up the spur, which has several more easy outcrops before arriving at the summit.

MULLWHARCHAR 692m

OS Landranger 78   (NX 454 866)   Map p398

A bit of a lump from a distance but with a rough and craggy north-east flank. Please check for seasonal bird restrictions before visiting.

210 Tauchers Couloir   Moderate   *
Alt 400m   Ht Gain +150m   (NX 457 875)   Map p398

The first recorded climb in Galloway, back in 1909. This deep slot usually contains a waterfall but is mostly on good clean rock with lots of positive holds. Much better than it looks from below.

DUNGEON HILL 401

Approach

The shortest approach is from Loch Doon. Park at 476 941 and take the track to the head of the loch then turn right on a forestry track. Where this ends bear right to reach a bridge over the Gala Lane, then follow the far bank upstream until below the cliffs. There are three main craggy areas, a tiered cliff on the right, the pillared Organ Pipes high up on the left and the Giant's Staircase centrally with the Couloir being the obvious slot on the left side of the last mentioned.

The Route

The lower stream is easy, so better is to scramble up a series of ribs of very rough granite to the left (Grade 2), joining the Couloir where it steepens into its first gorge. Easy steps lead up this to the main slot. A subsidiary groove round to the left provides an escape here, up good rock and steep heather. The main slot is easy at first, then a steeper 10m pitch intervenes before more easy but atmospheric scrambling take you to an exit left just below the top.

DUNGEON HILL 610m

OS Landranger 77   (NX 460 850)   Map p398

Not a spectacular hill, but very rocky, and set in the heart of some of the roughest country in Scotland. In addition to the described route the north spur has some good outcrops on its north end and a pleasant ridge above, while the south-west shoulder above the Nick of the Dungeon has some minor steps too.

211 East Shoulder   Grade 1,2 or 3   *
Alt 350m   Ht Gain+200m   (NX 464 851)   Map p398   Diag p402

A long but discontinuous scramble, mostly easy slabs but with short steeper sections, all avoidable.

Approach

The quickest approach is from the Craigencallie road end west of Clatteringshaws Loch (NX 503 778), largely on forest roads so a mountain bike is useful. Head north-west, turn right across the bridge after 1.5km then turn left for another 4km to Backhill of Bush bothy. Turn left across the stream just before this, then immediately right. Take the second gap on the left through recent tree felling to go out to the huge bog of the Silver Flowe. Follow the right edge of this past the Round Loch to the lowest craglet at the right-hand foot of Dungeon Hill (about 2 hrs). It is less distance but at least half an hour longer to approach from Glen Trool as for Route 212 as far as the Nick of the Dungeon. From here it is better to take goat paths down to about 350m then head north rather than making a descending traverse.

The Route

Clamber up piles of boulders then walk left to gentle slabs on the left edge

of the shoulder. Follow these until the spur runs out into the main hillside. Go up left to the skyline and zigzag up a steeper step (Grade 3 direct). A juggy rib on the right provides a way up the next outcrop, then more easy slabs and grass lead to a long steep wall. Pass this by steps on the right then continue up rightwards on outcrops of rough granite. A wide crack with a convenient jug is fun, with a Grade 3 finish or an escape left. More outcrops lead to a bigger final step which can be zigzagged up at Grade 2 or climbed direct. Minor craglets can be found all the way to the summit, as can a perched boulder pinnacle (worth V Diff for the final move, which of course has to be reversed).

CRAIGNAW 645m

OS Landranger 77   (NX 459 833)   Map p398

An extremely rocky hill surrounded by some very rough country. Much of the east face is slightly too steep for scrambling, as well as being very vegetated, but there are many other possibilities as well as the four described here.

212 North-West Slabs   Grade 2/3   *
Alt 350m   Ht Gain +100m   (NX 459 840)   Map p398   Diag p404

Slabs and outcrops of clean granite making a good way onto Craignaw from the west.

Approach
From the Bruce's Stone car park above Loch Trool (415 803) take the main track down to Buchan Farm, then just after crossing the bridge over the Buchan Burn take a smaller path left. This slants up into the valley of the Gairland Burn and up to Loch Valley. Cross the stream a little before reaching Loch Neldricken (or at its outlet) and continue round the east side of the loch. The path gradually becomes more fictional but a trail of sorts does lead up to the Nick of the Dungeon and a prominent cairn (454 843). Slant down south-east towards the cliffs on the flank of Craignaw's north ridge. On the right a line of slabs with a vertical right wall slants up rightwards. These can be padded up but better is to start 50 metres left at a short steep right-facing wall with more slabs above.

The Route
The short wall gives an optional hard start (Diff), then move left and go up easy slabs to slightly steeper slabs. Where these steepen again they also conveniently start to develop cracks. Pull onto a large flake and move delicately up left to ledges. More easy slabs follow, then a steeper tower, which forces you to use the flanking vegetation in places. The broad crest now breaks up into a chain of outcrops of rough granite with lots of possible routes before arriving at a big easy angled slab backed by a long steep wall. A grassy rake slants up rightwards across the wall. Pull onto this and follow

212. North-West Slabs — Grade 2/3 *

North-West Slabs Craignaw (Route 212, Grade 2/3).
Scrambler: Paddy Earle. Photo: Iain Thow.

it for 10 metres or so (it continues to the top of the wall), then move up left to a narrower rake. Sidle awkwardly right on this then step left to climb a final slab. Walking angle rock above leads to the deep slot of the Wolf's Slock, best crossed near its left end. The craggy summit of Craignaw is not much further on.

213 North-East Shoulder   Grade 3   **
Alt 350m   Ht Gain +200m   (NX 463 840)   Map p398   Diag p402
A long scramble on good granite, mainly slabby but quite varied.

Approach
As for Dungeon Hill (Route 211) to the Silver Flowe. Cross the north edge of this between the two Lochs of the Dungeon and bear left to slabs on the east side of Craignaw's blunt northern spur. The Silver Flowe itself is an SSSI, as well as being very hard going, better to avoid it on both counts.

The Route
Start up an easy angled clean rib with a sharp right edge, just left of big blocks. Move left to its obvious continuation then climb a broader slab. Gain a steeper rib from the right using a good flake. Short slabs and grass lead to a bigger slab capped by an overlap, avoided on the left. Traverse in above the overlap and go up to a substantial buttress with a vertical right wall. Climb a vegetated groove just left of the arête, then make an awkward step up to more slabs. Go up the right arete of these on lovely rock. Climb a short wall by a steep curving scoop then go out left and up more slabs. Climb a steep prow using square holds on a left slanting pegmatite vein. The general angle now eases but there are many small outcrops above to provide more fun. An exposed ramp out left to a nice step up and a step off a pinnacle onto slabs are both worth finding. Walking angle slabs lead almost all the way to the top of Craignaw, with the gash of the Wolf's Slock adding some unexpected interest.

214 Dow Spout   Grade 2/3
Alt 300m   Ht Gain +150m   (NX 465 829)   Map p398   Diag p402
A slabby waterfall, only sensible in a dry spell. Quite a tricky crux but escapable almost anywhere.

Approach
Come in from Craigencallie as for Dungeon Hill (Route 211) but about 2km south of Backhill of Bush turn left and ford the Cooran Lane (often tricky and sometimes impossible). Dow Spout is the obvious waterfall descending the east face of Craignaw about halfway along. It can also be reached by slanting down northwards from the top of the next route.

The Route
The lower slabs are easy, avoiding the water where possible. At a steepening go up right and continue right of the stream to a shelf below a vertical wall.

Wolf's Slock, Craignaw (Route 213, Grade 3).
Scrambler: Paddy Earle. Photo: Iain Thow.

Climb a chimney on the right, stepping left at the top. More easy slabs lead to the much more sustained top section. Zigzag up left and right then tiptoe delicately left across the stream to reach good holds up the middle of the slabs (or avoid this section on the right). Avoid the wet vertical wall above by going up right and climbing a short corner behind a big block. The final rise is in the stream but easy angled, fairly clean and on positive holds.

215 Snibe Hill Rib   Grade 2   *
Alt 300m   Ht Gain +100m   (NX 466 814)   Map p398   Diag p408

A series of outcrops on excellent granite.

Approach

From the Glen Trool road end (NX 415 803) go down the track to Buchan Farm and just after the bridge fork left on the smaller track that slants up into the valley of the Gairland Burn. Cross very rough ground along the south side of Loch Valley and cut across to the rocky foot of Snibe Hill, the south-east spur of Craignaw. On the bottom right-hand side of the face is an easy angled spur. This point can also be reached from Craigencallie (503 780), crossing the bridge at 496 793 and fording the Cooran Lane about 2km south of Backhill of Bush (only feasible in dry weather).

The Route

Climb the spur past a huge block and where it steepens go left and up jugs. Where the spur ends walk up to the face on the right and climb a groove on the left edge. Walk horizontally left below a steep wall to a larger face. Climb a groove and go left up steps, then continue left to go up a slabby arête. This gradually breaks up into shorter steps, then climb a bigger block either delicately on the left or up on the right (easier). Minor rocks lead to the top.

Other Southern Uplands Routes

Most of the Southern Uplands outside Galloway is unsuitable for scrambling but there are a few exceptions. Screel Hill near Dalbeattie (NX 779 552) is scattered with outcrops where the greywacke has been baked by a neighbouring intrusion so is much more solid than usual. These provide plenty of fun clambering, although they don't line up to make continuous scrambles (a great place to go with adventurous kids).

Hang Gill on Swatte Fell near Moffat (NT 141 098) provides a short easy stream scramble that fits naturally into a route up the hill. The crags on the East Face higher up though consist mostly of bilberry, despite the crag markings on the OS maps.

The gorge of Crichope Linn near Thornhill (NX 914 953) has been scrambled up, but this is mostly wading – well worth a visit though.

By far the best Southern Upland scramble outside the Galloway heartland though is to be found higher up Nithsdale at Glenwhargan Craig.

GLENWHARGAN CRAIG

216. Glenwhargan Craig — Grade 2

GLENWHARGAN CRAIG 482m

OS Landranger 78 (NS 763 035)

Hidden away up the Scaur Water in the unfrequented grassy hills west of Nithsdale are a number of cliffs, the largest of which is Glenwhargan Craig. Although 100m high it is quite broken and vegetated, with some short steep rock climbs and one good scramble.

216 Glenwhargan Craig   Grade 2
Alt 300m   Ht Gain+200m   (NS 762 030)   Map ibc   Diag p410

A roadside crag, but with a long winding drive to reach it. Not really worth a special visit but fun if you happen to be in the general area. The rock is quite lichenous in places and very slippery if wet, but sound underneath.

Approach
Park a little beyond the crag at a gate. Walk up right then clamber up small outcrops and up the left-hand edge of scree to the main crag.

The Route
Climb the lowest rib and continue up a groove in the crest. At a steeper band go up left, then back right delicately to the arête. Go up left to the edge of a clean slab and up to a heather shelf. An easy spur leads to more heather, then go up left to a bigger buttress. Gain the crest of this from the left above its steepest part, then go up the crest to the top. The flanks of the crag are very shattered so it is better to descend by going over the top of the hill and coming down well wide of the cliff.

INDEX OF ROUTES – listed mainly by nearest mountain or crag

A' Chailleach	275
South Face	275
A' Chir	391
A' Chir Ridge Traverse	394
Boundary Ridge	391
Ainshval	70
Forgotten Ridge	70
Harris Face	72
North Ridge	70
An Caisteal	83
South Face	83
Aonach Beag	225
North-East Ridge	225
Aonach Dubh	
see Stob Coire nan Lochan	
Aonach Eagach	271
Aonach Eagach Traverse	271
Clachaig Rib	274
Aonach Mòr	227
An Cùl Choire Headwall	227
Golden Oldy	229
Askival	61
East Ridge	63
North Ridge	
via Askival Pinnacle	61
North Ridge Easy Route	63
South Ridge	64
West Ridge	64
Barkeval	55
Broad Buttress	55
Descent Spur	61
Honeycomb Arête	59
Narnia Arête	59
North-West Flank	55
Beinn nan Aighenan	342
North-East Face	342
Ben Alder	215
Long Leachas	217
North Buttress	215
Short Leachas	217
Beinn an Aodainn (Ben Aden)	88
East-North-East Ridge	88
South Face	90
Beinn Beag	112
East Face	113
Beinn a' Bheithir	323
Sgòrr Bhan, North-East Ridge	323
Sgòrr Dhonuill,	
Sgòrr a' Chaolais	323
Beinn a' Bhùird	183
Addition Buttress	185
Dividing Buttress	185
M & B Buttress	187
Ben Buie	135
Juniper Buttress	137
Sròn Dubh Spur	135
Sròn Dubh Central Slabs	135
Summit Buttress	137
Beinn na Caillich	77
South-East Slabs	77
Beinn a' Chaorainn	205
East Ridge	205
Beinn Chreagach Mhòr	133
South-West Face	133
Beinne a' Chrùlaiste	278
Pink Rib	281
Split Buttress	278
Summit Buttress	278
Ben Cruachan	355
Stob Dearg, North Ridge	355
Beinn Fhionnlaidh	325
North-West Slabs	327
South Face	325
Beinn Gharbh	95
North-West Face	97
Ursainn Slabs	97
Beinn Macduibh	181
Coire Sputan Dearg,	
Crystal Ridge	181
Creagan a' Choire Etchachan,	
Quartzvein Edge	181
Ben More	134
Northern Circuit	134
Beinn Narnain	369
Restricted Crack	371
Spearhead Arête	369

INDEX

Ben Nevis	232
Castle Ridge	236
Creag Coire na Ciste,	
Central-North Route	244
Garadh Buttress	244
Ledge Route	239
Number 4 Gully Buttress	242
Observatory Ridge	251
Raeburn's Easy Route	246
South Trident, Upper Arête	244
Tower Ridge	246
Beinn Resipol	123
South-West Flank	124
Beinn na Seilg	131
Hebrides Rib	131
Beinn Sgulaird	330
South-West Slabs	330
Beinn Sgùrrach	202
North-West Ridge	202
Ben Starav	344
Leac nam Fionn	344
Red Man's Rib	345
Slabathon	348
Beinn Trilleachan	335
Coire Crìche Slabs	335
Ben Vorlich	359
South Face, Central Rib	359
South Face, Right-hand Rib	361
Bidean nam Bian	317
Diamond Edge	319
Binnein Mòr	269
North-East Ridge	269
Binnein Shuas	206
Ardverikie Rib	209
Braeriach	171
The Black Pinnacle	173
Near East Buttress	171
Broad Cairn	197
Broad Cairn Slabs	197
Buachaille Etive Beag	294
Creag nan Cabar,	
North-East Buttress	297
Stob nan Cabar,	
Alltnafeadh Buttress	297
Buachaille Etive Mòr	281
Broad Buttress	291
Chasm to Crowberry Traverse	283
Creag na Tulaich,	
North-East Spur	292
Crowberry Ridge Indirect	287
Curved Ridge	284
D Gully Buttress	284
Great Gully Buttress	289
Lagangarbh Buttress	292
North Buttress	289
South Buttress	283
Cairn Lochan	158
Fiacaill Ridge	158
Cairn Toul	175
Solitude Rib	175
Caisteal Abhail	375
Ceum na Caillich	375
Little Broomstick Ridge	378
Càrn a' Choire Bhoidheach	195
Stuic Buttress	195
Càrn a' Mhaim	178
Creag Coire na Poite	178
Càrn Mòr Dearg	232
Càrn Dearg Mheadhonach,	
East Ridge	232
Càrn na Nathrach	107
Left Spur	110
Right Spur	110
Cir Mhòr	385
Cubic Gully Spur	385
Cubic Ridge Indirect	385
East Shoulder	389
Lower South-East Slabs	389
Prospero's Prelude/Old East	388
Cnoc a' Bhac Fhalaichte	92
Tarbet Slabs	93
The Cobbler	363
South–North Traverse	363
Colonsay	372
Beinn nan Caorach, West Ridge	372
Craig Mellon	199
Craig Mellon	199
Craignaw	403
Dow Spout	406
North-East Shoulder	406

INDEX

North-West Slabs	403
Snibe Hill Rib	409
Creach-Beinn (Mull)	**139**
Loch an Eilein Shoulder	141
Creach Bheinn (Ardgour)	**120**
Coire Mheall Challuim Slabs	123
Meall a' Bhràghaid, Holly Tree Slabs	120
Creag an Airgid	**124**
Western Flank	124
Creag a' Chuir	**209**
Central Buttress	209
Creise	**348**
Inglis Clark Arête	350
Sròn na Creise	350
Stob a' Ghlais Choire, North-East Spur	352
The Devil's Point	**176**
Corrour Slabs	176
Dungeon Hill	**401**
East Shoulder	401
Garbh Bheinn	**113**
Eagle's Nest Slabs	113
Great Ridge	116
Pinnacle Ridge	119
Sròn Lag nan Gamhna	119
Garbh Chìoch Mhòr	**92**
Coire nan Gall Slabs	92
Garbh Uisge Crag	**143**
Feith Buidhe Slabs	145
Feld Spur	145
Geal Chàrn	**213**
Aisre Cham Streamway	213
Lancet Edge	213
Geàrr Aonach *see* Stob Coire nan Lochan	
Glen Nevis	**255**
Scimitar Ridge (Polldubh)	257
Surgeon's Rib	255
Glenwhargan Craig	**411**
Glenwhargan Craig	411
Goatfell	**379**
Am Binnein, South Face	383
Bonus	380
Cioch na h-Oighe	379
Coire nam Meann Slabs	383
North Goatfell, West Ridge	380
Hell's Lum Crag	**147**
The Escalator Right-hand	147
Islay	**373**
Dun Athad	373
Ladhar Bheinn	**79**
An Dìollaid	79
Làirig Ghrù (North)	**166**
Lairig Ridge	166
Lochnagar	**191**
Central Buttress	191
Black Spout Buttress	193
Black Spout Left-hand Branch	193
Lurcher's Crag	**158**
Arctic Monkeys Ridge	166
Collie's Ridge	160
Doorway Ridge	162
Drystane Ridge	160
Ptarmigan Ridge	162
Summit Buttress	165
Sweep	165
Meall Coire Choille-rais	**206**
East Ridge	206
Meall Cumhann	**257**
Traverse of Meall Cumhann	258
Meall nan Eun	**85**
Cannonade	85
Meall Odhar	**339**
Epiphany Arête	339
Meall Sanna	**127**
West Flank	129
Meall an t-Suidhe	**253**
Central South-west Buttress	253
Right-hand South-west Buttress	255
Meall na Teanga	**100**
Meall Dubh, Central Buttress	100
Meall Dubh, Right-hand Buttress	103
Milldown	**400**
North-East Spur	400
Mullach Buidhe	**397**
North-West Ridge	397
Mullach nan Coirean	**259**

INDEX

Gendarme Ridge	259
Mullwharchar	400
Tauchers Couloir	400
Rum Cuillin (Traverse of)	75
Main Ridge Traverse	75
The Saddle	153
Saddle Slabs	153
Sgòr Gaoith	169
Corner Ridge	169
Sgòr an Lochain Uaine	175
Angel's Ridge	175
Sgòrr Craobh a' Chaorainn	104
Meall na h-Airigh, West Ridge	104
Sgùrr Dhomhnuill	112
Druim Garbh, Left-hand Slabs	112
Sgùrr an Eilein Ghiubhais	93
Right-hand Rib	93
Sgùrr nan Gabhar	127
North-East Rib	127
Sgùrr Ghiubhsachain	107
North Ridge	107
Sgùrr nan Gillean	72
Dibidil Face	72
Sgùrr Innse	218
South-East Slabs	218
Sgùrr a' Mhaim	265
Ring of Steall	265
Sròn a' Choire Ghairbh	99
Sean Mheall, South Face	100
Stac an Fharaidh	152
Broad Buttress	152
Stag Rocks	147
Afterthought Arête	147
Final Selection	152
Serrated Rib	150
Stob Bàn (Grey Corries)	221
Giant's Staircase	221
Stob Bàn (Mamores)	262
North Buttress, East Ridge	262
Stob a' Chearcaill	81
North-East Ridge	81
Stob Coir' an Albannaich	342
Coire Glas Headwall	342
Stob Coire nam Beith	319
Number 1 Buttress	319
Number 3 Buttress	321
Stob Coire nan Lochan	300
Aonach Dubh, East Face	306
Barn Wall Route	306
Far East Buttress, Left Edge	308
Far East Buttress, Right Edge	306
Aonach Dubh, West Face	312
A Minus Buttress	314
B–D Buttress	316
B–F Buttress	317
Dinner-time Buttress	312
Rhyolite Romp	314
Coire nan Lochan	308
Lochan Approach, Left-hand	308
Lochan Approach, Right-hand	310
Geàrr Aonach	303
The Nose	303
The Zigzags	303
North Face	310
Dorsal Arête	312
Summit Buttress, Left Flank	310
Stob Coire Sgreamhach	298
Eilde Rib	300
Sròn na Lairig	298
Stob Coire an t-Sneachda	153
Fingers Ridge	155
Pygmy Ridge	155
Stob Daimh	357
Stob Garbh, North-East Ridge	357
Stob an Fhuarain	333
Bealach Fhionnghaill Buttress	333
Stob Ghabhar	352
Aonach Eagach	352
Lochnan Buttress	353
Stùc a' Chroin	361
North-East Buttress	361
Trollabhal	66
East Ridge	66
South Flank	66
West Ridge	68

Scottish Mountaineering Club

Established in 1889, the Scottish Mountaineering Club is at the forefront of climbing and mountaineering in Scotland. We want our guidebooks, covering hillwalking, scrambling and climbing, to be the first book you reach for when you head for the cliffs, hills and outcrops of Scotland.

www.smc.org.uk/publications

Scottish Mountaineering Press

The Scottish Mountaineering Press exists to promote and share Scotland's natural wonders. We do this by embracing the creativity and art born out of an explorer spirit. Whether it's poetry, photography or prose, our publications capture the moments when nature stuns us into silence and stops us in our tracks.

www.scottishmountaineeringpress.com

Scottish Mountaineering Trust

All profits from Scottish Mountaineering Press books go to help fund the Scottish Mountaineering Trust, a charity that provides grants to projects and organisations that promote recreation, knowledge and safety in the mountains, especially the mountains of Scotland.

www.thesmt.org.uk